AN UNFINISHED REVOLUTION

AN UNFINISHED REVOLUTION

Women and Health Care
in America

Edited by

Emily Friedman

United Hospital Fund of New York

Printed in the United States of America.

Library of Congress Cataloging-in-Publication Data

An unfinished revolution: women and health care in America/Emily Friedman, editor
p. cm.
Includes bibliographical references.
ISBN 1-881277-17-8: $20.00
1. Women in medicine. 2 Women-health and hygiene.

R692.T35 1994
610'.82—dc20   94-5940
                                                                    CIP

For information, write, Publications Program, United Hospital Fund, 55 Fifth Avenue, New York, NY 10003.

Dedicated to

Ruth M. Rothstein,
Director, Cook County Hospital, Chicago,

for a lifetime of service
to women and their health

and to the memory of

Andrea Boroff Eagan

who worked tirelessly to
improve the health of women and to strengthen
their relationship with the health care system

Contents

Foreword

LONG THE MAJORITY of caregivers and patients, women have not exerted a proportional influence on the practice of medicine. Beginning in the 1970s, however, women in the health care consumer movement drew attention to the kinds of care women were (or were not) receiving, and called into question the traditional scx-typcd relations between patients and health care providers. As a result of their efforts, patients today are more likely to have access to good information about their treatment options, and researchers are paying more attention to women's health issues.

At the same time, women began making inroads into medicine and health care administration. Female physicians, projected to number 200,000 by 2010, are shaking deeply ingrained gender stereotypes and helping to reshape the practice of medicine. And slowly but surely, as women rise to leadership positions in academic medicine, health care administration, hospital governance, and politics, they are bringing to the system their unique perspectives and experiences as caregivers, neglected for too long.

At the United Hospital Fund, a century-old research and philanthropic organization dedicated to improving health care in New York City and across the nation, we knew that it would be impossible to understand the future of health care without considering questions of gender. To analyze the changing relations between women and the health care system, we sponsored a one-day conference, "Taking Care: The Impact of Women on Health Care," in 1990. The conference grew out of a suggestion by health policy writer and analyst Emily Friedman that was enthusiastically acted on by Bruce C. Vladeck, then president of the Fund. The conference brought together health care providers, administrators, policymakers, advocates, and researchers from across the country to explore these pivotal issues. Conference participants brought deeply felt personal perspectives on the issues, drawing on their own experiences as health care professionals, "informal" caregivers for aging parents, and trailblazers in traditionally masculine worlds. The result was a day that was not only extraordinarily informative, but also often quite moving.

So enthusiastic was the response to the conference that the Fund undertook to publish this book, drawing on and developing the ideas presented at the conference. With sections on women as patients, family caregivers, health care providers, and health care leaders, the book provides a comprehensive look at the issues confronting women today.

Both the conference and the book owe their existence to many people's dedication and hard work. We are especially grateful to the 19 authors who contributed chapters to the volume. We have much to learn from their insights and experiences, which cast new light on women's health care needs and their interactions with the health care system.

Our most profound debt of gratitude is to Emily Friedman, without whom the book would not exist. Her commitment to women's issues and sharp insights into the workings of the health care system set the tone and standard for the volume. Her grasp of the complex forces that have led women to where they stand today and her urgent sense of the battles still to be fought—so eloquently described in Chapter 1—serve as a challenge and inspiration to us all.

At the United Hospital Fund, David Gould and Deborah Halper helped plan the conference; Phyllis Brooks, Sally J. Rogers, Melvin I. Krasner, Avery Hudson, and Barbara Kancelbaum reviewed the manuscripts; and Toni Heisler and Shelley Yates provided invaluable research support. Liza Buffaloe handled the typesetting of the book with her usual style and proficiency.

Both a progress report and a call to action, *An Unfinished Revolution* reminds us that much work remains if we are to create a system that takes good care of women and men alike, while making best use of their respective strengths. When the revolution is finished, we will all enjoy a better, more equitable health care system.

JAMES R. TALLON, JR.
President
United Hospital Fund of New York

Note from the Editor

NO BOOK WITH 19 authors is a snap to produce; however, *An Unfinished Revolution* was an especially challenging project for all who worked on it. I was constantly traveling and being sidetracked by other work; Bruce Vladeck left the leadership of the Fund in mid-book, to be replaced by the eminent James Tallon, Jr.; one of our authors died, and others changed jobs and locations. The book, at times, much as we loved it, became an editor's nightmare.

Four people in particular deserve the credit for this book seeing the light of day. The first is Bruce Vladeck, whose wholehearted commitment and enthusiasm were invaluable. Jim Tallon continued that high level of support from the moment he joined the Fund. Sally Rogers kept the ship on course, providing counsel, making contacts, offering suggestions, talking me out of giving up, and always keeping her eye on the prize.

And my deepest thanks go to Phyllis Brooks, editor *extraordinaire* at the Fund, whose book this is, far more than mine. For years, she read every manuscript in every revision, kept contact with all the authors, conveyed often-complex editorial remarks from me to author and back again, kept track of the progress of every chapter, and constantly kept me informed of where we stood. She solved every problem, dealt with the production people and the printers, and brought us all through.

She would soothe ruffled feathers one day and have to track me down to fax something to some distant location the next, but she never lost her temper, was never ill-mannered, and maintained her patience to the bitter end—no mean feat when the alleged editor of the book was always traipsing around somewhere, working on something other than this project. The book could easily have been dedicated to her.

However, we dedicated it to two other people. Andrea Boroff Eagan, one of our authors and a tireless crusader for women patients' rights, died on March 9, 1993, after a heroic fight with cancer. We regret that she will not see the finished product, but are grateful that her work is part of it.

Ruth Rothstein—hospital executive, civic leader, mentor of women, champion of social justice, a woman so valued in Chicago that the city named a street after her—holds a special place in the story of this book. As one of the speakers at the 1990 conference that inspired *An Unfinished Revolution*, she spoke not only of the need for more women health care leaders, but also, most movingly, of her years of struggle to care for her beloved disabled husband. When the audience rose in a standing ovation, there were few dry eyes. It is thus fitting that we dedicate this volume to her, in the hope that we are moving toward a time when women will face fewer and less formidable obstacles than those she has overcome as a patient, a caregiver, and a health care leader.

EMILY FRIEDMAN

AN UNFINISHED REVOLUTION

1

Women and Health Care: The Bramble and the Rose

Emily Friedman

See how the bramble and the rose intertwine?
Love grows like the bramble and the rose;
'round each other we will twine.
—Traditional folk song

A History as Healers

WOMEN AND HEALING have a long shared history. Eons before anyone thought in terms of formal "health care," women in hunter-gatherer societies bore and tended the children, created and protected the home, and cooked (and often garnered) the food. Because of these roles, women were probably more likely than men to be the guinea pigs of trial-and-error methods that taught human beings about both poisons and healing plants. Indeed, although it was not true in the United States after European immigration began, women in many early cultures became *shamans*, or healers. They still serve in that role in some societies.

In the West, the coming of Christianity produced religious communities that provided both safe haven and what passed for medical care at the time. It is no accident that the terminology that evolved within these communities—"Father," "Brother," "Sister," "Mother"—mimicked that of the family, the most personal of human communities. Nuns excelled as nurses; their expertise placed them among the primary healers of post-Middle Ages Europe. The image of the nurse as nun, in fact, became so much a part of European health care that until recently, in some nations, nurses were still referred to as "sisters" and hospital administrators as "matrons." The nurse's cap with the short veil, so common until World War II, paid homage to the sister-nurses of earlier days.

Yet in more recent times, the relationship of women with health care, in this country as well as others, has been decidedly ambivalent. What began as voluntary (*somewhat* voluntary, anyway) family service and then broadened into social service hardened over the centuries into rigidly defined, gender-bound roles that gradually eroded much of the power that women once held as healers. Women traditional healers may have lingered on in some places, but the healing mission of women largely fell under the control of others.

In fact, as professionalism permeated hospital administration and medicine in this century, women (who had been poorly represented in medicine but were often administrators) lost ground rapidly. Medical schools and hospital administration programs generally would not accept them; if accepted, female graduates in either discipline (but especially the latter) often could not find work.

Nursing remained the province of women, however, and it was guarded jealously—not always with positive results. For example, it is one of the ironies of history that the only nursing schools that would admit men in the late 1800s and early 1900s were the black schools that opened as a response to white schools' refusal to accept African-American applicants.

During and after the Vietnam War, when male military medical corpsmen with extensive combat experience sought to become nurses, they were told that they would have to undertake a complete nursing school education, as though they were novices.[1] The result, in the opinion of some analysts, was the rise of the profession of physician assistant, which to this day often finds itself in conflict with nursing over issues involving scope of practice and professional competence.

But if nursing was female, medicine was male. The first formally educated American woman physician, Elizabeth Blackwell, was admitted to Geneva Medical College in New York in 1847[2]—82 years after the first colonial medical school opened in Philadelphia in 1765. Her sister Emily was rejected by 11 medical schools before being accepted by Rush Medical College in Chicago in 1852.[3] As late as 1970, only 6 percent of U.S. physicians were women, although the situation has changed greatly since; nearly one in five U.S. physicians is female now.[4]

Women Patients: A Difficult Road
Women's history as patients has been more egalitarian, at least on the surface. Indeed, one of the great successes of health care in this century has been a massive reduction in maternal mortality, which helped transform the United States from a nation of widowers to a nation of widows. Even in this half-century, the rate of women dying in childbirth dropped from 73.7 per 100,000 live births in 1950 to 7.2 in 1991.[5] However, the rate for African-American women in 1991 was 18.1.[6] (It is not surprising that we lack federal statistics for African-American maternal mortality in 1950; little attention was directed to that population in that era.)

Women patients have often trod a difficult road, however; sometimes, in fact, they were required to serve as patients and as providers simultaneously. Among those condemned to the dubious charity of the almshouse in seventeenth, eighteenth, and nineteenth century America were prostitutes and women who were pregnant out of wedlock. In 1810, Ezra Stiles Ely, a Presbyterian minister, described a New York City almshouse-hospital as "a grand receptacle of blasted, withered, dying females," most of them prostitutes.[7] When the New York Hospital closed its maternity ward in the 1840s, representatives of the New York Society for the Asylum for Lying-in Women fretted that there would be no recourse for "virtuous" pregnant women but the almshouse, where they would be companions of "degraded, unmarried mothers."[8] From among these outcast women, as (and if) they recovered, were recruited nurses; they were expected to earn their keep, as it were, by caring for those sicker than themselves. In 1835, the Board of Guardians for the Poor in Philadelphia suggested that four women's wards in the almshouse be arranged: "aged and helpless women in bad health, aged and helpless women who can sew and knit, aged and helpless women who are good sewers, [and] spinners."[9] This was certainly rooted in a different philosophy than the diagnosis-specific hospital wards and departments of later times.

That peculiar bit of history illustrates two truths of American women's health care experiences: First, women were expected to be informal healers as well as formal ones, which is still true today, especially in terms of care for family members. Second, the humble origins of hospital nursing might explain, in part, why the profession has had a difficult time gaining respect from other providers such as physicians and administrators, despite its high standing with the public.

But being a "respectable" woman patient in a private hospital was no guarantee that respect would be forthcoming from providers. Women patients historically have often been at a disadvantage in terms of the resources and autonomy allowed them by the health care system; they have been disproportionately victimized by unnecessary care as well as dismissal of symptoms as nothing more than emotional turmoil or menses. Even the rights and wishes of women patients in persistent vegetative states have been ignored far more often by the courts than the preferences of male patients in similar situations.[10]

Discrimination against women patients lingers today. Much of it, probably, was and is unintentional and involuntary. Nonetheless, a significant part of the history of health care's treatment of women is a tale of neglect and paternalism.

A Lingering Doubt

Today, women patients have become far less tolerant of discrimination, intentional or not. What has been perceived as providers' overuse of procedures such as cesarean section and mastectomy and undertreatment for women's cancers and cardiac conditions has led to changes in both policy and attitude.

The change has been striking. In 1975, the late Rose Kushner, founder of the campaign against unnecessary mastectomy, was booed off the stage while attempting to speak to a group of oncological surgeons; in 1990, at the time of her death from breast cancer, that same group was planning to present her with an award. Her memorial service was held at the National Institutes of Health (NIH).

Representative Patricia Schroeder (D-CO) and other women in Congress have made a public issue of the exclusion of women from clinical research trials, and forced a change in policy at the NIH, which today supports an Office of Research on Women's Health (ORWH). In 1993, its first year of operation, ORWH identified several areas of women's health for "special consideration" in funding, including depression; alcohol use and appropriate interventions; abuse and violence; lung cancer in women; antiprogestins and reproductive health, cancer, or meningioma; and risk factors for disease in women of different racial, ethnic, and/or economic groups.[11]

However, there is so much need among women in the United States that there are pitifully few laurels to rest on. The 1993 Commonwealth Fund Survey of Women's Health found that in the previous 12 months, more than one-third of American women did not have a Pap smear, a breast examination, a pelvic examination, or a complete physical.[12] Of all women, 13 percent did not receive needed care; 44 percent of women aged 50 or older had not undergone a mammogram in the previous year; 40 percent of women reported experiencing severe depression; and 6 percent of women reported having considered suicide.[13] A Kaiser Family Foundation survey has found that although 55 percent of non-Hispanic white women receive preventive health services, 57 percent of African-American and Latino women do not.[14]

Furthermore, women are less likely to have private insurance, although they are more likely to receive Medicaid, largely because Medicaid is targeted to extremely low-income persons receiving Aid to Families with Dependent Children; these families make up more than 70 percent of the Medicaid population. The program also subsidizes long-term care for low-income elderly patients, the vast majority of whom are women.[15] Of the nearly 11 million Americans who spend more than 10 percent of their total income on health care, 69 percent are women.[16]

The fact that women dominate the over-65 and especially the over-85 population means that they are more vulnerable than men to excesses, abuses, and inequities in long-term care insurance and services. One cannot help but wonder if the low priority assigned in most health care reform proposals to long-term care services reflects not only the very difficult financial and actuarial issues involved, but also the fact that 80 percent of the beneficiaries of such services are elderly women. Nancy Jecker has suggested, in fact, that calls for rationing of health care based on patient age would automatically (and perhaps not unintentionally) seriously discriminate against women, and that another, fairer criterion would be preferable.[17]

Changes—Quick and Slow
Today, women are in a curious position, standing at yet another of the many crossroads that delineate women's history in this country. There were 127.5 million women in 1990—51 percent of the population.[18] The earnings of women who worked year-round in 1992 averaged $21,440; the comparable figure for men was $30,358.[19] Women con-

tinue to be overrepresented in service professions such as clerical, administrative, and health care (they are 77 percent of the work force in these areas), and underrepresented in production, craft, repair, and labor occupations, at 9.5 percent.[20]

They continue to make progress in health care. In 1988, women earned 32.8 percent of degrees from medical schools (the rate is higher now), an estimated 28.2 percent of degrees from osteopathic medical schools, 27.2 percent of degrees from dental schools, 37.3 percent of degrees from schools of optometry, and 50.1 percent of degrees from schools of veterinary medicine.[21] By contrast, in 1949-50, those figures were, respectively, 10.4 percent, 5.5 percent, 0.7 percent, 1.1 percent, and 1.5 percent.[22]

However, on other rungs of the health professions ladder, women have progressed only marginally since 1985, when Irene Butter and her colleagues published their landmark work on the health professions and gender.[23] They found health care heavily gender-segregated. Women dominated in virtually all job categories that the study dubbed "psycho-social," whether they involved high, moderate, or little autonomy. These included the professions of nurse practitioner, medical social worker, most nursing jobs, and most aides.

In "somatic-diagnostic curing" professions that have greater autonomy, such as medicine and osteopathy, women were in a distinct minority. In other professions in this category where autonomy was lower, such as physical therapy, dietetics, and respiratory therapy, women predominated. In technical health professions, women's representation depended on the degree of autonomy the work involved. The ranks of opticians and pharmacists, who enjoy high autonomy, included few women. However, women represented the vast majority of technical workers with lower autonomy, such as medical secretaries and medical records specialists. Indeed, there did not appear to be any male medical secretaries at all.[24]

Yet there is evidence that a revolution is in the making. Dozens of women were elected to Congress in 1992; many analysts attributed this, in part, to the bitter confirmation hearings for Clarence Thomas as an associate justice of the U.S. Supreme Court, and the controversy over Professor Anita Hill's allegations of his sexual improprieties. These new senators and congressmen have been prominent in debates over health care reform, Medicaid, women's health, and gun control. It will be interesting to see how many of them retain their seats in the next election.

Women are flooding into medical schools and may well represent the majority of medical practitioners by the year 2020, if not before. Nursing seems destined to garner more power, and broader clinical autonomy, as a result of public policy interest in making primary care the basis of the health care system (difficult as that will be to achieve in reality).

Consumerist women (and several bitter public fights) have made medical researchers far more sensitive to the need for gender equity in research priorities, funding, and ethics. Whatever comes of recent scandals involving the validity of research on the relative value of lumpectomy versus mastectomy in the treatment of breast cancer, it seems inevitable that future studies using women patients will be far less cavalier in the collection and reporting of data. Women's causes have also benefited, ironically, from recurring scandals over dubious treatment of women patients, including the widespread use of allegedly unsafe silicon breast implants. Perhaps the world is changing, after all.

But even if there is a revolution in some places, the health care world is not changing for all women. Those at the bottom of the employment ladder remain disproportionately female and minority, lacking chances for advancement, and often vulnerable to reduced wages and benefits, relegation to part-time work, and layoffs as the health care field reconfigures itself. Aging women are at greater risk of losing private health insurance than ever before. Women, because they are the ones who get pregnant, remain the targets of complex and increasingly ugly public battles over abortion, reproductive rights, and fetal health. The women's health care revolution is far from over.

Furthermore, greater statistical representation for women in this or that health care profession or research cohort represents only one kind of equity. There is another kind that has long been sought: societal consensus that women contribute to health care in the same way and to the same degree as men (if not more). Although success in this quest would be extremely helpful to women seeking equal pay for equal work, the fact is that women's contributions to health care are strikingly different from those made by men, and always have been.

Are Women Different?

Women have debated for decades—probably centuries—what it is that they bring to health care. One contribution is thought to be a more sensitive practice style. Since the flowering of American feminism, it has been widely thought that women physicians and nurses are more caring and more receptive to women's concerns than are men.

However, even if this perception is accurate, the fact remains that three-quarters of American women physicians are younger than 45; is their more patient-sensitive practice style the result of gender or of age? We may never know. On the other hand, it is unquestionable that women health care professionals and women patients share an exclusive bond: after all, no male obstetrician ever gave birth. Women patients, especially younger ones, may seek such a bond with their physicians, and that, in turn, would likely lead to a more trusting patient-physician relationship.

Yet women physicians' relations with women nurses are often as contentious as those of male physicians,[25] and women obstetricians seem to get sued at the same rate as men.[26]

It has also long been argued that women who serve on health care boards are more patient-oriented. However, as has been pointed out by Mary Jane Anderson, a Seattle hospital trustee, women on boards bring both advantages and problems. The advantages include a tendency (both trained and innate) to indeed be publicly compassionate and caring—an opportunity often denied men by society or by men themselves. But men are also taught, on the sporting field and elsewhere, to compete, win or lose, and then forget their differences; women, taught to compete in arenas with bigger stakes, such as protection of their children, tend to hold grudges long after the debate is over.[27] This kind of bitterness can compromise the effectiveness of a board.

Perhaps the most convincing (if not the most politically correct) argument is that women bring both unique gifts and unique drawbacks to health care, as caregiving professionals, as informal caregivers, and as patients. On the positive side, most women have more intimate childrearing experience than men (although this is said to be changing), and thus come to health care with more knowledge of the fears and concerns of vulnerable individuals. Women are also the primary health educators in their homes. Women are allowed by society to express emotion, to discuss delicate subjects with strangers, and to touch people they do not know, including members of their own sex, without the kind of questioning or recrimination that such behavior by men might provoke.

At least in recent decades, women have been better educated about their bodies, and can talk about bodily functions more easily. Women are also far more likely to be able to talk about serious or uncomfortable issues—pregnancy, birth control, severe or terminal illness—with each other than are men. And women, when concerned or angry, can be tenacious advocates and foes, as the history of women's health care consumerism has shown.

However, the capacity for emotional expression that makes women good caregivers can also become a capacity for emotional overexpression, which at times is inappropriate or even disruptive. Women, especially in organizations, are more likely to commit the opposing sins of being either too passive or overly aggressive. This is nowhere so true as in professional associations dominated by women, such as nursing groups, which have often been self-destructive in terms of their internal bickering.

Women in health care also tend to emulate some of the worst habits of men in health care, such as arrogance, hierarchical thinking, and lack of accountability. Nursing education, for example, adopted most of the worst elements of medical education, including a pecking order in which nonpracticing academics disdain practitioners. White women who occupy most of the limited number of top-level slots in health care held by their sex have not done nearly enough to aid their minority sisters in less prestigious jobs, who often have been left untouched by women's progress toward the top of the heap.

And for all the legitimate gripes women patients have about male (and sometimes female) physicians' patronizing ways, it must be noted that women patients often do not speak up, do not ask the hard questions, and do not demand the respect that is due them. A health care culture that historically has relegated women to second-class citizenship is not going to change unless prompted to do so. Too often, women have accepted their lower status all too willingly, whether as patients or as providers.

In the end, the fact is that women's contributions to and problems with the health care system are neither automatically more important nor less important than those of men. They are simply different.

This is to be expected. The health care system, since its inception, has mirrored society's values and preferences. When society sought to segregate and punish women who did not follow its rigid rules, so did hospitals. When men rose to control positions of power and influence in society, so men rose to control similar positions in health care. When women were relegated to extraordinarily meaningful and productive, but nonetheless underpaid and underrecognized, roles in society, the same thing happened to them in health care, a field that, centuries before, they had dominated.

And as men and women in the larger society grapple with basic issues of justice, equality, role delineation, and uniqueness of gender, so the same struggles are being played out in health care. When one hears a woman pilot address the passengers on a commercial airliner, or the husband of a governor describe his experiences, one is reminded that the gender-based revolutions that are shaking parts of the world of healing are occurring in other fields as well.

In the public mind, however, there is a difference when it comes to health care. To the average person today, as in earlier times, health care has a female character. Those traits associated (accurately or not) with women—nurturing, visible emotion, unconditional love, acceptance of flaws, strength in the face of adversity—are traits that the sick or injured person wants in a health care provider. The hopes and expectations associated with that preference are not likely to change.

So the issue of how women and health care interact is more than a question of turf or gender-blindness. It is a question of extending woman-associated virtues throughout the field. Just as some men asked, when women's health centers sprang up across the land, if there might be a similar flowering of men's health centers, so we might ask if the positive values women are thought to bring to health care could be broadly disseminated by men and women alike. These values are not the exclusive province of women; men can express them in their health care work. It may simply be a matter of society giving them permission to do so.

In 1873, Father Damien de Veuster, a young Belgian-born priest, voluntarily settled on the Hawaiian island of Molokai to minister to the Hansen's disease (leprosy) patients who had been exiled there.[28] He lived a heroic but often lonely existence until, in the late 1880s, Mother Marianne Kopp, a Franciscan nun, joined him.

She shared his work, ministered to his spiritual needs, and was in many ways his salvation until he died of Hansen's disease in 1889. She continued their work for many years after that. Theirs was a partnership that immeasurably improved the lot of thousands of sick people condemned to live out their lives in miserable exile. That partnership of a caring and heroic man and a caring and heroic woman, both de-voted first and foremost to their patients, is a model deserving of emulation today.

Women and health care are inextricably intertwined, like a bramble and a rose. The good and the bad come with the territory. Health care has both used women and benefited them. It has largely excluded them from professions where they could do much good, yet it gave them, in nursing, one of the most beloved professions in American society. It has often been paternalistic toward their diseases and concerns, yet it has also largely eliminated some of the horrible scourges that claimed the lives of women over the centuries. It has been extraordinarily dependent on women workers, and has succeeded because of them, but has often relegated them to positions of powerlessness.

The relationship of women and health care is rich, complex, and fraught with risk on both sides; each threatens the other's status quo. But the fact is that, at the end of the twentieth century as it was in the Middle Ages, women and health care are stuck with each other. Women will always need to work in health care, and health care will always need women to do so. Women will always need health care, and women in health care will always provide it. Outside of the formal system, women will remain the primary providers of health care in families, and women, especially in their later years, will be the primary beneficiaries of that old kindness. As a new millennium dawns, our challenge is to see to it that this strange but inevitable partnership between a form of caring and those who care and are cared for becomes stronger—and more equal.

Notes

1. E. Friedman, "Troubled Past of 'Invisible' Profession," *Journal of the American Medical Association* 264(22)(1990):2851-2856.

2. Ruth J. Abram, *"Send Us a Lady Physician": Women Doctors in America* (New York: W.W. Norton & Co., 1985).

3. Ibid.

4. E. Friedman, "Changing the Ranks of Medicine: Women MDs," *Medical World News* 29(8)(1988):56-68.

5. National Center for Health Statistics, "Maternal Mortality Rates for Complications of Pregnancy, Childbirth, and the Puerperium, According to Race and Age: United States, Selected Years, 1950-1990," in *Health, United States, 1993* (Hyattsville, MD: U.S. Public Health Service, 1993).

6. Ibid.

7. Charles E. Rosenberg, *The Care of Strangers* (New York: Basic Books, 1987).

8. Ibid.

9. Ibid.

10. S. Miles and A. August, "Courts, Gender, and 'the Right to Die,'" *Law, Medicine, and Health Care* 18(1-2)(1990):85-95.

11. Rosemary Torres, "A Vision for Women's Health Research in the 21st Century," *NAWHP Focus* (Fall 1993):1.

12. Louis Harris and Associates, *The Commonwealth Fund Survey of Women's Health* (New York: The Commonwealth Fund, 1993).

13. Ibid.

14. Women's Research and Education Institute, *Women's Health Insurance Costs and Experiences* (Menlo Park, CA: Henry J. Kaiser Family Foundation, 1994).

15. Ibid.

16. Ibid.

17. N. Jecker, "Age-based Rationing and Women," *Journal of the American Medical Association* 266(21)(1991):3012-3015.

18. Bureau of the Census, "Facts from the Census Bureau for Women's History Month" (press release), March 4, 1994.

19. Ibid.

20. Ibid.

21. Health Resources and Services Administration, U.S. Department of Health and Human Services, *Minorities and Women in the Health Fields*, 1990 Edition, HRSA-P-DV 90-3, June 1990.

22. Ibid.

23. Irene Butter et al., *Sex and Status: Hierarchies in the Health Workforce* (Washington, DC: American Public Health Association, 1985).

24. Ibid.

25. Friedman, 1988.

26. "Malpractice Risk the Same for Female, Male OB/GYNs," *Medical Staff Leader* 21(12)(1992):3.

27. E. Friedman, *Women on Health Care Boards: Their Changing Role* (Chicago: Hospital Research and Educational Trust, 1987).

28. Gavan Daws, *Holy Man* (Honolulu: University of Hawaii Press, 1973).

I

WOMEN AS USERS OF HEALTH SERVICES

Women are the primary users of the health care system. They average one-third more physician visits, one-fourth more hospital discharges, and 5 percent more hospital days of care than men. Of all nursing home residents, 75 percent are women, as are 81 percent of those over the age of 85. Women represent 60 percent of Medicare beneficiaries and the vast majority of adults who receive Medicaid benefits.

Yet as the chapters in this section attest, women's relationship with the health care system has not always been a comfortable one. There is abundant evidence that suggests patterns of discrimination against women patients, intentional or not. Certainly controversies over high rates of cesarean section, less timely and comprehensive diagnosis and treatment of women with heart disease, and the use of mastectomy for breast cancer have grown from clinical disagreements to public crusades. The exclusion of women from most clinical trials and unequal funding for research into problems that affect mostly women have also led to heated public policy debate—and changes in policy. The courts, too, have been accused of bias against women in areas such as reproductive rights and termination of treatment.

However, it is also true that the health care system is changing in terms of its attitudes and practices regarding women. Dedicated centers for women's health, targeted programs for the frail elderly (the majority of whom are women), and efforts to equalize women's standing in research activities are all becoming part of the health care landscape. Much remains to be done, however, especially in terms of vulnerable populations, such as low-income women of color and aging women. The changing relationship between women and the providers that treat them is destined for yet more change.

2

The Women's Health Movement and Its Lasting Impact

Andrea Boroff Eagan

IN JANUARY 1970, Senator Gaylord Nelson presided over hearings in the U.S. Senate concerning the content of an informational sheet to be packaged with a woman's monthly prescribed dose of birth control pills. The safety of the pill, which had then been on the market for less than a decade, was not the central issue of these hearings, even though such questions had been raised a few months earlier with the publication of Barbara Seaman's book *The Doctors' Case Against the Pill* (P.H. Wyden, 1969). The issue was just how much information women consumers really needed about the product they were beginning to use by the millions. Only male doctors testified. Some reported adverse effects of the pill and argued that full information be provided to women. More typically, one prominent professor of gynecology, arguing that information itself could have harmful side effects, opined: "If you tell a woman she may get a headache, she'll get a headache."[1]

The hearings were most remarkable, however, for an event that occurred during the proceedings, which extended over several months. A group of women from Washington Women's Liberation repeatedly disrupted the hearings, protesting the fact that all those testifying were men (rather than women who had some first-hand experience with the drug in question) and objecting to the tone of much of what was said. The hearing room had to be cleared several times. So began the women's health movement.

Andrea Boroff Eagan died in 1993. This chapter, written in 1990, reflects her keen understanding and grasp of the rapidly changing field of health care consumerism.—EF

The Beginnings of the Movement

In the ferment of the larger women's movement of the early 1970s, among the discussions of sex and art and housework, were many about health and medicine. Often these discussions were little more than information sharing and referrals, and some never went beyond the most superficial level. But many women's groups included nurses, other medical professionals, and women who had some serious interest in health and medical matters. And some of these women went on to a more sustained and organized connection with medicine.

Some groups began to do research, to pool information, and to produce health-related literature of their own. One such group, the Boston Women's Health Course Collective, was composed of groups of women who shared knowledge, did research, discussed the information they found, checked it against their own experiences, and then wrote it all up. The product of this collective effort was a 136-page newsprint book called *Women and Their Bodies*, issued in 1971. The book covered topics ranging from basic sexual and reproductive anatomy to birth control, abortion, childbirth, sexuality, and dealing with medical professionals and institutions. Its price was 30 cents. One year later, 65,000 copies were in print, and the book's title had achieved its final form: *Our Bodies, Ourselves*. Today, at 352 pages and published by Simon & Schuster, the book is still in print and still the fundamental source of information for women who want to learn about themselves for themselves. It remains a collaborative effort (the collective eventually changed its name to the Boston Women's Health *Book* Collective), with contributions by scores of women, many of them self-educated in a particular area.

Similar courses were initiated in other parts of the United States. In New York, "Know Your Body" courses educated a generation of women. Some teachers and students coalesced into the Women's Health Organizing Collective and HealthRight, which published pamphlets on topics ranging from vaginal infections to abortion, as well as a quarterly newsletter that addressed topics from genetic engineering to home birth. In San Francisco, the Coalition for the Medical Rights of Women did education and political work. In several cities, informal self-help groups obtained training and opened women's clinics, eventually forming the Federation of Feminist Women's Health Centers. By 1977, there were 1,200 women's health groups, of varying sizes, with varying agendas, operating in the United States.

Making Abortion Safe and Legal

In many states before the *Roe v. Wade* decision in 1973, the women's movement was heavily involved in the campaign to legalize abortion. At the same time, some groups helped women to obtain safe, though illegal, abortions. In Chicago, where abortion was illegal until 1973, members of a group called "Jane" referred women to licensed physicians who would perform abortions, accompanied women to the physicians' offices, and eventually performed abortions themselves. In New York, where abortion was illegal until 1970, the Women's Health and Abortion Project and the Clergy Consultation Service referred women to physicians around the country who would perform abortions.

The women who made referrals quickly realized that they were in a position to make demands—concerning both price and quality of service—of the doctors to whom they referred. Thus, they could assure the women who sought their assistance of high-quality medical care, they were able to negotiate reasonable prices, and they could persuade the doctors to whom they referred to provide a number of free or very low-cost abortions for women who needed them.

In those states, like New York and Colorado, where abortion was legal before 1973, and in other states after the Supreme Court decision, many women went to work as practitioners, counselors, and ancillary staff at newly established abortion clinics. In New York, among other states, pre-procedure and birth control counseling was mandated by law as an integral part of the abortion procedure. Women's movement activists, working as counselors, took the opportunity to instruct their patients about the struggle to legalize abortion and the significance of the very existence of a legal abortion clinic, as well as about the medical particulars of the procedure they would undergo. Abortion was viewed by these counselors as a positive step in a woman's life, an opportunity for her to take control and make sound decisions, as well as a point of entry into the larger women's movement.

Some of the clinics became alternative models for health care for women. They were not, of course, comprehensive, but within the limits of the services that were provided, women were treated with respect, their questions were answered, they were given full information about such things as medical procedures and contraceptive choices, and they were encouraged to make responsible decisions. The high quality of some of these services encouraged women who were involved with them to apply the standards established for abortion clinics to other medical institutions.

Childbirth as a Natural Phenomenon

At the same time in the early 1970s, the natural childbirth movement, which overlapped the women's health movement, was gaining strength. As the women's health movement took as its guiding books *Our Bodies, Ourselves; The Doctors' Case Against the Pill;* and *Witches, Midwives and Nurses: A History of Women Healers* (Feminist Press, 1972), the childbirth movement had Grantly Dickread's *Childbirth Without Fear* (HarperCollins, 1979) and Marjorie Karmel's *Thank You, Dr. Lamaze* (Harper & Row, 1981). Although both books had been originally published years earlier, the movement they sparked did not really take off until the 1970s.

Women began demanding some control over routine hospital birth procedures, in the hope of "demedicalizing" what they considered a normal, healthy process. They demanded that the use of anesthetics and other drugs be minimized and that they be permitted to have a husband or other support person with them through the delivery. Some doctors joined enthusiastically in the natural (or prepared) childbirth movement, recognizing that birth was usually an uncomplicated event. In other cases, however, husbands had to handcuff themselves to their wives and threaten hospital personnel with assault charges to avoid "standard" treatment.

Some women opted out of the medical system altogether, and home birth increased in popularity. Sometimes, attendants were nurse-midwives, with the standard training that was still available in a few places. In other cases, women were attended by lay midwives—some with extensive on-the-job training, some with relatively little skill—or simply by family and friends. Very few physicians have supported home birth under any circumstances, however, and some feminists have questioned the earth-mother romanticism of some advocates of home birth.

However, at the same time that the natural childbirth movement was gaining strength, new technological advances such as fetal monitors and a rising rate of cesarean sections seemed to be pulling in the other direction. In part because the Lamaze method gained ascendancy over other styles of childbirth preparation, and because most Lamaze teaching stressed the importance of the woman's (voluntary) cooperation with the physician, doctors were usually able to persuade women in labor of the need (as the doctor saw it) for drugs, monitoring, or surgery. The cesarean section rate, which was around 5 percent in the United States in 1970, rocketed to 25 percent nationally in 1988, reaching almost 50 percent in some hospitals. Two new groups, one opposing unnecessary cesarean sections and the other encouraging vaginal birth after cesarean section, were called forth.

Healthy Skepticism
At the same moment that these diverse movements were gaining strength, other events conspired to alert women medical consumers to the inadvisability of relying on physicians without question. The adverse reports in 1969 and 1970 on the safety of the birth control pill were only the first blow. Those were followed, in 1971, by the revelation that diethylstilbestrol (DES), used by millions of women over almost a quarter century to prevent miscarriage and "to make a healthy pregnancy healthier," had caused an array of problems, including sometimes fatal vaginal cancers in the daughters of the women who had taken the drug.

In 1974, it was revealed that the Dalkon Shield, an intrauterine contraceptive device, was the cause of severe pelvic infections in many of its users. The Dalkon Shield had been particularly recommended for women who had not yet borne any children, many of whom were rendered sterile by these infections. Within another few years, it became clear that many doctors and the manufacturer of the shield had been aware of the problems it was causing, but did nothing to warn women who already wore it or to remove it from use. Dalkon Shield "survivors" organized support networks, sued in great numbers, and were eventually recognized as affected parties when the shield's manufacturer, the A.H. Robins Company, declared bankruptcy. The Dalkon Shield revelations resulted in pressure from women's health organizations on the U.S. Food and Drug Administration (FDA) to include medical devices, not only drugs, in its review procedures. The change in FDA practice was in fact made, resulting in regulatory oversight of a range of products, including intrauterine devices, pacemakers, and cosmetic and reconstructive implants.

In 1975, the *New England Journal of Medicine* published an article reporting that the use of estrogen by menopausal women caused a 5- to 14-fold increase in the rate of uterine cancer in its users.[2] These and similar though less stunning revelations—of the dangers of certain drugs used in obstetrics, the high rates of dilation and curettage (D&C) and hysterectomy, the widespread practice of prescribing Valium and other tranquilizers to women who complained of a variety of physical symptoms—alarmed and alerted women to potential problems with their medical care. In keeping with the spirit of the 1970s, women began questioning and challenging their doctors, especially their obstetricians and gynecologists. Relying on what was by then becoming a vast amount of educational material, most of it consumer-written, women in ever-greater numbers began asking doctors about side effects and alternatives and questioning the necessity of many procedures.

The Battle over Breast Cancer

In 1975, a book titled *Why Me?* (Saunders), by Rose Kushner, a well-established medical writer, explored the state of breast cancer treatment in America. Kushner, herself diagnosed with breast cancer, was outraged by standard practice at the time and by the attitudes of many of the surgeons and oncologists she encountered. Customarily, at that time, women were taken in for breast biopsy, and if the lump proved on frozen section to be malignant, a mastectomy—usually a Halsted radical mastectomy—was performed immediately. The Halsted radical, originated in the 1920s, involved the removal of the entire breast, all the axillary lymph nodes, and the underlying chest wall muscle; a thin layer of skin was left to cover the rib cage. Some surgeons excised the subclavicular nodes, as well. Women awoke to face not only a diagnosis of cancer but disabling and disfiguring surgery.

Kushner, aware of the dismal survival statistics for women with breast cancer, investigated alternatives such as lumpectomy, already widely available in Europe, and new forms of chemotherapy. She attacked the practice of simultaneous biopsy and mastectomy as medically unnecessary, since there was no evidence that a delay of up to two weeks between the procedures contributed at all to morbidity or mortality. In addition, she argued, the practice kept women from participating in the decision as to what kind of surgery to have or even in the choice of which surgeon would perform the procedures after the biopsy. She questioned medicine's reliance on standard practices that were without adequate scientific foundation, and she believed that giving a woman a full role in the decisions concerning her treatment could only improve her prognosis.

Kushner's book was a bombshell. Although her arguments had the support of only a few prominent breast surgeons and faced the sometimes strong resistance of others, women began demanding changes in practice. Many surgeons were willing to consider the data objectively and to accede to the demands of their patients for less radical surgery. Kushner's presentation of the evidence that radiation following a radical mastectomy decreased the chances of survival was the death knell of that particular practice. The Halsted radical fell out of favor relatively quickly, since there was no evidence that removing the chest muscle did anything to improve the chances of survival, and most women, once they knew of an alternative, objected strenuously. Nonetheless, the modified radical mastectomy—in which the breast and some or all of the lymph nodes are removed—remains popular (at least with surgeons). To this day, in many parts of the United States, mastectomy is routinely recommended for most breast cancer patients, despite evidence that in the great majority of cases, it confers no survival benefit.

In the mid-1970s, publication of the results of major European studies of combination chemotherapy for breast cancer began to bring treatment into the modern era. Kushner and other writers, in magazine articles, books, and television appearances, brought these advances to the attention of women. By the late 1970s, large-scale clinical trials of various surgical and chemotherapeutic regimens were begun and the results—issued periodically in the professional literature and publicized in the popular media—accelerated the changes in practice.

To come full circle, women with breast cancer, inspired by groups such as ACT-UP, an organization active on behalf of people with AIDS, have recently begun organizing to demand changes in the way they are treated. Although there have long been support groups for cancer patients, they have been primarily concerned with helping patients cope with the emotional and physical impact of their disease and their treatment. These new groups, Breast Cancer Action and CAN-ACT among them, focus on public education and political advocacy. Among their urgent concerns are the slow pace of research into new treatments for breast cancer and the long delays in getting new advances to the patients who need them. Their public education campaigns are intended to inform breast cancer patients directly of new treatments, the results of studies, and the relative merits of various regimens. With the rising incidence of breast cancer, the groups are also concerned with research into causes and prevention of the disease.

Deconstructing the Doctor-Patient Relationship
As women became aware of the imperfections in the medical care they were getting, some began to offer a critique of the dynamics of the doctor-patient relationship. An attitude that many women felt was all too typical was expressed by one doctor during the Congressional hearings about the birth control pill in 1970. In opposing labeling that would enumerate the risks of the pill, he said: "A misguided effort to inform such women leads only to anxiety on their part and loss of confidence in the physician . . . They want [the doctor] to tell them what to do, not to confuse them by asking them to make decisions beyond their comprehension . . . The idea of informing such a woman is not possible."

Our Bodies, Ourselves and the other works and courses that it spawned, as well as the whole women's health movement, were informed by the belief that women had the right to full and accurate information concerning diagnosis, treatment, and treatment alternatives; that women should be full partners in making decisions about their health; and that they were capable of making reasonable decisions given adequate, accurate information. Women also knew that the doctor-patient relationship, in its common form, was unequal. Although everyone expected and accepted that doctors had special expertise, no one liked being patronized, having questions and concerns dismissed, or being advised to allow the doctor to decide what was best. Again, this subject was raised informally in groups and in conversation. In addition, the doctor-patient relationship was formally deconstructed, first in popular works, such as *For Her Own Good: One Hundred Fifty Years of Expert's Advice to Women*, by Barbara Ehrenreich and Deirdre English (Doubleday, 1989), and later in a host of academic studies that examined both the form and the content of communication. Over and over, the findings confirmed what women knew: Questions were answered, if at all, at a lower level of complexity than they were asked. Real symptoms were deemed imaginary (providing one explanation for the huge number of tranquilizer prescriptions). Physicians resented having their judgment questioned or their recommendations challenged, sometimes becoming openly hostile.

Poor communication was more than just irritating. Inadequate information resulted in unnecessary surgery, as documented by a number of studies, among them Sue Fisher's study of decision making in hysterectomy cases.[3] Fisher found that most patients were inadequately informed of their diagnoses and their options, which led to a number of procedures that might have been avoided.

Doctors' training, which reflected general social attitudes, reinforced negative stereotypes. One popular gynecology text, in widespread use up through the 1970s (when most doctors now practicing were trained), stated in a discussion of pelvic pain: "Perhaps the greatest diagnostic aid is the patience to listen to the patient's complaints and the intelligence to sift out fact from fancy." Pharmaceutical advertising for tranquilizers, sedatives, and treatments for menopause in medical journals regularly portrayed women as emotional, irrational, irritable, dependent, unreliable, and prone to psychosomatic complaints. This advertising did not escape the notice of women's health activists, who often wondered publicly and in widely read articles about its probable effect on impressionable young physicians.

Symptoms that would occasion thorough workups in men were often dismissed when they occurred in women. In one study conducted at the University of California at San Diego in 1979, 52 men and 52 women complained to physicians of symptoms such as chest pain, fatigue, headaches, and dizziness. The men, in *every* case, were given more thorough workups than the women.

Women, paradoxically, were often overtreated, as well. Hysterectomy (one-third to one-half, in most studies, were deemed unnecessary), D&C, and the increasingly popular cesarean section are frequently cited as particularly abused. Prescription of drugs whose side effects were unknown or ignored—tranquilizers, hormones, DES, birth control pills—without adequate history or workup was also cause for criticism and alarm.

As women learned to assert themselves in other spheres, their new behavior inevitably carried over into the doctor-patient relationship. Middle-class women, better educated and better paid than their mothers and older sisters, were often unwilling to tolerate long waits in the doctor's office, being called by their first names, or having their concerns dismissed. They asked questions, took notes, and did research on their own. Some doctors resisted the change; others tried to find a more positive response.

The New Medical Training
The women's movement, antidiscrimination lawsuits, and affirmative action programs created in response began to change the makeup of

medical school classes. In the early 1970s, women constituted 5 to 10 percent of entering medical school classes. Today, almost half of medical students are women (see Chapter 8, "Women in Medicine," and Chapter 9, "The Woman Physician"). Their presence has changed the style and the content of medical education. Some of the gross sexism has been muted or disappeared, and, according to a handful of studies on the subject, the presence of relatively large numbers of women has increased the valuation of communication skills in doctors in training.

The "new" medical training, in doctor-patient communication and psychosocial issues, as well as—in some instances—courses in literature or art, has been incorporated into the curricula of almost all the nation's medical schools. In residency programs, such training is frequently an integral part of the education of young doctors in internal medicine, family practice, and pediatrics. Training in the medical interview involves observation skills, learning to look at body language, to assess the patient's tone and demeanor. Doctors learn to ask open-ended questions at the beginning of the interview and to focus only gradually on specific symptoms. They also learn not to interrupt, since patients often have a lot to contribute to their own diagnosis. Practicing physicians, trained in continuing education seminars, have also begun applying these new techniques.

For Women Only

In the 1970s, some women, not content with simply critiquing existing medical institutions and impatient with the prospects of changing them, began providing medical care on their own. Freestanding clinics were established in many cities, some grouped into the Federation of Feminist Women's Health Centers. They provided clinical care, birth control, abortions, education, and training in self-help techniques. Some provided menstrual extraction; some offered artificial insemination. The centers also furnished a locus for political activism on issues such as access to health care, abortion rights, and product safety. All these clinics shared a fundamental philosophy: that the woman herself should have control over her health care.

Only a few of these original clinics still exist. Many fell victim to the financial pressures created when public funds for family planning and abortion services were restricted in many states; others had difficulty finding physicians who would serve under a board made up primarily of lay women. In some areas, local medical societies pressured physicians not to work at the centers. In Florida, one Feminist Women's Health Center successfully sued the local medical society for restraint of trade.

Despite their problems, the clinics were popular with many women. In addition to offering a wide range of services, many had hours that suited the schedules of working women with children; on-site child care was usually available. Many of the services were provided by midwives, nurses, physician assistants, and lay people. The atmosphere was nonauthoritarian and nonthreatening. Young women, single women, women of color, and lesbians could feel comfortable. For many women, it was the first example they had ever found of an institution in which they were not made to feel like second-class citizens.

For some women, the feminist health centers offered an entry point into the system as providers, as well. Some women went on to get degrees as nurses, midwives, physician assistants, or physicians. Others eventually found their way into administrative positions in more traditional institutions.

In the 1980s, the feminist clinics served as a model for women's medical centers established as adjuncts to hospitals in many communities. These centers provide primary care and take referrals for many conditions from doctors and clinics at the sponsoring institution, as well as refer patients to the parent institution for surgery and other services not available at the satellite facility. Most provide comprehensive primary care, prenatal and postpartum care, birth control counseling, and, where possible, abortion. They are usually staffed largely or exclusively by women, often utilizing the skills of nurses, physician assistants, and midwives, along with women physicians. Many have evening and weekend hours and child care on site.

The difference between these new hospital-affiliated centers and the feminist model lies at the policy-making level and in the fundamental philosophy. The former are under the control of the hospital administration, not independent groups of women, including providers and consumers. At the feminist health centers, practice evolved from the conviction that every woman has a right to control her body and to be the primary decision-maker about questions affecting her own health and care. At the hospital-affiliated centers, the fundamental feminist concept of health care for women and by women is usually lost. The new centers may do little more than provide routine services that some physicians find tedious, such as breast exams and birth control counseling, and serve as sources of referrals for other, often male, specialists. Their existence may serve to provide uninformed patients for services deemed questionable by some, such as "preconception care," progesterone treatment for premenstrual syndrome, and osteoporosis screening. As many women have come to express a preference for female physicians, a women's health center may also help a hospital in recruiting women doctors to practice at the institution. Nonetheless, the potential of these centers—not only as profit-makers for their parent institutions, but as a center for women's empowerment and education and the delivery of top-quality primary care—is considerable.

Research, Development, and Activism

Another area in which the women's health movement and consumerism have had a significant impact on health care is drug research and approval. Consistent with its beginnings at the U.S. Senate hearings on the birth control pill, the women's health care consumer movement has never lost interest in the safety of drugs and devices, both those already on the market and those awaiting approval. Numerous groups— the National Women's Health Network and the Public Interest Health Research Group chief among them—have testified again and again before the FDA, Congress, and other bodies. These groups were involved, in the wake of the Dalkon Shield disaster in the mid-1970s, in lobbying to have the FDA's mandate extended to cover devices as well as drugs. They have taken positions on subjects ranging from breast implants to birth control pills. These consumer groups have been instrumental in blocking approval for some products, sometimes to the chagrin of the pharmaceutical manufacturers.

Some organizations that began as patient support groups, such as DES Action (for women whose mothers had been given DES) and the Endometriosis Association, have evolved into strong, vocal national groups that lobby, provide information and education, and even support research. These and other groups that grew out of the self-help movement of the 1970s form another important strand in the fabric of consumerism.

The number of women's health groups and the level of their activism have certainly declined since the 1970s. But the concerns of the women's health movement and the changes that it demanded and effected have become part of the fabric of women's health care in this country. The acceptance of husbands and partners in labor and delivery, the official scrutiny of medical devices, the routine appearance of both lay and professional women at FDA and Congressional hearings on medical matters, the existence of thousands of self-help and support groups for women facing a variety of medical problems, the growing emphasis on empathy and communication as important skills for the physician, women's insistence on being treated as full-fledged adults in the medical encounter—all virtually unknown 20 years ago—have become unremarkable elements in today's medical care. All this is testimony to the powerful and pervasive influence of the women's health movement, one of the most lasting and effective forces to emerge from the 1960s and 1970s.

Notes

1. Dr. Frederick Robbins, quoted in Barbara Seaman, *The Doctors' Case Against the Pill* (New York: P.H. Wyden, 1969).

2. D.C. Smith, R. Prentice, D.J. Thompson, and W.L. Herrmann, "Association of Exogenous Estrogen and Endometrial Carcinoma," *New England Journal of Medicine* 293(23) (1975), 1164-1167.

3. Sue Fisher, *In the Patient's Best Interest: Women and the Politics of Medical Decisions* (New Brunswick, NJ: Rutgers University Press, 1986).

3

Women, Health Care, and the Law: Birth, Death, and In Between

George J. Annas

THE EXPERIENCES OF WOMEN as patients are fostering a virtual revolution in health law and patient rights. This should come as no surprise. Women are, of course, primary in reproduction, and the most important health law case of the century, *Roe v. Wade*,[1] which declared most laws restricting abortion unconstitutional, has had an overwhelming impact on privacy in other areas of medicine as well. Both men and women die, but male doctors tend to experience more "rescue fantasy" with female patients, believing, falsely, that medical intervention can save lives by preventing death. Thus, the cases of women patients, most notably Karen Ann Quinlan, Elizabeth Bouvia, and Nancy Cruzan, have defined and refined our laws and practices concerning all dying patients. And "in between" women make disproportionate use of medical services. Four of the six most commonly performed surgical procedures, for example, are done exclusively on women: cesarean section, hysterectomy, diagnostic dilation and curettage of the uterus, and fallopian tube occlusion procedures. Adding abortion, the most commonly performed surgical procedure in America, to this list would make it five of the top six procedures.

Since the typical patient is a woman, the way women patients are treated is the way in which almost all patients will be treated. Unfortunately, women have been treated badly; and paternalism in medicine refers not only to male physicians treating women patients as children, but also to the tendency of physicians (both male and female) to patronize patients. How have the experiences of women patients helped shape the current contours of health law and patient rights, and what changes might we reasonably expect in the future?

Pregnancy and Childbirth

The bodies of pregnant women have served as the battlefield over which major constitutional cases have been fought for more than two decades. The primary fight has been over abortion rights, but pregnant women have become convenient scapegoats, and thus targets, in many arenas where public officials have refused to deal with real social problems directly. Examples include the cocaine epidemic (in which it is suggested that women who give birth to cocaine-addicted babies be charged with criminal behavior to protect fetuses) and the AIDS epidemic (in which experimental drugs have been until recently withheld from pregnant women, and in which women are blamed for the birth of HIV-infected children).

In the late nineteenth century, the medical profession succeeded in medicalizing childbirth and taking it out of the hands of women and midwives. Since then, home birth has become unusual, and in-hospital birth routine. In fact, the most common reason people are admitted to the hospital in the United States is for childbirth (4 million admissions annually, or more than 10 percent of all admissions).

Women have resisted the complete medicalization of childbirth, although it remains firmly in the hands of physicians. Over the past two decades especially, due in part to pressure from patients, hospitals have added birthing rooms and tried to make the atmosphere in the hospital more homelike. Fathers are now routinely invited into the delivery room, and birth is at least somewhat of a family experience instead of simply another medical procedure.

On the other hand, the epidemic of cesarean sections is continuing cause for concern. Approximately 25 percent of all births are by cesarean section in the United States, and this percentage has risen one full percentage point per year—from 10 percent in 1975 to 25 percent in 1990—with no end in sight. With about one million cesarean sections annually, the operation has become the most common surgical procedure (other than abortion) performed in the United States. Consumer groups, and even some medical groups, acknowledge that perhaps half of these operations are unnecessary, but no one seems to know how to decrease this unnecessary trauma to women. One group of researchers reports:

> The forces driving the increasing rate of cesarean childbirth in the United
> States are not well understood. Much discussion has centered around

medicolegal issues [malpractice litigation]. However, the 1980 consensus conference concluded that, "Although commonly cited, there is no evidence that fear of litigation and the possible consequent practice of defensive medicine is a major cause of the increased cesarean birth rate."...Recently a call was made for the increased use of committee reviews of institutional cesarean birth rates [with no effect]...mandatory consultation prior to cesarean [which is used in 43 percent of hospitals resulting in a 4 percent lower rate].[2]

The way in which the cesarean section epidemic is ultimately stemmed will likely serve as a model for dealing with all unnecessary procedures that physicians have a personal and financial interest in performing on their vulnerable patients.

Although the vast majority of pregnancies end with childbirth, about 27 percent are terminated with abortion. Until 1973, states had the constitutional authority to make this common medical procedure a crime, and most did. In 1973, however, the U.S. Supreme Court ruled that a woman had a fundamental constitutional right, under the "right of privacy," to enlist a physician to terminate her pregnancy. The Reagan–Bush administrations made the recriminalization of abortion a major part of their agenda, and both President Reagan and President Bush appointed judges who appeared to be on the threshold of gutting the constitutional rights of women guaranteed by *Roe v. Wade*.

Physicians generally sat on the sidelines in this debate about whether to again grant state legislatures the power to control the reproductive lives of women citizens. This was unfortunate for two reasons: the first is that recriminalizing abortion would convert the doctor–patient relationship into a criminal–victim relationship; the second is that the right to privacy, although primarily an individual right of women in this circumstance, also protects physicians and the doctor–patient relationship itself.[3] The election of Bill Clinton and the subsequent appointment of Ruth Ginsberg to the U.S. Supreme Court have meant that the case of *Roe v. Wade* is safe and previability abortions are unlikely to be criminalized.

Roe v. Wade balanced a woman's freedom with governmental interests in abortion and permitted states to regulate the procedure to protect maternal health after the first trimester and to protect potential life after the second trimester (even by proscribing abortion where it would not threaten maternal health or life). Yet, a central focus of *Roe* is the nature of the doctor–patient relationship and the degree of protection that it deserves from state interference. *Roe* and its companion case *Doe v. Bolton*⁴ recognize that the interests of the doctor and the patient are usually the same and that the state should seldom be permitted to interfere with their joint decisions to perform or undergo standard medical procedures. The importance of granting the doctor–patient relationship a measure of constitutional protection can be demonstrated by examples of legislative attempts to interfere with treatment decisions made by patients and their physicians.

As recently as 1965, the state of Connecticut prohibited married couples from *using* contraceptives.⁵ It was also a crime to assist, abet, or counsel a person to commit any offense. Pursuant to these laws, the executive director of the Planned Parenthood League of Connecticut and the physician who served as the medical director of the league were arrested and convicted of giving "information, instruction and medical advice to married persons as to the means of preventing conception." The executive director and the medical examiner had examined a woman and prescribed the best contraceptive device or material for her use. The U.S. Supreme Court, in reversing the convictions, struck down this statute, stating, "We deal with a right of privacy older than the Bill of Rights—older than our political parties, older than our school system" (*Griswold v. Connecticut*). In explaining this "fundamental" constitutional right of privacy, the Court recognized that there are decisions that are so personal and so private, and that so profoundly affect the individuals who must live with the consequences, that the state has no power to interfere in those decisions, absent a compelling state interest. Thus, the constitutional right of privacy is primarily a liberty interest, which preserves a sphere of individual decision making free from governmental compulsion.

In *Roe v. Wade*, the Court explained how the right of privacy protects the doctor–patient relationship. *Roe* ensured a woman's right to make reproductive decisions, but it also recognized that a pregnant woman's decision is ordinarily made with the advice and counsel of a physician and that a woman could not implement the decision without the assistance of a physician. If a woman is to be free to make reproductive decisions, her physician must be similarly free to advise her and to act on that advice without unwarranted state regulation. Thus, in *Roe* the Court found that during the first trimester, "The *attending physician*, in consultation with his patient, is free to determine, without regulation by the State, that, in his *medical judgment*, the patient's pregnancy should be terminated" [emphasis added]. During the first trimester, the Court said, "the abortion decision and its effectuation must be left to the medical judgment of the pregnant woman's attending physician." The Court declared that its decision "vindicates the right of the physician to administer medical treatment according to his professional judgment" up until the point that compelling state interests justify intervention. The Court concluded that the abortion decision is "inherently, and primarily, a medical decision" for which "basic responsibility" rests with the physician. These are very strong statements of physicians' rights that, when coupled with the right given to women, form a powerful barrier against state intrusion into the doctor–patient relationship.

One method legislatures, and the Bush administration with the "gag rule" (which President Clinton rescinded shortly after taking office), have tried to use to control the doctor–patient decision-making process in the area of abortion has been to interfere with the ability of doctors to freely communicate with their patients. Rules have been created that either require physicians to make specific statements or silence them altogether. These attempts strike directly at the heart of the doctor–patient relationship. For example, the City of Akron passed an ordinance requiring physicians to recite what the Court referred to as a "parade of horribles" regarding fetal development and the effects of abortion on the fetus and the woman.[6]

There is no more central attack on the practice of medicine than an attack on communication in the doctor–patient relationship. Information concerning health risks that are caused or exacerbated by pregnancy and information concerning possible fetal genetic or congenital disorders are squarely among the categories of information that a physician is obliged by law and ethics to disclose to a pregnant woman to facilitate knowledgeable decisions about her pregnancy. It is good and accepted medical practice for a physician to inquire into the genetic and medical history of a prospective mother and father who consult him or her for care and advice concerning family planning, contraception, and pregnancy evaluation. Legislation that directly or indirectly attempts to silence certain physicians prevents them from performing their ethical and legal obligations to their patients consistent with existing medical science, and thereby deprives patients of information they need in order to decide whether to have a child. It promotes ignorance, viewing an uninformed patient as a desirable result.

In the summer of 1992, the U.S. Supreme Court surprised almost all observers by refusing to overrule *Roe v. Wade*. In its *Casey* opinion, although upholding parental consent and a 24-hour waiting period requirement, the Court reaffirmed the central holding of *Roe:* states cannot make abortion a crime prior to fetal viability. The Court also struck down a provision of the Pennsylvania statute under review that required spousal notification prior to abortion, saying that this put an "undue burden" on the woman's decision to terminate her pregnancy. Perhaps most remarkably, the Court reconsidered its previous emphasis on the physician's right to practice medicine (and the state's limited ability to interfere with it), and instead concentrated on the rights of the woman, saying:

> Whatever constitutional status the doctor–patient relationship may have as a general matter, in the present context it is derivative of the woman's position. The doctor–patient relation does not underlie or override the two more general rights under which the abortion is justified: the right to make family decisions and the right to physical autonomy.[7]

This shift in emphasis, from the physician to the patient, should be applauded. It *is* the woman, not the physician, who is pregnant, the woman who is making the decision, and the woman who is responsible for the decision. Reemphasizing the centrality of the woman in the abortion decision should help other courts reemphasize the centrality of the patient in all decisions made in the context of the doctor–patient relationship, and thus enhance the rights of all patients.

In Between

Although almost all communication between physicians and family members responsible for patient decision making (parents, spouses, siblings) is between physicians and women, most of the important cases articulating the rights of patients and their surrogates regarding informed consent have involved male patients. This is not surprising. Male judges may well expect male physicians to explain more things to male patients (especially middle-aged white male patients) than to female patients. Regardless of the traditional paternalistic logic, however, the fact is that the two leading informed consent cases in the United States both involved male patients who sued their physicians for failure to adequately inform them of the risks of surgery prior to the operation. (In Great Britain, the leading informed consent case involved a woman, which may explain why British law, already more physician-oriented than American law, is even more so in this area.[8]) Both courts articulated the doctrine of informed consent in this setting, one noting that the "fiduciary relationship" inherent in the doctor–patient relationship required the physician to give the patient certain information prior to asking for consent to operate. This information includes:

    1. a description of the proposed procedure;
    2. the risks and benefits of the proposed procedure;
    3. the alternatives (and their risks and benefits);
    4. the major problems anticipated during recuperation.[9]

It is also reasonable to tell the patient what the probability of success is, what success means to the physician, and the cost of the procedure.

Informed consent, associated as it is with the concept of autonomy, is "male-based," but women undergo most of the operations in the United States. It is an operation that is performed exclusively on women, surgery for breast cancer, that has been used as the primary example to explain the underlying rationale of the informed consent doctrine: self-determination. Jay Katz, for example, has shown that although historically physicians had no evidence on which to base their claims for radical mastectomy as the treatment of choice, they nonetheless insisted it was the only possible treatment for decades. Even today, although we now know about many alternative treatments, we still do not know which is best. But as Katz notes:

> Of importance to decision making between physician and patient is the fact that, if they are so inclined, physicians now can make clearer distinctions between what they know and do not know. Thus, they can offer patients a variety of treatment options based on pieces of evidence from available clinical data. *There is no certainty about the available knowledge, but its uncertainty can be specified.* This crucial point holds true for the treatment not only of breast cancer but for many other diseases as well.[10]

Since 1979, more than a dozen states have passed informed consent statutes that require that women with breast cancer be told of all medically acceptable alternatives. A 1981 study commissioned by the American College of Surgeons on the frequency of lumpectomies in

Massachusetts and California (states with consent statutes) and New York (a state without a statute) concluded that the number of lumpectomies was directly related to the existence of an informed consent statute. Figures for wedge excisions of tumors under 1 cm as a percentage of the total were as follows: national average, 4.8 percent; Massachusetts (2-year-old law), 18 percent; California (1-year-old statute), 10 percent; New York (no law), 2 percent.[11]

The issue of patient self-determination has probably been best explored in all its complexities by poet Marcia Lynch in her *"Peau d'Orange"*:

> We barter the difference
> between black and gray
> "Surgery, radiation or
> death," you say and leave
> the decision to me,
>
> while I insist you are the gods
> I believed in as a child.
> I prayed you to pull magic
> out of your black leather bag
> to wave away the rattling
> in my bones.
>
> I accept your calling
> my breast an orange peel,
> let you lay hands on this fruit
> my mother said no man
> must touch. In this disease
> there is no sin.
>
> If you lift the chill
> that unravels my spine,
> I will send you stars,
> from the Milky Way,
> sending them spinning down,
> dancing a thousand-fold. Please
> let me grow old.[12]

Death

The discussion of cases involving women has thus far focused on the uniqueness of their bodies and their reproductive ability. Death, of course, has no such uniqueness. Thus it is both surprising and instructive to see that almost all the major cases involving decisions where treatment refusals would likely lead to death that have been vigorously challenged by physicians have involved women.[13] Some of the most famous and useful examples are the cases of Karen Ann Quinlan, Mary O'Connor, and Nancy Cruzan.[14]

The story of Karen Ann Quinlan is a modern parable. Severely brain-damaged in an accident, Quinlan was "successfully" resuscitated in a hospital emergency department and put on a mechanical ventilator that breathed for her. When it became clear that she would never regain consciousness, her parents asked her physician to remove the ventilator and let her die. Worried about possible civil and criminal liability, Quinlan's physician asked her parents to obtain legal immunity for him in court. A lower court refused, but in 1976 the New Jersey Supreme Court ruled that if she were competent, Quinlan would have a constitutional right to refuse continued medical treatment, and that her parents could exercise this right on her behalf. Quinlan's ventilator was thereafter removed—although she survived another decade in a coma, able to breathe on her own.

Almost all Americans have said, "I never want to be like Karen Quinlan." We intuitively, if not rationally, recognize that such expensive and intensive medical intervention is both pointless for us and cruel for our families. Since 1976, more than 50 courts in almost 20 states have reviewed cases dealing with the right to refuse treatment. All but two have agreed with the basic analysis and conclusion of the New Jersey Supreme Court. The two that disagreed merit brief mention.

The first was a New York case in which the state's highest court rejected the previously expressed wishes of a 77-year-old widow to refuse a nasogastric tube proposed to deliver nourishment to her body.[15] Mary O'Connor was severely demented and profoundly incapacitated as a result of a series of strokes that left her bedridden, paralyzed, unable to care for herself, and with no hope of any significant improvement. Her husband had died of brain cancer, and the last two of her nine brothers had also died of cancer. A former hospital administrator, she had visited them regularly when they were hospitalized and had cared for them at home. During this time, she had several conversations with hospital coworkers and her daughters, saying, among other things, that it was "monstrous to keep someone alive ...by using machines and things like that when they were not going to get better" and that she "would never want any sort of intervention, any sort of life-support system." Her two daughters, both nurses, had no doubt that their mother would not want the nasogastric tube. Nonetheless, the hospital went to court to force treatment.

The lower court denied the hospital's petition, but the New York Court of Appeals, in a cruel opinion, granted the hospital's request on the basis that O'Connor had not been specific enough in expressing her desires. For example, the court noted that her husband and brothers had died of cancer, whereas she "is simply an elderly person who as a result of several strokes suffers certain disabilities." The court also observed that almost everyone has made similar statements: "Her comments...are, in fact, no different than those that many of us might make after witnessing an agonizing death."

The fact that almost everyone has made similar statements is no reason to ignore them; indeed, it is the reason to take them seriously. It is precisely because medical technology is being used indiscriminately that most elderly citizens have had to witness the painfully and pointlessly prolonged dying process of friends and relatives and have consequently expressed their wishes not to be similarly abused. My guess is that most of us would rather have our courts err on the side of protecting our liberty rather than prolonging our lives in similar situations. In this regard, death, Patrick Henry's "second choice," remains preferable to being treated as an inanimate object without personality, family, or history.

The second aberrant case, that of Nancy Cruzan, is more important because it was decided by the U.S. Supreme Court. This case is essentially identical to the case of Karen Ann Quinlan, with one exception: Cruzan, a young woman in a permanent coma as a result of an automobile accident, required only tube feeding (rather than a mechanical ventilator and tube feeding) to continue to survive. Her parents believed she would not want to have the tube feeding continued in such circumstances, and she herself had said that she would not want to continue to live if she could not be "at least halfway normal." Unlike the court in the *Quinlan* case, however, a lower court granted the family's request to have Cruzan's tube feeding discontinued, and the Supreme Court of Missouri reversed.

The Missouri Supreme Court's opinion disregarded Cruzan herself, treating her like an abstraction who embodied all the nursing home patients in Missouri and who must be kept alive for their sake. Although conceding that if Cruzan were competent, she herself could refuse even such simple medical interventions as feeding tubes, the court rejected the idea that her parents could exercise her rights on her behalf. Instead, the court stressed the personal nature of informed consent and required that Cruzan *personally* make a decision to reject artificial feeding in circumstances like those in which she found herself, and with the knowledge that such a refusal would result in starvation.

The Missouri court was able to arrive at its opinion only by viewing Cruzan as a disembodied woman who could not be hurt and who had no interests in either autonomy or dignity, and no family that cared for her. The U.S. Supreme Court affirmed the right of competent individuals to decide for themselves what medical treatments to undergo, but also permitted the state of Missouri to require "clear and convincing" evidence of an incompetent patient's wishes before a proxy could make termination of treatment decisions.[16]

The one woman then on the U.S. Supreme Court, Justice Sandra Day O'Connor, opined that had Cruzan simply stated that she wanted her mother to make medical decisions for her when she was unable to make them herself, this decision would have been a constitutionally protected delegation of authority. This powerful suggestion energized a national movement to encourage adults to designate proxy decision makers through a document called a health care proxy. Thus, the only two women involved in the legal proceedings from the trial court to the U.S. Supreme Court in the Cruzan case, Nancy Cruzan herself and Justice O'Connor, shaped both the dispute and the resolution, and the ultimate outcome was one that encourages communication, caring, and cooperation at the level of family decision making for incompetent persons.

What can be done to help make sure patients' individuality survives incompetence, and that they are not used as biological exhibits by the state, or thoughtlessly preserved by guilt-ridden relatives? There are no certain measures, but some steps will help:[17]

Providers and others should encourage patients and others to discuss death and medical treatment issues with their families and physicians so that they know what relatives and patients want regarding medical treatment. The more specific such discussions, the better. Relatives should not have to guess about what people would decide in various circumstances; they should know.

Hospitals and other providers should encourage everyone—patients, employees, and others—to appoint someone they trust, through a document called a "health care proxy" or "durable power of attorney for health care," to make health care decisions on their behalf when they are no longer able to make them for themselves.

Hospitals and nursing homes should make forms necessary for completing a "living will" (written statement of directions regarding treatment in the event of incompetency) and "durable power of attorney for health care" routinely available to all patients upon admission (or prior to admission if the admission is elective), so that thinking about dying and making decisions about treatment during incompetency become matters that *must* be confronted and are seen as the personal responsibility of each of us.

Health care providers must routinely give patients sufficient pain medication to keep them pain-free. Patients have no obligation to suffer, and doctors do have an obligation to alleviate suffering, even if doing so shortens life.

Health care providers should be *required* to honor a patient's directions regarding treatment refusals (or to find quickly another physician who will) under penalty of license revocation and malpractice charges.

Refusal of treatment by family members on behalf of incompetent patients should be honored unless the health care providers believe such requests are contrary to the patient's wishes, and themselves obtain a court order to continue treatment.

The core legal and ethical principle that underlies all human interactions in medicine is autonomy, the right of the individual to decide whether to undergo any proposed medical intervention. The "right to decide" has been given legal status in the doctrine of informed consent, the requirement that a physician describe a proposed procedure and disclose its risks of death and injury, its benefits, the alternatives that exist, and the anticipated results and likely course of recuperation before the physician subjects a patient to a procedure that carries risk of injury. Since competent adults must consent to medical procedures before the procedures can legally and ethically be performed on them, they also have the *right to refuse*. If this right did not exist, the doctrine of informed consent would collapse into a "right" to agree with one's doctor.

The Future of Patient Rights

Informed consent is often seen as a male, rights-based approach to medical care, as opposed to a female, communitarian-based approach. The history of medical care related to reproduction, surgery, and dying, however, indicates that this is a false dichotomy. Compared to men, women have as much at stake, if not more, in controlling their own bodies and their own destinies, and the failure of physicians to acknowledge autonomy has not led to more communitarian-based medicine, but has served only to perpetuate paternalism and a health care system that leaves more than 30 million Americans, mostly women and children, uninsured.

However, it is time to stop focusing narrowly on male- or female-based ideologies, and to focus on the problems of cost, quality, and access to care for all Americans. In this regard the lessons we have learned from the experiences of women in the health care setting are ones that can and should guide us in making medical care a patient-centered activity where decisions are made jointly by physicians and patients, and where patients have the final decision about what will or will not be done with their bodies.

It is of course not for a male lawyer to tell women what their rights as patients are. I am, however, honored that the authors of *Our Bodies, Ourselves*, the premier book on women and the health care system in America, have in every edition reprinted the model Patients' Bill of Rights that I developed in 1975 for *The Rights of Hospital Patients*, and revised for the 1989 edition of the same book, retitled *The Rights of Patients*. This model Patients' Bill of Rights (Appendix) provides a useful summary of patient rights and an agenda for action in all settings where they are not currently honored.

Appendix: A Model Patients' Bill of Rights

Preamble: As you enter this health care facility, it is our duty to remind you that your health care is a cooperative effort between you as a patient and the doctors and hospital staff. During your stay a patient rights advocate will be available to you. The duty of the advocate is to assist you in all the decisions you must make and in all situations in which your health and welfare are at stake. The advocate's first responsibility is to help you understand the role of all who will be working with you, and to help you understand what your rights as a patient are. Your advocate can be reached twenty-four hours a day by dialing ———. The following is a list of your rights as a patient. Your advocate's duty is to see to it that you are afforded these rights. You should call your advocate whenever you have any questions or concerns about any of these rights.

1. The patient has a legal right to informed participation in all decisions involving the patient's health care program.

2. We recognize the right of all potential patients to know what research and experimental protocols are being used in our facility and what alternatives are available in the community.

3. The patient has a legal right to privacy regarding the source of payment for treatment and care. This right includes access to reasonable medical care without regard to the source of payment for that treatment and care.

4. We recognize the right of a potential patient to complete and accurate information concerning medical care and procedures at our facility.

5. The patient has a legal right to prompt attention in an emergency situation.

6. The patient has a legal right to a clear, concise explanation in layperson's terms of all proposed procedures, including the possibilities of any risk of mortality or serious side effects, problems related to recuperation, and probability of success, and will not be subjected to any procedure without the patient's voluntary, competent, and understanding consent. The specifics of such consent shall be set out in a written consent form and signed by the patient before the procedure is done.

7. The patient has a legal right to a clear, complete, and accurate evaluation of the patient's condition and prognosis without treatment before being asked to consent to any test or procedure.

8. The patient has a right to designate another person to make health care and treatment decisions for the patient, and based on the patient's own directions and values, in the event the patient is unable to participate in decision making. The health care facility agrees to recognize the authority of an individual so designated.

9. The patient has a right to know the identity, professional status, and experience of all those providing service. All personnel have been instructed to introduce themselves, state their status, and explain their role in the health care of the patient. Part of this right is the right of the patient to know the identity of the physician responsible for the patient's care.

10. The patient has a legal right not to be discriminated against in the provision of medical and nursing services on the basis of race, religion, national origin, sex, or handicap.

11. Any patient who does not speak English, or who is hearing impaired, has a right to have access to an interpreter.

12. The patient has a right to all the information contained in the patient's medical record while in the health care facility, and to examine the record on request.

13. The patient has a right to discuss the patient's condition with a consultant specialist, at the patient's request and expense.

14. The patient has a legal right not to have any test or procedure, designed for educational purposes rather than the patient's direct personal benefit, performed on the patient.

15. The patient has a legal right to refuse any particular drug, test, procedure, or treatment.

16. The patient has a legal right to privacy of both person and information with respect to: the staff, other doctors, residents, interns and medical students, researchers, nurses, other health care facility personnel, and other patients.

17. We recognize the patient's right of access to people outside the health care facility by means of visitors and the telephone. Parents may

stay with their children, and relatives with terminally ill patients, twenty-four hours a day.

18. The patient has a legal right to leave the health care facility regardless of the patient's physical condition or financial status, although the patient may be requested to sign a release stating that the patient is leaving against the medical judgment of the patient's doctor or the staff.

19. The patient has a right not to be transferred to another facility unless the patient has received a complete explanation of the desirability and need for the transfer, the other facility has accepted the patient for transfer, and the patient has agreed to the transfer. If the patient does not agree to the transfer, the patient has the right to a consultant's opinion of the desirability and necessity of the transfer.

20. A patient has a right to be notified of impending discharge at least one day before it is accomplished, to a consultation by an expert on the desirability and necessity of discharge, and to have a person of the patient's choice notified in advance.

21. The patient has a right, regardless of the source of payment, to examine and receive an itemized and detailed explanation of the total bill for services rendered in the health care facility.

22. We recognize the right of a patient to competent counseling from the facility staff to help in obtaining financial assistance from public or private sources to meet the expense of services received in the health care facility.

23. The patient has a right to timely prior notice of the termination of eligibility for reimbursement by any third-party payer for the expense of care.

24. At the termination of the patient's stay at the health care facility the patient has a right to a complete copy of the information contained in the patient's medical record.

25. We recognize the right of all patients to have twenty-four-hour-a-day access to a patient rights advocate who may act on behalf of the patient to assert or protect the rights set out in this document.

Notes

1. *Roe v. Wade*, 410 U.S. 113 (1973).

2. P.H. Shiono, J.G. Fielden, D. McNellis, et al., "Recent Trends in Cesarean Birth and Trial of Labor Rates in the United States," *Journal of the American Medical Association* 257(1987):494-497.

3. This section is taken from George J. Annas, Leonard H. Glantz, and Wendy K. Mariner, "The Right of Privacy Protects the Doctor–Patient Relationship," *Journal of the American Medical Association* 262(1990):858.

4. *Doe v. Bolton*, 410 U.S. 179 (1973).

5. *Griswold v. Connecticut*, 381 U.S. 479 (1965).

6. *Akron v. Akron Center for Reproductive Health*, 462 U.S. 416 (1983).

7. *Planned Parenthood v. Casey*, 112 S. Ct. 2791 (1992). For a complete discussion of *Casey*, see G.J. Annas, *Standard of Care: The Law of American Bioethics* (New York: Oxford University Press, 1993), 54–60.

8. *Sideway v. Bethlehem Royal Hospital Governors*, 1 ALL ER 1018 (1984).

9. *Cobbs v. Grant*, 502 P.2d 1 (Cal. 1972). The other case is *Canterbury v. Spencer*, 464 F.2d 772 (D.C. Cir. 1972).

10. J. Katz, *The Silent World of Doctor and Patient* (New York: Free Press, 1984).

11. Dabice and Cordes, "Informed Consent Heralds Change in Breast Treatment," *Medical World News* (Nov. 11, 1985):1.

12. J. Mukand, ed., *Sutured Words* (Brookline, MA: Aviva Press, 1987),124.

13. See generally, S. Miles and A. August, "Courts, Gender, and 'The Right to Die,'" *Law, Medicine, and Health Care* 18(1990):85–94.

14. See G.J. Annas, *The Rights of Patients* (Carbondale, IL: Southern Illinois University Press, 1989).

15. G.J. Annas, "Precatory Prediction and Mindless Mimicry: The Case of Mary O'Connor," *Hastings Center Report* 18(6) (Dec. 1988):31–33.

16. *Cruzan v. Director, Missouri Department of Health*, 110 S. Ct. 2841 (1990).

17. See G.J. Annas, "Life, Liberty and Death," *Health Management Quarterly* (Jan. 1990):5.

4

Health, Health Care, and Women of Color

Risa J. Lavizzo-Mourey and Jeane Ann Grisso

IT IS A FAMILIAR SCENE at a big city hospital: a resident chastising a woman of color as she seeks health care. The harsh words may be for choosing the emergency room instead of a clinic, for waiting too long to seek medical care, or for failing to comply with a prescribed treatment. All too often, the words are delivered by someone who recognizes that the woman is not realizing the optimal outcome of our health care system, and is frustrated by that observation. However, instead of examining the flaws in our system or the gaps in medical knowledge that might account for this tragedy, the well-intentioned health care provider too often blames the victim. The sick and humiliated woman, on the other hand, probably blames the system.

To be sure, health care for women of color in the United States is wanting. Whether the chosen measure is health status, access to care, or utilization of services, there is an inappropriate gap between women of color and white women. The reasons women of color use fewer health care services despite bearing a heavier burden of disease than other groups are complex, and represent an interaction among economic, cultural, and historical factors, including rising poverty, more limited access to health insurance, a health belief system that is not exclusively based on the biomedical model, and a history of denied access to health care services. This chapter will provide an overview of the health status of women of color and explore the health system characteristics and health beliefs that contribute to their unacceptably low health status.

Sociodemographic Factors

Over the last decade, there have been striking increases in the proportion of women living in or near poverty. Women of color have been particularly affected. In general, few data are available on Asian women, and information on Hispanic women has become available only recently from the Hispanic Health and Nutrition Examination Survey (HHANES). From these data, it appears that Hispanic women are similar to African-American women in many demographic factors. In the United States, African-American, Mexican-American, and Puerto Rican women are much more likely than white women to live in female-headed households;[1] of these households, 43.8 percent of African-American, 45.4 percent of Mexican-American, and 57.3 percent of Puerto Rican are below the poverty level, in contrast to 22.3 percent of the households headed by white women.[2]

More than one-third (36.4 percent) of Mexican-American women and 13.2 percent of African-American women have completed eight years of education or less, in contrast to 8 percent of white women.[3] Although 59.5 percent of African-American women are employed,[4] only 46 percent of Puerto Rican women are in the labor force.[5] Finally, most white women in the United States (61.6 percent) are married, in contrast to only 40.6 percent of African-American women and 35.7 percent of Puerto Rican women.[6]

The socioeconomic characteristics of women of color have implications for health status. Data from the National Health Interview Survey indicate a positive correlation between income and health status. Thus, the low socioeconomic status of large portions of women of color suggests that they may suffer disproportionately from chronic illnesses and disabilities.

Health Status
The morbidity and mortality statistics for women of color are distressing. Virtually every comparison of mortality rates for women of color and white women reveals excess mortality for women of color. (Excess mortality is defined as the difference between the number of deaths observed in a subgroup and the number that would have been expected if that subgroup had the same age-specific death rates as the entire population. In this case the subgroups are women representing various non-white racial and ethnic groups.) African-American women have excess deaths for cardiovascular disease, cancer, cirrhosis, diabetes, injuries, and homicide. Fortunately, excess mortality due to cardiovascular disease and cancer has not been observed for the other racial or ethnic subgroups. Excess deaths occur in Mexican-born and

Native American women for diabetes and homicide, while Asian women (when considered as a single group) do not have excess mortality for any of these conditions.[7] While at first glance the situation for Asian women may seem encouraging, it must be emphasized that in this country, the Asian population consists of eight to ten subpopulations, and that health statistics predominantly report the status of the Chinese, the most affluent and numerous of the subpopulations. Thus, there may be excess mortality buried in these "good" statistics.

Among African-American women little progress has been made over the years in reducing excess mortality caused by the traditional killers such as cancer and cardiovascular disease. Now AIDS has added to the problem. Although death rates for heart disease and cerebrovascular disease declined in both African-American women and white women, African-American women still have a 50 to 80 percent greater risk of dying of these conditions than white women, and the mortality ratio has not changed substantially over the last 40 years. The most marked mortality ratio is for AIDS; African-American women are more than nine times as likely to die of AIDS than white women. Other major differences are found for diabetes and homicide, for which death rates are 2.5 and more than 4 times as high among African-American women as among white women. Of note, death rates for cancer have increased for African-American women. The breast cancer death rate for African-American women now surpasses that for white women (27.6 percent versus 22.5 percent).[8]

Perhaps even more striking than the data on excess mortality due to chronic illness are the data on maternal mortality. That women are still dying in childbirth is a cruel anachronism that strikes African-American women more than three times more frequently than white women. According to recent statistics, the maternal death rate per 100,000 live births is 5.0 for white women and 18.1 for women of color. The rate has decreased steadily since 1940 for all women, falling from 376 per 100,000 live births in 1940 to 7.2 in 1991.[9] However, the difference in maternal mortality rates between women of color and white women over the last 50 years has remained constant at best and may be increasing. In 1940 the maternal mortality rate among women of color was 2.4 times that of white women, as compared to 3.6 in 1991.[10]

Similarly, survival rates for commonly occurring cancers are poor for women of color. Compared to African-American women, white women have better five-year survival rates for virtually every cancer. For example, for the period 1983-90 the overall survival rate was 59.8 percent among white women but only 45.5 percent among black women. Even more striking are the rates for uterine cancer; the survival rate for white women was 84.9 percent, while the rate for black women was only 55.2 percent.[11]

Since illness does not always kill, mortality data are not the only measure of health status. Morbidity data capture the number of diseases or health problems and nonfatal consequences of disease. Like the mortality data, morbidity statistics indicate limitations in health status for African-American and Hispanic women. Obesity is more common in black women than in white women irrespective of age. The proportion of Hispanic and African-American women who are overweight is extremely high. Nearly half of African-American women and Mexican-American women are significantly overweight, compared with 33.5 percent of white women.[12] Diabetes and hypertension are also more prevalent among African-American women and Hispanic women than among white women. The prevalence of diabetes in persons 45 to 74 years of age is extremely high for Mexican-Americans (24 percent) and Native Americans (21 percent) compared with white persons (12 percent). Previously, it was assumed that Mexican-Americans had high rates of diabetes due to genetic admixture with Native American populations, in which there is a high prevalence of diabetes. However, a report from HHANES of the very high prevalence of diabetes in Puerto Ricans (26 percent), a population that does not have such an admixture, was a major surprise, and means that the previously held theory has to be re-examined.[13] This is an example of how much can be learned from evaluating each ethnic and racial group separately.

An additional reason for examining each ethnic group separately is that health status and health practices may differ widely among subpopulations of Hispanic and Asian women. Stroup-Benham et al. report that nearly twice as many Cuban-American women (27.1 percent) rate their health as excellent as Mexican-American women (14.0 percent) or Puerto Rican women (14.4 percent). The researchers also report that reproductive characteristics vary widely. Compared with Cuban-American women, Mexican-American and Puerto Rican women have higher frequencies of miscarriages and stillbirths. Mexican-American women are almost twice as likely to use oral contraceptives

(15.7 percent) as their Puerto Rican (8.7 percent) and Cuban-American (8.2 percent) counterparts, while Puerto Rican women have very high rates of sterilization (23.0 percent) compared with Cuban-American (15.4 percent) and Mexican-American (14.8 percent) women.[14] Thus, health statistic reports for Hispanic women as a whole will not reflect the true picture for each ethnic group or the diversity among groups.

In addition to suffering a greater burden of chronic illnesses, minority women are also disproportionately affected by infectious diseases, such as tuberculosis and sexually transmitted diseases, and violence. Although violence against women affects all racial and ethnic groups, the rates reported in an urban African-American population were two to three times greater than in a predominantly white population in northeastern Ohio.[15] In fact, African-American women are more likely to die from homicide than white men in the United States.[16] Although little is known about violence among other ethnic groups, immigrant Asian women may be particularly vulnerable if they are brought to the United States through arranged marriages. Many of these women are faced with the choice of remaining with an abusive husband or risking deportation. A recent article in the *New York Times* reported that thousands of immigrant women and children are terrorized by domestic violence.[17]

Perhaps for no other disease is the contrast between minority women and white women as striking as it is for AIDS. Minority women constitute more than 70 percent of all AIDS cases among women, with African-American women making up over half (56 percent) of all cases. Although Hispanics constituted only 9.3 percent of the U.S. population in 1991, they accounted for 16 percent of AIDS cases among women. The cumulative incidence rate for AIDS is 14.0 and 5.9 times higher for African-American and Hispanic women, respectively, than for white women.[18] In short, women of color are burdened with higher incidence of disease, as well as worse outcomes.

Women of color as a group represent a population with special health needs because of the disparity in health status between them and other U.S. populations. *Healthy People 2000*, the national health promotion and disease prevention objectives, describes three goals for the nation:

1. Increase the span of healthy life for Americans.

2. Reduce health disparities among Americans.

3. Achieve access to preventive services for all Americans.[19]

The reduction of disparities has particular relevance to women of color because of their compromised health status. Understanding the reasons for the disparity is essential to closing the gap. The factors underlying the increased burden of disease can be grouped into four categories: poor access to care, poor care, cultural attitudes and beliefs, and deficiencies in medical knowledge.

Limited Access to Health Care

Use of health care is affected by perceived health care needs, insurance status, income, culture, language, available health services, and other factors. Although utilization reflects the complex interaction among these factors, information on utilization of health care services suggests that women of color may well have more limited access to health care than other populations in the United States. The most direct evidence is the data on prenatal care utilization from the National Center for Health Statistics. Many groups of women of color receive less prenatal care than white women. In 1991, 79.5 percent of white women received prenatal care in the first trimester, but only 61.9 percent of African-American, 59.9 percent of Native American, 58.7 percent of Mexican-American, 65 percent of Puerto Rican, and 63.4 percent of Central and South American women received such care.[20] What may be more important in explaining the high maternal and infant mortality rates among women of color is the percent of women who receive prenatal care only in the last trimester or not at all, which is 4.7 percent for white women, 5.7 percent for Asian women, 10.7 percent for African-American women, and 12.2 percent for Native American women. The rate for Hispanic women (selected states) is 12.2 percent for Mexican-American women, 12.2 percent for Puerto Rican women, and 9.5 percent for Central and South American women.[21] There can be little doubt that women of color have less access to prenatal care than white women.

The importance of prenatal care as an indicator of access to health care for women of color relates to its role in the birth of healthy babies. There is little argument among health care providers that good prenatal care is strongly related to low infant mortality rates. There-

fore, there is no dispute about the appropriateness or necessity of prenatal care; such is not the case for many other health care services. All
women should get prenatal care, and get it early in their pregnancy.
That thousands of women of color do not is an irrefutable failing of
the system with direct impact on women of color.

Less direct indicators of limited access to care for women of color
can be found in other health care utilization statistics. Overall, Hispanics are more likely to be uninsured than either whites or African-
Americans.[22] Data indicate that 34 percent of Hispanics were uninsured in 1992 as compared to 22.3 percent of African Americans and
16.1 percent of whites.[23] Among Hispanics, Mexican Americans, the
fewest of whom have insurance, visit physicians least often. About half
as many Hispanics as whites have a regular source of health care.[24]
They are twice as likely as whites to use the emergency department as a
source of primary care. Similarly, a study of Vietnamese women living
in Iowa found that 40 percent did not have a personal physician, 26
percent did not have medical insurance, and there was a highly significant correlation between having medical insurance and having had
more than one prenatal visit.[25] Although statistics on health care utilization are patchy, those that are available underscore the notion that
women of color have limited access to health care.

The Health Interview Survey indicates that for every age group, the
number of discharges from short-stay hospitals is higher for those living below the poverty line than for those whose resources place them
above poverty.[26] For example, the discharge rate is 137 per 1,000 for
families with an annual income of less than $14,000 but 62.5 per 1,000
for those with an income over $50,000. The most common explana-
tions for these statistics are that poor people have a greater burden of
illness and a greater tendency to substitute inpatient care for outpatient care than do people who are better off financially. If these were
the only explanations, one would expect poor people of color to have
the highest utilization of short-stay hospitals. Rather, poor whites have
the highest rates. For example, among all age groups living below the
poverty line, whites have a discharge rate of 16 per 100,000, while
people of color have a rate of 14.2. (The rates for whites and nonwhites living above poverty are similar: 10.8 per 100,000 and 10.3 per
100,000, respectively.) These statistics suggest that both race and poverty are factors in access to health care services. Women of color are
likely to have limited access to health care because of the combination

of race, low socioeconomic status, and lack of insurance. However, limited access to care is not the only reason why women of color may suffer a low health status. There is increasing evidence that women and people of color receive a different standard of care once in the system.

Access to Poor Care

It makes every health care provider uneasy to consider the existence of more than one standard of care, but data from a variety of sources suggest that such is the case and that women, particularly women of color, may find themselves deprived of the best available care. Three conditions—cardiovascular disease, breast cancer, and hip fractures—are worth highlighting because they illustrate the differences in treatment received by people of color as compared to whites in this country.

Race and gender are factors in the use of high-technology treatment modalities for patients hospitalized for cardiovascular disease, especially myocardial infarction. In 1989, Ford et al., using data from the National Hospital Discharge Survey, reported that more whites than blacks received coronary artery bypass surgery and coronary angiography.[27] The ratio of myocardial infarction among black and white men was 0.77. Since myocardial infarction is an indication for coronary angiography and bypass surgery, one would expect the ratios for these procedures to be similar to those for myocardial infarction. However, among men, the ratio of blacks to whites receiving angiography and bypass surgery was 0.53 and 0.35, respectively. Among women the results were even more striking. While the ratio of black to white women discharged with a diagnosis of myocardial infarction was 1.03, the ratio of black to white women receiving coronary angiography or coronary artery bypass grafting was 0.81 and 0.48, respectively. Among blacks, men had more myocardial infarctions (1.9) and angiography (1.6), but substantially more bypass surgery (3.0). A more recent study compared the types of treatment women and men received for a myocardial infarction, but did not stratify by race. This study reported similar patterns for the use of surgery and angioplasty.[28] Gittelsohn et al. analyzed discharge abstracts collected by the Hospital Services Cost Review Commission for Maryland for the years 1985 to 1987. They found that although admission rates for cardiovascular disease were similar for African Americans and whites, African Americans were half as likely to undergo angio-plasty or coronary bypass surgery; this pattern held true for both men and women.[29] Of course, such studies do not tell us who is getting appropriate care and who is receiving substandard care. However, in our health care system, where high technology is equated with high quality, the inaccessibility of high-technology procedures and treatments to women, particularly women of color, must be viewed as a potential contributor to the disparity in health status.

In order to analyze whether racial differences in health care are due primarily to differences in income and insurance status, Hadley and colleagues analyzed 1987 hospital discharge abstracts nationwide and compared uninsured and privately insured hospital patients. They found insurance status was a major predictor of in-hospital deaths for both African-American men and women. Insurance status was also highly correlated with the likelihood of undergoing discretionary cardiac procedures.[30] Thus, it appears that socioeconomic status may be a major determinant of the health care minority women receive.

Breast cancer provides another illustration of access to poor care among women of color. As was mentioned earlier, black women have lower survival rates for breast cancer than do white women. Access to health care is felt to be part of the problem, along with low mammography rates.[31] However, there is also evidence that black and white women do not get the same treatment. In 1989, Diehr reported that black women with breast cancer were less likely to get progesterone receptor assays and post-operative rehabilitation, and more likely to receive liver scans and radiation in situations deemed less appropriate.[32] These differences persisted even after age, type of health insurance, type of hospital, and physician characteristics were controlled for. The authors concluded that such differences in patterns of care may help to explain the differing survival rates. Studies exploring these questions in other diseases for which there is a disparity in survival or morbidity are lacking, as is documentation of health care services received by other (non-African-American) women of color. Such studies should be done, but they will not tell the whole story.

Over 75 percent of hip fractures occur to women. Although hip fracture rates are greater in white women than in African-American women, hip fractures are a significant public health problem among African-American women, affecting up to 1 percent of elderly African-American women each year. Furthermore, death rates after hip fracture are considerably higher among African-American women than among white women. A comparison of the hospitalization experiences of African-American and white hip fracture patients found that African-American hip fracture patients were less likely to receive surgery, experienced greater delays to surgery, and were significantly more likely to be nonambulatory on discharge.[33] Despite these differences, none of the African-American hip fracture patients were discharged to a rehabilitation setting. Although African-American hip fracture patients were sicker, with a greater number of chronic illnesses, the racial difference persisted after age and chronic illness were controlled for. Thus, it appears likely that differences in health care, especially the differential access to rehabilitation services, may explain part of the racial differences in survival after hip fracture.

Cultural Practices and Beliefs
Another factor in the disparity in the health status between women of color and white women is the difference in health behaviors practiced by the various groups. Healthy behaviors such as maintaining ideal body weight, abstaining from smoking, and seeking immunizations and screenings for cancer are practiced to varying degrees by people of color. Because of the burden of illness among people of color, there is particular interest in improving healthy behaviors in minority communities. Without an understanding of the beliefs that underlie health behaviors, however, there can be little hope of changing health-related practices, much less of delivering sensitive, compassionate care. Because women of color in this country represent more than a dozen different ethnic and racial groups, it would be impossible to describe their belief systems exhaustively here. Rather, some examples will be used to illustrate the differences between the dominant biomedical belief system that drives most health care providers' decisions and the beliefs held by women of color. The examples are chosen to demonstrate the potential relationship among health beliefs, practices, and outcomes.

At the heart of one's belief system are one's views on the causes of disease, which, of course, influence therapeutic actions. If one believes, as health care professionals do, that diseases are infections or derangements in a system such as the immune or cardiovascular system, medical treatments seem logical and worthy of compliance. However, if one has an alternative belief system, other behaviors follow. For example, a study of beliefs about the causes of hypertension among southern, rural African-American women found that the beliefs fell into two categories. Some women believed that hypertension was due to an expanded blood volume, and referred to the disease as "high blood." Others felt that hypertension was caused by excessive stress or tension and tended to use the word "hypertension" in describing the disease. The women conceptualizing the disease as high blood tended to be more compliant with prescribed pharmacologic therapy, while the other women tended to seek stress reduction strategies and were less compliant with medical therapy. After all, why should one take a medication for a disease caused by stress if that drug does nothing to reduce stress or if one has managed to reduce the sources of anxiety and stress?

Another illustration of the implications of health beliefs can be found in the opinions expressed by African-American women about AIDS. Medical research supports the view that AIDS is caused by a virus that is transmitted only through contact with infected body fluids. If one believes this view, behaviors consistent with medically recommended therapeutic and preventive strategies should follow. However, many African Americans (and Hispanics) believe that illnesses fall into two categories: natural and unnatural.[34] Natural illness occurs when a person is unprotected against the forces of nature or engages in excessive behaviors, whereas unnatural illness is caused by evil forces. By implication, natural illness can be healed by practicing moderation, using appropriate protection, or taking medication. Unnatural illness, on the other hand, can be cured only by religion or the supernatural (e.g., charms, potions). When African-American participants in Los Angeles County's Women, Infants and Children (WIC) program were surveyed about their AIDS-related beliefs and practices, only 3 out of 22 women felt that transmission of the AIDS virus occurred only through contact with infected body fluids. A majority felt that AIDS was a punishment for sin, and several indicated that they thought it could be contracted as a result of natural exposures such as to unclean surroundings or cold temperatures.[35] These beliefs justify a far different set of behaviors and practices than does the biomedical literature. In fact, a recent survey of women of color reported that the majority believed they had little or no chance of contracting HIV despite the disproportionately high prevalence of AIDS among people of color.

Similarly, the health beliefs of Asian women living in the United

States are quite different from those of the dominant culture. Understanding the belief systems of Asian women is particularly challenging because of the diversity of ethnic groups. Although, as stated earlier, the majority of Asian people living in this country are of Chinese descent, recent immigrants represent many different groups, particularly Koreans and southeast Asians. When asked to state the causes of illness, Vietnamese women who had settled in the Midwest cited weather or temperature (48 percent), bad food or water (11 percent), fatigue (7 percent), germs (5 percent), the supernatural (4 percent), mental state (3 percent), not covering one's head (1 percent), and personal actions (1 percent).[36] One can speculate that these beliefs are the result of previous experiences with disease in a country lacking adequate housing and sanitation. Irrespective of the underlying rationale for the belief system, however, someone who believes that illness is caused by germs only 5 percent of the time is less likely to seek treatment with antibiotics than someone who believes that germs are the major source of illness.

To take another example, information gathered through in-depth interviews with Korean women revealed a belief that health was the result of physical, psychological, and spiritual factors, with 45 percent believing that faith in God was a force in maintaining health. These same Korean women strongly believed that during the post-partum period, a woman should rest for 30 days, eat brown seaweed soup, and avoid anything cold.[37] Once these beliefs are appreciated, it is easy to see how instructions for post-partum care that do not acknowledge these commonly practiced behaviors would lack credibility and would therefore be ignored.

These examples of the diversity of health beliefs among women of color and the distinctions between them and those of the dominant culture demonstrate the importance of health beliefs in understanding health care utilization. Professionals' lack of knowledge of these health beliefs plays a role in the poor health status of women of color, just as inadequate access to care and access only to poor health care do. Even though there is a growing body of literature in each of these areas, our knowledge is incipient and ignorance prevails.

Inadequate Knowledge
The gaps in our knowledge can be put into four categories: statistics; pathophysiology and mechanisms of disease; the significance of race,

ethnicity, gender, and class; and ways to narrow the disparity in health status among groups. Each of these areas is important, because it is essential in the formulation of solutions. Resources cannot be redirected if we do not know which groups need them most. Cures cannot be found if the underlying mechanisms of disease remain a mystery. Finally, the gaps in health status cannot be eliminated if we do not know how race, ethnicity, social class, and gender contribute to the gaps.

This last question—what to measure—is fundamental to all the others. Certainly, there are genetic differences between males and females and among the races, but there are also social differences. Which is more important in explaining the differences in health status? A recent study investigated the relationship between skin color and severity of hypertension among African Americans and found that there was a correlation, but not for everyone.[38] The relationship existed for men but not for women, and only for men from lower socioeconomic groups. Thus, the study, which started with the assumption that larger doses of the genes responsible for hypertension would result in more severe disease and that black people who had less admixture with whites (as measured by skin color) would have larger doses of the gene, was unable to prove a positive relationship between skin color and severity of hypertension for either men or women, or across social classes. It may be that skin color is not a good proxy for race, but it is also likely that the severity of hypertension is related to social class as well as race. In this country, race and social class confound each other, and until we are able to sort out the relative contribution of each, the contributions of race will remain a mystery. Such is the case with gender and ethnicity as well.

Essential to the effort to understand exactly what is being measured when data on race, ethnicity, or gender are collected are reliable health statistics. At present, our information is patchy because we lack data on many ethnic groups. Some health statistics are collected with only three racial classifications: white, black, and "other." As a result, many details, particularly about Asian and Hispanic populations' health status, remain largely unknown. Further, the information collected on Hispanic and Asian populations often does not distinguish ethnic groups. Rather, the subpopulations are combined, even if the statistics on the individual groups are not similar. For example, when statistics on Chinese and Laotian peoples are lumped together, the Laotians' problems are masked, and our ability to understand the role of ethnicity is compromised. Although statistics are most complete for blacks, gaps remain, as does the potential for even greater gaps in the future. Because of immigration from African and Caribbean countries, the black population is beginning to have substantial ethnic heterogeneity. Health statistics that do not report ethnicity among blacks ignore the increasing heterogeneity of this racial group, which may be a factor in health status.

Since we are barely able to measure the differences among groups, it should not be a surprise that our understanding of the reasons underlying the differences among racial and ethnic groups is rudimentary. Explanations for the marked differences in mortality rates among ethnic and racial groups vary. Although poverty does not correlate completely with minority health differentials, socioeconomic status remains a powerful predictor of morbidity and mortality. Factors such as family structure, community supports, and cultural values also need to be examined. Kumanyika describes the process of chronic disease emergence that is characteristic of modern, affluent societies, in which different ethnic groups acquire different disease patterns as they adopt the lifestyles of the dominant (Caucasian) population.[39] In fact, studies of Hispanic populations have shown that health status is lower among the more acculturated (as measured by bilingual speech patterns). Like populations in some developing countries, members of some U.S. racial or ethnic minority groups have less cumulative exposure to characteristic western sedentary life-styles and high-fat diets. Thus, a Hispanic woman who still speaks only Spanish may not have added fast food to her diet or begun smoking cigarettes. Other studies suggest that as Hispanic women become more acculturated, their health status worsens. Hispanic women who are more acculturated are more likely to smoke than their less culturally adapted counterparts, and researchers link smoking with the near doubling of lung cancer rates among Hispanic women. Another study reported that as Hispanic women become more acculturated, their risk of giving birth to low birthweight babies increases and the likelihood that they will breastfeed their infants decreases.[40] Researchers postulate that as these groups adopt the dominant lifestyles, obesity emerges first, followed by increased rates of diabetes, hypertension, cardiovascular disease, and cancers associated with dietary factors, such as breast cancer and colorectal cancer.

So What?

If solutions are not found soon, what is now a minority issue will soon become a majority issue. Hispanics are the fastest growing minority in the United States, a result of high birthrates and immigration. Compared with other populations, Hispanics have a higher fertility rate (approximately 100 per 1,000 women aged 15-44, as compared to 85 per 1,000 among African Americans and 67 per 1,000 among whites),[41] give birth to children at younger ages, and have more children. By the year 2000, Hispanics will number an estimated 31 million and will constitute the largest minority group in the United States.[42] We must improve our understanding of where the gaps in health status exist between women of color and other groups. More importantly, we need a better understanding of the reasons for these disparities and we must use this knowledge to close the gaps.

In order to turn knowledge about health status into improved health status, we need to know what works. Without high-quality health services research involving minority populations, we will, as a nation, continue to grope for solutions as the health problems of people of color worsen. As we move into an era of practice guidelines, quality assurance, and emphasis on medical outcomes, there is no excuse for not evaluating these measures *vis à vis* race, ethnicity, and gender. Should the guidelines for the treatment of breast cancer be different for women of color, and is the treatment the same for black and Hispanic women? We don't know. Will the same strategies to reduce maternal mortality work for black and Hispanic women? We don't know. Yet these are the kinds of questions we must be able to answer if the disparities and scenes such as the one described in the opening of this chapter are to be eliminated.

Notes

1. U.S. Bureau of the Census, *Statistical Abstract of the United States: 1993*, 113th ed. (Washington, DC: U.S. Government Printing Office, 1993), 56.

2. U.S. Department of Commerce, *1990 Census of Population, Social and Economic Characteristics, United States* (1990 CP-2-1) (Washington, DC: U.S. Government Printing Office, 1993), 93, 94, 137.

3. *1990 Census of Population, Social and Economic Characteristics*, 57, 58, 125.

4. Ibid., 44.

5. Patricia Montgomery, *The Hispanic Population in the United States*, Current Population Reports, Population Characteristics, P20-475 (Washington, DC: U.S. Government Printing Office, 1994), 14.

6. *Statistical Abstract 1993*, 53.

7. *Health, United States, 1993*, 93-94.

8. Ibid., 94.

9. *Statistical Abstract 1993*, 1874.

10. *Health, United States, 1993*, 127.

11. Ibid., 152.

12. Ibid., 166.

13. Hispanic Health and Nutrition Survey.

14. C.A. Stroup-Benham and F.M. Trevino, "Reproductive Characteristics of Mexican-American, Mainland Puerto Rican, and Cuban-American Women," *Journal of the American Medical Association* 265(2)(1991):222-226.

15. Jeane Ann Grisso, Amy R. Wishner, Donald F. Schwarz, Barbara A. Weene, John H. Holmes, and Rudolph L. Sutton, "A Population-Based Study of Injuries in Inner-City Women," *American Journal of Epidemiology* 134(1):59-68.

16. *Health, United States, 1993*, 93-94.

17. Marvine Howe, "Battered Alien Spouses Find a Way to Escape an Immigration Trap," *New York Times*, August 25, 1991.

18. *Health, United States, 1993*, 143.

19. U.S. Department of Health and Human Services, *Healthy People 2000: National Health Promotion and Disease Prevention Objectives*, (Washington, DC: U.S. Department of Health and Human Services).

20. *Health, United States, 1993*, 70.

21. Ibid.

22. Council Report, "Hispanic Health in the United States," *Journal of the American Medical Association* 265(2)(1991):248-252.

23. *Health, United States, 1993*, 240.

24. "Hispanic Health in the United States," 1991.

25. S.E. Bell and M.B. Whiteford, "Tai Dam Health Care Practices: Asian Refugee Women in Iowa," *Social Science Medicine* 24(1987):317-325.

26. *Current Estimates from the National Health Interview Survey, Center for Health Statistics, Vital Health Statistics* 10(181), 1991.

27. E. Ford, R. Cooper, A. Castaner, B. Simmons, et al., "Coronary Arteriography and Coronary Bypass Surgery among Whites and Other Racial Groups Relative to Hospital-based Incidence Rates for Coronary Artery Disease: Findings from the National Hospital Discharge Survey," *American Journal of Public Health* 79(1989):437-440.

28. S. Tunis, "Variation in Utilization of Procedures of Peripheral Arterial Disease: A Look at Patient Characteristics," *Bass Archives of Internal Medicine* 153(8)(1993):991-998.

29. A.M. Gittelsohn, J. Halpern, R.L. Sanchez, "Income, Race, and Surgery in Maryland," *American Journal of Public Health* 81(11)(1991):1435-1441.

30. J. Hadley, E.P. Steinberg, and J. Feder, "Comparison of Uninsured and Privately Insured Hospital Patients," *Journal of the American Medical Association* 265(3)(1991)374-379.

31. L.W. Bassett, "Social Class and Black-White Differences in Breast Cancer Survival," *American Journal of Public Health* 76(12)(1986):1400-1403.

32. P. Diehr, J. Yergan, J. Chu, P. Feigl, et al., "Treatment Modality and Quality Differences for Black and White Breast-Cancer Patients Treated in Community Hospitals," *Medical Care* 27(10)(1989):942-954.

33. Anne-Linda Furstenberg and Mathy D. Mezey, "Differences in Outcome between Black and White Elderly Hip Fracture Patients," *Journal of Chronic Disability* 40(10)(1987):931-938.

34. K. Huckshorn, "Minority Women Heard on Health Issues," *Philadelphia Inquirer* (September 12, 1991).

35. J.H. Flaskerud and C.D. Rush, "AIDS and Traditional Health Beliefs and Practices of Black Women," *Nursing Research* 38(4)(1989):210-215.

36. S.E. Bell and M.B. Whiteford, "Tai Dam Health Care Practices: Asian Refugee Women in Iowa," *Social Science Medicine* 24(1987):317-325.

37. K.-J.Y. Park and L.M. Peterson, "Beliefs, Practices, and Experiences of Korean Women in Relation to Childbirth," *Health Care for Women International* 12(1991):261-269.

38. W.W. Dressler, "Social Class, Skin Color, and Arterial Blood Pressure in Two Societies," *Ethnicity and Disease* 1(1)(1991)60-77.

39. Shiriki K. Kumanyika and Patricia M. Golden, "Cross-Sectional Differences in Health Status in U.S. Racial/Ethnic Minority Groups: Potential Influence of Temporal Changes, Disease, and Life-Style Transitions," *Ethnicity & Disease* 1(1)(1991):50-59.

40. R. Scribner and J.H. Dwyer, "Acculturation and Low Birthweight among Latinos in the Hispanic HANES," *American Journal of Public Health* 79(1989):1263-1267.

41. *Health, United States, 1993.*

42. U.S. Bureau of the Census, Current Population Reports, P25-1092, *Population Projections of the United States by Age, Race, and Hispanic Origin*, 1992-2050 (Washington, DC: U.S. Government Printing Office, 1992), 29.

II

WOMEN AND INFORMAL CAREGIVING

Once we are born, it is likely that much of the health care we receive as children and adolescents will be provided by our mothers. In the years immediately before our deaths, it is likely that much of the health care we receive will come from women—mothers, daughters, daughters-in-law, neighbors, and friends. Although much is made of the approximately 1.5 million residents of nursing homes, we forget that an equal number of frail Americans who might otherwise qualify for nursing home care are instead supported and cared for at home by a large and too-often invisible army of women caregivers. Almost always a labor of love, it can also be a crushing burden for women who must balance work and other family responsibilities with constant caregiving of a vulnerable, dependent human being. Often that human being is older; but increasingly, informal caregivers are tending younger patients as well. Sometimes it is the work of a lifetime, involving a child injured at birth or born chronically ill, who may live for decades. This is health care of a crucial kind—but it is too often taken for granted, thus endangering an often-heroic but nonetheless fragile safety net.

5

Women as Unpaid Caregivers: The Price They Pay

Elaine M. Brody

MANY WOMEN IN HEALTH care have parallel, less visible careers as unpaid caregivers to the disabled elderly. During the same time span in which women's roles in the health care enterprise have been changing, dramatic changes in their roles as unpaid health providers also have been occurring. About one-quarter of all persons in the U.S. labor force, the vast majority of them women and most of them adult daughters, are now providing unpaid health services to at least one disabled elderly family member.[1] These cross-sectional data do not reveal the number of such women who have had parent-care responsibilities in the past or will have them in the future. Nor do they include those women who have left their jobs because they could not manage paid and unpaid caregiving simultaneously.

Women who work outside the home and those who do not are both feeling the stunning impact of massive demographic and socioeconomic trends that have converged to make elder care a normative life experience.[2] In a situation unprecedented in history, their traditional roles as wives, homemakers, mothers, and grandmothers have been augmented not only by roles as unpaid caregivers to the vastly increased population of older people, but also by roles as paid workers in the labor force. In trying to respond to the multiple demands on their time and energy and to sort out their priorities, many are under severe strain and bewildered by the dilemma in which they find themselves.

Some of the material in this chapter is abstracted from E.M. Brody, *Women in the Middle: Their Parent Care Years* (New York: Springer Publishing Co., Inc., 1990).

Such women are "women-in-the-middle." They are most often in their middle years; they are, in the main, a middle generation in three- or four-generation families; and they are caught in the middle of the requirements of their various roles.[3] Many are also caught between competing values: the deeply rooted traditional value that care of older people in the family is women's responsibility and the newer value that it is all right—even necessary—for women to work.

The focus in this chapter on daughters and daughters-in-law is not meant to deprecate the commitment and efforts of other family members. Spouses, sons, grandchildren, and other relatives become caregivers to older people. Elderly spouses, in particular, are enormously loyal to each other when one of them becomes disabled. (Because of the discrepancy in life expectancy between men and women, most caregiving spouses are wives.) Daughters are the largest group of helpers for the most disabled elderly, however, because most of these elderly are in advanced old age and are widowed (they are usually women), and thus do not have a spouse on whom to rely. Daughters outnumber sons by about four to one as primary caregivers to severely disabled parents and in sharing their homes with those who can no longer manage alone.[4] When "sons" are named as the main caregivers, "sons" is often a euphemism for the sons' wives, the daughters-in-law, who provide the actual hands-on care.

Women vary widely in age and stage of life during their parent-care years. The 1982 U.S. Long Term Care Survey found that almost two-thirds of caregiving daughters were between the ages of 45 and 64, but one-quarter were under 45 years of age, and 13 percent were 65 years of age or older.[5] One-fourth still had children under 18 living at home, while others undoubtedly had reached the theoretical "empty-nest" stage. Those over the age of 65 exemplify the growing number of situations in which one generation of older people takes care of members of a still older generation.

Parent-caring women are extremely diverse in other ways too: in socioeconomic and ethnic backgrounds, marital status, personality, adaptive capacity, personal circumstances, and the quality of their relationships with their parents. Some have lived traditional lives as homemakers; some worked when young, then gave up their jobs for marriage and motherhood; others have worked all of their adult lives; and still others move in and out of the labor force as their own needs, and those of their families, dictate. Most women work because they and their families need the money, others because of commitment to careers or because their jobs give them various kinds of satisfaction. Most have combinations of those reasons.

How It Happened

Powerful demographic and socioeconomic trends have intersected to make today's situation very different from that of earlier times. Those trends developed in the context of values and behavior that remained constant. The notion that the extended family has been replaced by the isolated nuclear family has been conclusively refuted. Research, beginning with the national and cross-national studies of Ethel Shanas and colleagues,[6] has shown definitively that ties between the generations continue to be strong and viable. The aged give as well as receive the garden-variety kinds of help that family members exchange on a day-to-day basis, and families have been steadfast, even heroic, in caring for the disabled elderly. When families are unable to care for their older members, a constellation of personal, social, and economic factors are at work.

So too has the misconception that older people are dumped into nursing homes been disproved.[7] In the overwhelming majority of situations, permanent placement occurs only after families have endured unrelenting strains for many years. Five percent of the elderly are in nursing homes at any given time: half of this group are there temporarily; the rest are in advanced old age and are severely disabled physically and mentally (most have Alzheimer's disease or another form of dementia). Those in nursing homes have fewer family members than the noninstitutionalized; a small minority have a surviving spouse, many are childless, and those with children have fewer children and—significantly—fewer daughters. When there are family members, they continue to do what they can, to visit regularly, and to monitor the care of the older people. Against that background of continuing family cohesion and loyalty, two of the major trends that created women's current predicament have been demographic: the vast increase in the aging population and the falling birthrate. A third trend has been the increasing needs of older people for help in their daily lives (see Chapter 6, "Caring for Women in Older Age"), and a fourth, the large-scale entry of women into the workplace.

Demographic Trends

The steady growth in the number and proportion of older people in our population was brought about by public health measures, improved welfare programs, better nutrition and sanitation, antibiotics, and discoveries that prevent epidemic diseases such as cholera, smallpox, diphtheria, and poliomyelitis. As a result, more people survive to old age (Exhibit 1).

Affecting filial care even more directly are the number and proportion of *very* old people, those aged 75 or older, which have increased more rapidly than the total older population. This shift is attributable to high-technology medicine, coupled with Medicare (enacted in 1965), which made such care available to the aged. At present, more than 40 percent of all older people are aged 75 and older, and that proportion will increase.[8]

The declining birthrate has made the shift in the ratio between the old and the younger generations even more pronounced. In 1900, the average family with children had four children; today the average family has fewer than two children. Thus, a woman who is now very old has fewer children than her mother did in old age. Fewer children

Exhibit 1
People Aged 65 Years and Older
United States
1900–2030

	Number (Millions)	Percent of Total Population
1900	3.1	4.1
1930	6.7	5.4
1960	16.7	9.2
1990	31.2	12.5
2010	39.7	13.3
2030	69.8	20.2

Sources: U.S. Department of Commerce, Bureau of the Census, *Historical Statistics of the United States: Colonial Times to 1957; Statistical Abstract of the United States* (Washington, DC: U.S. Government Printing Office, 1990 and 1992); J.C. Day, *Population Projections of the United States, by Age, Sex, Race, and Hispanic Origin: 1992–2050* P25-1092 (Washington, DC: U.S. Government Printing Office, 1992).

means fewer daughters. Because many women are daughters-in-law as well as daughters, they have greatly increased chances of being called upon for parent or parent-in-law care, or both. Moreover, a shorter period of parent care was needed 90 years ago since people were more likely to die at younger ages from acute, short-term illnesses.

In the future, more people will be caring for very old persons after they themselves have reached retirement age. Between 1900 and 1967 the number of middle-aged couples with two or more living parents increased fivefold: from 10 percent to 47 percent.[9] By 1980 there were about 9 persons aged 85 years and older per 100 persons aged 60 to 74, a ratio predicted to reach 33 per 100 by 2050, when the large number of people in the "baby boom" reaches 85 and over. At that time, every third person between the ages of 60 and 74 could have a surviving parent! These radical changes portend a continuing increase in the need for filial care, since the very old are the most vulnerable to the chronic illnesses that lead to disability and dependence on others.

In addition, rates of widowhood soar as people move toward advanced old age, so that fewer of the very old have a surviving spouse on whom to depend. Even when a spouse is present, he or she is also likely to be in advanced old age, to have health problems and be less able to provide care, and therefore to rely on adult children for help in doing so. And while more caregiving adult children will be old or approaching old age in the future, the growing proportion of births to women in their thirties means that there will also be more women providing elder care while they still have young children at home. With more families having two generations in the aging phase of life, adult grandchildren may find themselves helping both parents and grandparents—a situation that is not uncommon even now. Some grandchildren need to provide care for grandparents when the death of the latter's adult child creates a gap in the generational chain.

Changing Needs of Older People

As health care professionals know well, by the 1960s, the health care needs of the elderly had shifted radically from acute care to chronic or long-term care (see Chapter 6 for data).[10]

The family responded to the new needs of the elderly by inventing long-term care. Nearly three-quarters of the noninstitutionalized disabled elderly rely solely on the family for the assistance they receive and most of the remainder depend on a combination of family care and paid help.[11] Only 15 percent of all helper days of care come from non-family sources, and only a tiny minority of the elderly receive all their care from such providers. In short, the family members who constitute the unpaid informal systems of health care far exceed paid health workers from the formal system in providing long-term care.

Families nowadays provide more care and more difficult care to more older people over much longer periods of time than has ever before been the case. Women may begin by spending a few hours weekly in helping minimally disabled parents or parents-in-law, but ultimately may provide help around the clock when the old person becomes severely disabled. Almost half of caregiving daughters have been providing care for one to four years, and one out of five has been doing so for more than five years.[12] Some spend more years in parent care than in raising their own children. Moreover, parent care often is not a one-time episode in their lives. Many women have what may be called caregiving careers in that they help more than one older person simultaneously or sequentially.[13]

Women's Changing Lifestyles
While the demography and the kinds of help needed by the aged were changing, and while women were rising to the occasion to provide that help, their lives were taking increasingly diverse paths. Patterns of marriage, divorce and remarriage, and childbearing have been changing rapidly. Since there is a tendency for an elderly parent to rely on the child with the fewest competing responsibilities,[14] the fact that 44 percent of parent-caring women are not married[15] is probably due to the increase in the proportion of women who do not marry or who divorce, as well as to the high rates of widowhood during the parent-care years.

One of the most visible lifestyle changes affecting women has been the vast increase in the number who are employed outside the home. Contributing to that trend have been economic pressures, a lower birthrate (meaning fewer children to keep women at home), increased educational levels (to stimulate career interests), a high divorce rate, later marriage and childbearing, and changes in attitudes about gender-appropriate roles.

In 1930, 10 million women, or 24 percent of all working-age women, were in the labor force (22 percent of the total work force).[16] By 1985, seven of every ten women 25 to 54 years old were working

(44 percent of the total work force). By 1995, the proportion will rise to eight of ten women—nearly 60 million—and they will account for 46 percent of the work force.[17] Middle-aged women—those most likely to be caring for parents—entered the labor force much more rapidly than any other age group. Between 1920 and 1974, for example, the number of women workers between the ages of 18 and 34 increased by 115 percent, by 143 percent for those aged 35 to 44, by 266 percent for those aged 45 to 54, and by 352 percent for those aged 55 to 64.[18] By the 1980s almost half (43.5 percent) of daughters providing major help (i.e., personal care) to their parents were in the labor force.[19]

These changing roles, of course, hold potential for competing values. In a study of three generations of women,[20] for example, members of all generations were firmly committed to family care of the aged and large majorities also favored equal roles for men and women in child care and parent care. Despite their egalitarian views, and although two-thirds of the middle-generation women were working and although they endorsed in principle the acceptability of non-family (i.e., formal) services for many instrumental helping tasks, they were more likely to expect working daughters than working sons to adjust their work schedules for parent care. And they *behaved* in accordance with the "old" values about family care of the elderly and in accordance with the old values about women's roles: they were the ones who gave the bulk of the help to elderly mothers who were disabled.[21]

While challenging the old values in the workplace, these women are continuing to enact the old values at home. Although they have encountered gender bias, discrimination, and barriers to advancement in the workplace, their unpaid caregiving roles have not been disputed. They continue to provide care for those in their families who need it and have not been discouraged from taking more responsibility in parent care or other "gender-appropriate" roles at home.

Women who are employed in health care are not exempt from such value conflicts and values-based behavior. Working women, in general, continue to provide the bulk of child care. It was reported recently that 75 percent of all married female physicians perform all their household work.[22] (Nurses have known all about that for many years.) In short, while the massive changes triggered by Betty Friedan[23] were taking place, some conditions remained constant.

The Effects of Parent Care

To put the matter in perspective, it must be emphasized that the vast majority of women *want* to care for elderly parents and do so willingly. They derive satisfaction from fulfilling their perceived responsibilities, adhering to religious and cultural values, expressing affection, making sure that their parent is well cared for, and feeling that they are serving as a good model for their own children. A common theme in their stories is that they are returning the care they received as young children: "She cared for me and now it's my turn to care for her." Nevertheless, it is undeniable that many women pay in the coin of their mental health, physical health, income, and personal development.

By far the most pervasive and severe negative effects are the emotional strains. Study after study has shown that more than half of these unpaid health providers experience significant degrees of stress.[24] They report a litany of symptoms including depression, anger, anxiety, frustration, guilt, sleeplessness, demoralization, feelings of conflict caused by competing demands, feelings of helplessness, irritability, lowered morale, and emotional exhaustion. Time and freedom are often restricted, and some women are isolated and confined to the home. The care required of them may be physically demanding, uncomfortable, and even embarrassing. Mental and emotional problems head the list of caregivers' strains and are prominent among the characteristics of care recipients that predict these strains.[25] Mental disabilities of all types are especially stressful and difficult to deal with. The disruptive behavior associated with Alzheimer's disease and other dementias stands out in this respect, and is particularly important because of the increase in the number of elderly with such ailments. Such patients may present extraordinary difficulties because they need considerable personal care and have symptoms such as forgetfulness, incontinence, wandering, sleep disturbance, combativeness, and an inability to communicate or to provide appreciative feedback. Many adult children, who have a genetic stake in the matter, are frightened and anxious. "Will this happen to me?" they wonder. Perhaps most poignant is their feeling that they have "lost" the older person. Depression is a major problem among these unpaid caregivers.[26] They have been found to report three times as many stress symptoms as the general population, to take more prescription drugs, and to participate in fewer social and recreational activities.[27]

Depressions of the older people are another of the mental problems that have detrimental effects on their caregivers. Gurland and his associates found higher rates of depression among caregivers with depressed older people in their households, a phenomenon they characterized as the "contagion of depression."[28]

Some unpaid caregivers also pay with their physical health. Although research on such consequences of caregiving is in an early stage, a few studies have reported that caregivers of Alzheimer's patients use more health care and prescription medicines and have poorer health than those in a control group.[29] Some women speak of back problems from lifting and turning helpless old people and of stress-related ailments such as ulcers.[30] Research at Ohio State University indicates that impact of the chronic stress on such caregivers results in lower levels of immunological adaptations, which in turn may account for their greater susceptibility to physical health problems.[31]

The family also pays. There often are constraints on the lifestyle of the entire family: interference with social, recreational, and vocational activities; vacations; and even retirement. The caregiver's time and energy may be diverted to the older person. Many husbands of caregiving daughters report strain, and some even experience work interruptions as a result of the caregiving situation.[32] While there has been little research on the effects on the children of caregivers, anecdotal reports indicate that they do not go unscathed.[33] High on the list of factors associated with stress is sharing a household with a disabled elderly parent.[34] Many of the older people who live with children are severely disabled (that's why they moved in) and need heavier care; crowding and loss of privacy may result. Enforced close contact provides fertile ground for interpersonal conflicts. When the caregiver's nest also contains her own children (and there are about a million such households), the strains are intensified.[35] Some strains are relieved when the parent is placed in a nursing home, but then new ones appear, such as worry about the quality of care.[36]

Children who live at a geographic distance from a disabled parent also worry about the parent's decline and experience various emotional symptoms, albeit to a lesser extent. But they have unique problems, such as the need to make frequent and sometimes costly visits, an inability to respond to parents' needs in a timely fashion, a feeling that there is no one close at hand on whom the parent can rely, and guilt at not being able to do more to help.[37]

Unpaid caregivers pay an economic price, too. Based on government data, the cost of the average of 26 hours weekly they spend providing long-term care is estimated at $4,529 annually (calculated at minimum wage).[38] Economic costs that have been invisible until the past few years are the opportunity costs incurred when caregivers quit their jobs, reduce the number of hours they work, or refuse job promotions in order to take care of elderly relatives. In studies of parent-caring women who work outside the home and those who do not, 12 percent of the entire sample (28 percent of the nonworking women) had left their jobs in order to care for the parent.[39] In addition, 13 percent of the sample (26 percent of the working women) were considering quitting or had already reduced their work schedules for the same reason. Those women still working outside the home were anxious about the future, and were worried about what was happening to their parent while they were at work. Despite these pressures, their parents did not receive less care than the parents of nonworking women. What the women gave up was their own free time. Those who had left their jobs were often those who could least afford to do so. When they were depressed, their depressions were related to having given up their jobs for parent care, suggesting that work provides special gratification as well as some respite from parent care.

Results from the 1982 U.S. Long Term Care Survey about the proportions of women whose work lives are disrupted were strikingly similar to the findings of a study of the Philadelphia Geriatric Center. In that national representative sample, 11.6 percent of caregiving daughters had left their jobs for parent care, 23 percent had reduced their working hours, and 35 percent had rearranged their work schedules.[40] Similar reports about the problems of elder-caring workers have come from studies by industry in the United States and other industrialized countries. The Travelers Companies[41] found that 20 percent of their employees over the age of 30 (most of them women) were providing elder care. The American Association of Retired Persons[42] estimates that 14 percent of part-time workers had previously worked full time and that many of these workers were spending more than 20 hours weekly in caregiving. Such effects on women's work obviously incur opportunity costs for the family, often for those who need the money most. As a British review article pointed out, women do not work for pin money now.[43] And the opportunity costs these women incur today have implications for their own old age, since they also lose Social Security benefits and pensions they could be earning.

There is a growing awareness of the effects of elder care in reducing or eliminating work for some people. But it has been virtually unnoticed that some women *join* the labor force or *increase* the number of their work hours because of elder care. In early data from a study of parent care at the Philadelphia Geriatric Center, 10 percent of the daughters said that parent care had contributed to their taking a job, and 4 percent said that it had contributed to their increasing the number of hours they worked. Although information is not yet available about their reasons, anecdotal reports suggest that some of these women need the money to help meet the expenses of parent care and some need the respite that work provides.[44] This is consistent with data showing that among the factors predicting women's continued presence in the labor force is support of a child or an aged parent.[45] In another large survey, families reported average additional monthly expenditures of $117 related to caring for an elderly person.[46]

Finally, in addition to paying in dollars, in their physical and mental health, and in the well-being of their families, many women pay by foregoing or limiting their own personal development. Wished-for careers may disappear or goals may shrink. The satisfaction derived from doing useful, important, and enjoyable out-of-home work may dissipate. There are no measures to calibrate such losses.

Women who are paid health care workers may be in double jeopardy. Those caring for disabled elderly relatives may be doing the same work during their off hours as they do to earn their salaries. We hear a good deal about "burnout"—for example, among nursing staff in nursing homes—but the effects of their double exposure to personal and professional caregiving stress have not been studied.

The Subjective Experiences of Women in the Middle

Of particular relevance to the concerns of this volume is an intriguing aspect of parent and parent-in-law care: that it is primarily *women* who do this work, and that women experience more strain from caregiving than do men in the same role. Many women provide elder care for long years despite severe detrimental effects on themselves and their families, often going beyond what appear to be the limits of human endurance. In the stories they tell about their experiences, several illuminating subjective themes recur.[47] An overarching theme is the fundamental acceptance of parent care as a woman's role. The sexes are socialized quite differently in early life, with girls educated into the caregiving role (like their mothers), while boys learn early that work is their main role, to be the family breadwinner. Later in life, the powerful social value that adult children are responsible for the care of the old really means that daughters are held responsible. Gender-appropriate roles are so deeply ingrained that the possibility of their brothers being the caregivers to parents does not even occur to most daughters. Daughters-in-law often accept the same gender-role designation and become the caregivers when a parent-in-law does not have a daughter.

One reason that daughters experience more strain than sons is straightforward: daughters provide more help, and more help of the kind that requires hands-on care. Sons also love their parents and give them emotional and financial support when needed, but tend to become the main caregivers only when they have no sisters. They then receive more help from their spouses (the daughters-in-law) than women do. It is striking, however, that not only primary caregiving daughters, but sisters of those caregivers (both proximate and geographically distant) experience more stress than brothers. Moreover, daughters experience more stress from parent care than sons even after a parent has been institutionalized,[48] just as is true of those who provide home care. In short, being a woman means experiencing more strain from caring for a disabled older person.

Women's expectations of themselves increase their strains. They feel responsible not only for the needed tasks, but also for the emotional well-being of the older people and everyone else in the family. They feel, in effect, "I have to do it all, do it well, and see to it that they are happy." Since making people happy is an unrealistic goal, it is often doomed to failure. Guilt about that "failure" is intensified if the caregiver tries in any way to meet her own needs and in so doing perceives that she has failed to make the older person happy. Another source of guilt is that negative and positive feelings exist side by side: dislike and compassion, for example, and resentment and a sense of obligation.

Still another theme in women's subjective experiences derives from their stage of life. Parent care may be needed when a woman is anywhere from her thirties to her seventies. It may be experienced as what Bernice Neugarten has called an "off time"[49] (and therefore more stressful) event. Women in their thirties, who also may have young children at home, often say, "I'm too young for this." Those in their middle years (the theoretical "empty-nest" stage) say, "I thought I would be free at this stage of my life." Instead, their nests are refilled with the elderly parent and sometimes also with grown children who have returned to the parental home. Or, the nest may contain a developmentally disabled adult child. Women who are older and more likely to be experiencing the decrements of aging themselves, say, "I am too old for this; I'm old myself."

Family Relationships
Inevitably, parent care affects relationships throughout the family. Although what happens at this stage of family life depends on the historical quality of those relationships, the new pressures can exacerbate pre-existing problems. It is less of a strain to help a parent with whom one has a history of a warm relationship, but adult children provide the care the parents need even when relationships are poor. In most cases, one daughter becomes the principal caregiver and provides the bulk of help. Though she may feel resentment and a sense of inequity, and though intersibling conflicts may erupt, they are by no means inevitable. Sibling interactions range from extreme bitterness to amicable cooperation, with most families falling in between.

When the caregivers are married, they often feel conflicted by the pull of competing demands as they struggle to set priorities among the needs of parent(s), husband, and children. Though couples may experience conflict that focuses on parent care, sons-in-law are often unsung heroes who help their parents-in-law and provide considerable emotional support to their wives. The caregiver's children (and sometimes her grandchildren) can be a competing responsibility. Women have more mental health symptoms, for example, when three generations live under the same roof.[50] Such situations may be stormy, particularly when the grandchildren are adolescent. Then, the caregivers are in the middle in still another sense: in feeling that they must mediate conflicts among various family members. Grown children often act as a back-up system of care, however, providing emotional support and special help when needed, such as "sitting" to allow their mothers some respite or helping in emergencies. Women with many relatives often receive much emotional and instrumental support, though help from other family members supplements rather than reduces the amount of their help. At the other extreme, there are some women who quite literally have no one—who are not married, who are childless, and who are only children. Although they may not feel pulled by competing responsibilities, they often feel lonely and alone. Childless women who therefore have no potential caregivers for themselves have still another worry: "Who will take care of me when I am old?"

Family supports of daughters-in-law include *their* husbands: the sons of the elderly people being cared for. Often the women are even grateful to the men for helping to care for the latter's own parents! Such is the depth of women's socialization to the caring role and the social, cultural, and religious values that exert such powerful pressures to define and keep them in that role. Thus, helping an elderly in-law presents a special set of strains because there is no biological link to provide deep emotional bonds or the powerful motivation of reciprocity.

Continuing and New Trends

Indications are that the demands made on millions of parent-caring women will be intensified. Certain trends continue: the more vulnerable, very old population continues to grow, the falling birthrate continues to reduce the supply of filial caregivers, and the proportion of women in the labor force continues to rise. In looking to the future, however, one must be careful not to predict ever-increasing care needs of the elderly. Biomedical breakthroughs are already occurring that hold potential for reducing dependency among the aged by preventing or ameliorating age-related and disability-causing chronic ailments, particularly the dementias.

The high rates of divorce and lower marriage rates mean that in the future more women will not have husbands during their parent-care years. Because developmentally disabled people are living longer and because of the later ages at which many women are marrying and having their first child, more caregivers will experience "double dependency" in caring for their parents and their children—some of them disabled adults—simultaneously. Still another trend is an increase in geographic mobility, which creates special problems when distance separates parents and children.

And there are other trends that are newer still. Women's roles—their paid and unpaid jobs—continue to accumulate. Not only do grandmothers perform a significant proportion of child care for women who work, but there has been considerable publicity of late about the increased number of grandmothers who actually rear their grandchildren because of problems in generation two. And the number of women who have two or more paid jobs has risen sharply, with many of them belonging to the ranks of single women maintaining families who moonlight because of economic need.[51]

Implications

The predicament of those who care for the elderly is not only a salient personal issue, but one of major importance for older people, for all family members, for the health care system, and for society as a whole. The capacity of the family to provide the required assistance determines what services and supports should be provided or financed by government and social agencies. Government's role in long-term care has been and undoubtedly will continue to be hotly debated. It is now a common refrain among experts that the resources of families to provide long-term care have been exceeded and that we must have a federal system of long-term care insurance. The definitive report of the Brookings Institution stated unequivocally that most people could not afford privately purchased long-term care insurance.[52]

For those who fear that women would reduce or withdraw their caring services if more non-family help were provided, it may be reassuring to know that study after study has shown that the "service-substitution" hypothesis is unfounded. Non-family services complement and supplement, but do not substitute for, family help. Indeed, in a recently completed controlled study of a respite care intervention, family services increased in the course of the one-year study, regardless of whether respite intervention was received.[53]

There is no single or enduring solution, because change is a constant. The characteristics and needs of the elderly change as each successive cohort ages, as new scientific and social developments occur, and as the social and economic climate changes. But now and in the foreseeable future, the family—women, whether or not they are employed—simply cannot do it all. To say that the solution is for women to stay at home to care for the old ignores the facts. Setting aside the values that speak to women's right to work, such a "solution" would deplete the already inadequate cadre of workers in the health system. Moreover, in plain fact, most women work because they and their families need the money they earn—some for sheer subsistence and others to achieve a decent standard of living.

The now-hidden costs to the health care system remain virtually unexplored. That is, we know nothing about the dollar costs of physical and mental health care for caregiving women whose health suffers. Nor do we know the costs to the system when health workers caring for their relatives are deterred from entering the labor force, lose time from work, quit their jobs or work part-time, or are worried or interrupted while working because of what is going on at home. Interest has been generated in the business community as it has become aware of the extent to which employees are also caregivers. Some firms are taking steps such as considering the inclusion of elder day care as an employee benefit, holding caregiving fairs to disseminate information about services, and establishing referral services to service agencies. Other possible measures that can be considered are benefits similar to those wanted by workers with young children, such as flex time, sabbaticals, and job-sharing. And government's recognition of the problem has resulted in legislation mandating family leave.

A major imponderable is how the tension between changing and constant values will be resolved—that is, between the new values about women's roles and the enduring "old" values about care of the elderly being women's responsibility. Despite the influence of the new values, in the main the old values about gender-appropriate parent-care roles continue to be enacted. Even if men should participate in parent care to a greater extent, parent care and women's employment have created a larger package of responsibilities to be shared than existed before. And, despite the women's movement, children are still in the main being socialized into the familiar "gender-appropriate" roles. Values also influence our views as to what adult children *should* do. No yardstick can measure what is "right" or "good," however. There are no normative standards for parent-care behavior as there are for parenting young children, and perhaps there never can be such standards. (Parent care is, of course, qualitatively different from child care.) The complexities of setting such standards are compounded by a myriad of factors such as the variability in the extent and nature of old people's need for help, and the ages, health and economic status, and responsibilities of the adult children. Whatever one's values, what is possible now is different from what was possible in the past. It has been well established that what older people want most from their children is affection, contact, emotional support, and the sense that they have someone on whom to rely. Evidence is strong that they will continue to receive that kind of support. But their caregivers need help with the tangible services they cannot supply themselves in order to keep them from exceeding the limits of endurance and to prevent the reverberations from being felt down through the generations. In the final analysis, our values will be the determinants of what we do, or fail to do, to help the women who are the vast majority of unpaid health providers. And what is done for them will affect us all.

Notes

1. The Travelers Companies, *The Travelers Employee Caregiver Survey* (Hartford, CT: The Travelers Companies, June 1985); American Association of Retired Persons, *Care Givers in the Workplace, Survey Results, Overall Summary* (Washington, DC: February 1987).

2. E.M. Brody, "Parent Care as a Normative Family Stress," *The Gerontologist* 25 (1985):19-29.

3. E.M. Brody, "Women in the Middle and Family Help to Older People," *The Gerontologist* 21(1981):471-480.

4. R. Stone, G.L. Cafferata, and J. Sangl, "Caregivers of the Frail Elderly: A National Profile," *The Gerontologist* 27 (1987):616-626.

5. Ibid.

6. E. Shanas and G.F. Streib, *Social Structure and the Family: Generational Relations* (Englewood Cliffs, NJ: Prentice-Hall, Inc., 1965); E. Shanas, P. Townsend, D. Wedderburn, H. Friis, P. Milhog, and J. Stehouwer, *Old People in Three Industrial Societies* (New York: Atherton Press, 1968).

7. For a review, see E.M. Brody, "The Role of the Family in Nursing Homes: Implications for Research and Public Policy," in M.S. Harper and B. Lebowitz, eds., *Mental Illness in Nursing Homes: Agenda for Research* (Washington, DC: U.S. Government Printing Office, 1985), 234-264.

8. For descriptions of demographic developments, see C.M. Taeuber, *America in Transition: An Aging Society*, U.S. Bureau of the Census, Current Population Reports, Special Studies Series P-23, No. 128 (Washington, DC: U.S. Government Printing Office, 1983); U.S. Bureau of the Census, *Projections of the Population of the United States by Age, Sex, and Race: 1983 to 2080*, P-25, No. 952 (Washington, DC: U.S. Government Printing Office, 1984).

9. P. Uhlenberg, "Death and the Family," *Journal of Family History* 5(1980):313-320.

10. S.J. Brody, "Comprehensive Health Care for the Elderly: An Analysis," *The Gerontologist* 13(1973):412-418.

11. P. Doty, "Family Care of the Elderly: The Role of Public Policy," *The Milbank Quarterly* 64(1986):34-75.

12. Stone, Cafferata, and Sangl, 1987.

13. Brody, 1985.

14. E.P. Stoller, "Parental Caregiving by Adult Children," *Journal of Marriage and the Family* 45(1983):851-858.

15. Stone, Cafferata, and Sangl, 1987.

16. U.S. Department of Health and Human Services, Social Security Administration, *Women Social Security Beneficiaries Age 62 and Older, 1960-79*, Research and Statistics Note No. 8 (Washington, DC: Office of Research and Statistics, July 21, 1980).

17. U.S. Department of Labor, Bureau of Labor Statistics, Women's Bureau, *Facts on U.S. Working Women, Caring for Elderly Family Members*, Fact Sheet No. 86-4 (Washington, DC: October 1986).

18. B.A. Lingg, "Women Social Security Beneficiaries Aged 62 and Older, 1960-1974," *Research and Statistics Notes*, No. 13, September 29, 1975.

19. Stone, Cafferata, and Sangl, 1987.

20. E.M. Brody, P.T. Johnsen, M.C. Fulcomer, and A.M. Lang, "Women's Changing Roles and Help to the Elderly: Attitudes of Three Generations of Women," *Journal of Gerontology* 38(1983):597-607.

21. A. Lang and E.M. Brody, "Characteristics of Middle-aged Daughters and Help to Their Elderly Mothers," *Journal of Marriage and the Family* 45(1983):193-202.

22. *New York Times*, national edition, Sunday, February 18, 1990, 21.

23. B. Friedan, *The Feminine Mystique* (New York: W.W. Norton & Company, 1963).

24. See, for example, P.G. Archbold, "The Impact of Parent-caring on Women," *Family Relations* 32(1983):39-45; L.K. George, "The Burden of Caregiving: How Much? What Kinds? For Whom?" *Advances in Research*, Duke University, Center for the Study of Aging and Human Development, No. 8, 1984; B. Gurland, L. Dean, R. Gurland, and D. Cook, "Personal Time Dependency in the Elderly of New York City: Findings from the U.S.-U.K. Cross-national Geriatric Community Study," in *Dependency in the Elderly of New York City* (Community Council of Greater New York, 1978), 9-45; A. Horowitz, "Family Caregiving to the Frail Elderly," in C. Eisdorfer, M.P. Lawton, and G.L. Maddox, eds., *Annual Review of Gerontology and Geriatrics*, Vol. 5 (New York: Springer Publishing Co., 1985), 194-246; L.S. Noelker and S.W. Poulshock, "The Effects on Families of Caring for Impaired Elderly in Residence," *Final Report*, Administration on Aging No. 90-AR-2112 (Cleveland, OH: Benjamin Rose Institute, 1982).

25. P. Sainsbury and J. Grad de Alercon, "The Effects of Community Care in the Family of the Geriatric Patient," *Journal of Geriatric Psychiatry* 4(1970):23-41; J. Hoenig and M. Hamilton, "Elderly Patients and the Burden on the Household," *Psychiata et Neurologia* (Basel) 152(1966):281-293; J.R.A. Sanford, "Tolerance of Debility in Elderly Dependents by Supporters at Home: Its Significance for Hospital Practice," *British*

Medical Journal 3(1975):471-473; V.G. Cicirelli, "Relationship of Family Background Variables to Locus of Control in the Elderly," *Journal of Gerontology* 35(1980):108-114.

26. See, for example, D. Cohen and C. Eisdorfer, "Depression in Family Members Caring for a Relative with Alzheimer's Disease," *Journal of the American Geriatric Society* 36(1988):885-889; M.P. Lawton, E.M. Brody, and A. Saperstein, *Respite Services for Alzheimer's Caregivers: Research and Practice* (New York: Springer Publishing Co., 1990).

27. George, 1984.

28. Gurland, et al., 1978.

29. See, for example, W.E. Haley, E.G. Levine, L. Brown, J.W. Berry, and G.H. Hughes, "Psychological, Social, and Health Consequences of Caring for a Relative with Senile Dementia," *Journal of the American Geriatrics Society* 35(1987):405-411.

30. E.M. Brody, *Women in the Middle: Their Parent-Care Years* (New York: Springer Publishing Co., 1990).

31. J.K. Kiecolt-Glaser, R. Glaser, E.C. Shuttleworth, C.S. Dyer, P. Ogrocki, and C.E. Speicher, "Chronic Stress and Immunity in Family Caregivers of Alzheimer's Disease Victims," *Psychosomatic Medicine* 49(1987):523-535.

32. M.H. Kleban, E.M. Brody, C.B. Schoonover, and C. Hoffman, "Family Help to the Elderly: Sons'-in-Law Perceptions of Parent Care," *Journal of Marriage and the Family* 51(May 1989).

33. See Brody, 1990.

34. Horowitz, 1985; Lang and Brody, 1983.

35. E.M. Brody, M.H. Kleban, C. Hoffman, and C.B. Schoonover, "Adult Daughters and Parent Care: A Comparison of One-, Two-, and Three-Generation Households," *Home Health Care Services Quarterly* 9(1988):19-45; Noelker and Poulshock, 1982.

36. Brody et al., 1988; E.M. Brody, N.P. Dempsey, and R.A. Pruchno, "Mental Health of Sons and Daughters of the Institutionalized Aged," *The Gerontologist* 30(1990):212-219.

37. C.B. Schoonover, E.M. Brody, C. Hoffman, and M.H. Kleban, "Parent Care and Geographically Distant Children," *Research on Aging* 10(1988):472-492.

38. Doty, 1986.

39. Brody, "Parent Care...," 1985; E.M. Brody, M.H. Kleban, P.T. Johnsen, C. Hoffman, and C.B. Schoonover, "Work Status and Parent Care: A Comparison of Four Groups of Women," *The Gerontologist* 27 (1987):201-208.

40. Stone, Cafferata, and Sangl, 1987.

41. The Travelers Companies, 1985.

42. American Association of Retired Persons, 1987.

43. I. Allen, in collaboration with E. Levin, M. Sidell, and N. Vetter, "The Elderly and Their Informal Carers," in Department of Health and Social Security, *Research Contributions to the Development of Policy and Practices* (London: HMSO, 1983), 69-92.

44. Brody, 1990.

45. J.C. Henretta and A.M. Rand, *Labor Force Participation of Older Married Women*, Social Security Bulletin, 43 10 1980.

46. American Association of Retired Persons, 1987.

47. See Brody, 1990, for a fuller discussion of these inner aspects of parent care.

48. Brody et al., 1990.

49. B.L. Neugarten and G.O. Hagestad, "Age and the Life Course," in R.H. Binstock and E. Shanas, eds., *Handbook on Aging and the Social Sciences* (New York: Van Nostrand Reinhold, 1976), 35-57.

50. Brody et al., 1988.

51. P.T. Kilborn, "For Many Women, One Job Just Isn't Enough," *New York Times*, February 15, 1990, A-1, A-14.

52. A.M. Rivlin and J. Wiener, in *Caring for the Disabled Elderly: Who Will Pay?* (Washington, DC: The Brookings Institution, 1988).

53. M.P. Lawton, E.M. Brody, and A.R. Saperstein, *Respite for Caregivers of Alzheimer Patients* (New York: Springer Publishing Co., 1991).

6

Caring for Women in Older Age

Diane Rowland and Karen Davis

THE AGING OF THE AMERICAN population has especially significant implications for women. Women outlive men by an average of seven years.[1] A wife often cares for her husband through a long illness, and then spends a number of years living alone, without immediate assistance when her own health fails. The death of a spouse also typically brings a reduced standard of living, as savings are exhausted to pay medical and funeral expenses and income from pensions and Social Security is reduced.[2]

As the population ages, these problems will become more acute. By the year 2030, one in five Americans will be 65 years of age or older, up from one in nine today.[3] The absolute growth in the number of older people and the increasing proportion of older people over the age of 75 will lead to a substantial increase in the number of people needing long-term care. Most of these people will be women;[4] three-fourths of all nursing home residents are women.

For these reasons, a clear picture is needed of the health and long-term care needs of older women, and the steps this nation could take to assure them a better quality of life.

Profile of Older Women
In 1987 there were 16.6 million women 65 years of age and older in the United States, representing 59 percent of all older Americans. Women represent an even larger proportion (68 percent) of the very old, those aged 85 and over.

The authors wish to thank The Commonwealth Fund and The Brookdale Foundation for financial support, Barbara Lyons and Paula Grant for research assistance, and John Hanfelt for programming assistance.

Approximately one-third of all people aged 65 and older live alone (Exhibit 1). Older women are much more likely than older men to live alone; many are widows. Forty-four percent of older women live alone, compared with 19 percent of older men. This discrepancy reflects both the longer life expectancy of women, which makes it more likely that they will outlive their husbands, and the fact that women tend to marry men who are older than they are.

People living alone are particularly at risk as their health fails. Without someone immediately available to provide assistance, older people who have severe physical or mental limitations must rely on informal support from family members, obtain formal home care from a home care aide or agency, move in with family, or enter a nursing home or other type of sheltered living arrangement.

Older women are typically poorer than older men. The feminization of poverty holds true not only for younger families but for elderly people as well. Fifteen percent of older women are poor, compared with 8 percent of older men (Exhibit 1). Twenty-one percent of women over age 85 have incomes below the federal poverty level.

Women whose husbands are still alive fare much better than widows. The most vulnerable group is elderly women living alone, 27 percent of whom live in poverty—a poverty rate that is higher than that among children and almost five times as high as among women in other living arrangements (6 percent). While 44 percent of all elderly women live alone, 79 percent of poor elderly women live alone (Exhibit 1). Widowhood often drives women into poverty. A study by the National Bureau of Economic Research found that half of poor widows were not poor when their husbands were alive.[5]

According to future projections by ICF, Inc., by the year 2020 poverty among older people will be almost exclusively poverty among older women.[6] Although women have been entering the labor force in greater numbers and have increasingly become eligible for their own private pension and Social Security income, the poverty rate among older women is not expected to decline significantly between now and 2020. For example, the percentage of poor and near-poor men living alone will decline from 38 percent in 1987 to about 6 percent by 2020. The percent of poor and near-poor women living alone will decline only from 45 percent to 38 percent 25 years from now.[7] Increased participation in the labor market and improvements in pension coverage are projected to only modestly improve poverty rates among elderly women living alone.

Exhibit 1
Sociodemographic Characteristics of Persons Aged 65 and Over
United States
1987

	Total	Men	Women	Poor Men	Poor Women
Total	**100.0**	**100.0**	**100.0**	**100.0**	**100.0**
Years of Age					
65-74	60.7	64.8	57.8	52.9	47.7
75-84	31.0	28.7	32.6	35.6	38.7
85 and Older	8.3	6.5	9.6	11.5	13.6
Race					
White	88.8	88.9	88.7	68.1	71.3
Black	8.3	8.1	8.5	23.5	22.9
Hispanic	2.9	3.0	2.8	8.4	5.8
Income (Percent of Poverty Income)					
Less than 100%	12.2	8.4	14.9	100.0	100.0
100 - 199%	28.4	25.0	30.7	-	-
200% and Over	59.4	66.6	54.4	-	-
Living Arrangement					
Alone	33.4	18.7	43.8	47.0	78.8
With Others	66.6	81.3	56.2	53.0	21.2

Source: Estimates based on analysis of the 1987 National Medical Expenditures Survey.

The Supplemental Security Income (SSI) program, the federal program that provides cash assistance to low-income elderly and disabled persons, fails to lift all elderly people out of poverty for three reasons. First, half of those eligible for SSI fail to participate—largely because they do not know about the program or believe they are ineligible.[8] Second, the income eligibility level for SSI is set at 75 percent of the federal poverty level for a single person, and at 90 percent of the federal poverty level for an elderly couple.[9] Consequently, many poor single elderly people are not covered. Finally, SSI places severe restrictions on assets ($2,000 in liquid assets plus a home and car). As a result, low-income elderly people with modest assets may not qualify.

Health and Older Women

Health Insurance

The greatest concern of elderly people is the fear that they will experience a serious illness.[10] In the United States this fear is heightened by a health care financing system that provides inadequate protection against health care bills. As a result, older Americans also fear that medical expenses will exhaust their savings and they will not be able to afford needed care.

Nearly all elderly people are covered by Medicare. However, Medicare benefits are limited largely to hospital and physician services, and even these services are covered only after a substantial deductible is incurred. In 1994, Medicare beneficiaries are required to pay the first $696 of a hospital bill per spell of illness, and the first $100 annually of physician bills. In addition, Medicare beneficiaries must pay 20 percent of all physician charges in excess of the $100 annual deductible, as well as any charge the physician makes in excess of what Medicare deems a reasonable fee. Medicare beneficiaries must pay a monthly premium of $41.10 for Part B physician coverage.

Medicare does not cover prescription drugs or other services or equipment such as dental care, eyeglasses, or hearing aids. For patients with serious chronic conditions, these expenses can amount to several thousand dollars annually.

Medicare covers very little long-term care. It pays for home health services only for those elderly who are recovering from a condition such as a broken hip, who require the specialized services of a registered nurse or physical therapist, who are homebound, and who require intermittent care. Ongoing services, such as personal care for a person with Alzheimer's disease, are not covered. Payment for nursing home care is similarly limited to short-term convalescent care for patients requiring skilled nursing care following a hospitalization.

Because of these limitations in Medicare coverage, most Medicare beneficiaries obtain supplementary coverage from private health insurance or Medicaid. However, 12 percent of all Medicare beneficiaries rely solely on Medicare for assistance in paying their health care bills (Exhibit 2).

Since older women are more likely to be poor, a higher proportion of older women than men qualify for Medicaid. In 1987 12 percent of elderly women and 6 percent of elderly men had Medicaid to supplement Medicare (Exhibit 2). Medicaid pays the Medicare Part B premium and the deductible and coinsurance for Medicare-covered services. Medicaid is especially important in assisting elderly people in paying for long-term care services. About half of all nursing home expenditures are paid by Medicaid. Since older women are more likely to become impoverished and to live in a nursing home, this coverage is critical. Despite the fact that most Medicaid enrollees are low-income women and their children, 71 percent of all Medicaid outlays go to assist the elderly and disabled poor.[11]

Older men are somewhat more likely than their female counterparts to have private health insurance to supplement Medicare (80 percent vs. 78 percent). About half of this coverage is provided through employer health benefit plans for retirees. Married men, with their longer work history in better paying jobs, and their spouses are more likely to have retiree health benefits than single women. For elderly women living alone, 76 percent have private health insurance compared with 79 percent of women living with their spouse or others (Exhibit 2).

Private health insurance plans vary in the benefits they cover. Typically, however, such plans pick up the Medicare deductibles and coin-

Exhibit 2
Health Insurance Coverage, Persons Aged 65 and Older
United States
1987

	Total	Medicare Only	Medicare and Medicaid	Medicare and Private Insurance
Total	**100.0**	**12.1**	**9.2**	**78.7**
Men	100.0	14.4	5.6	80.0
Women	100.0	10.5	11.7	77.8
Women by Living Arrangements				
Alone	100.0	8.6	15.2	76.2
With Others	100.0	11.9	9.0	79.1
Women by Poverty Income				
Less than 100%	100.0	17.8	40.6	41.6
100 - 199%	100.0	12.3	12.1	75.6
200% and Over	100.0	7.4	3.6	89.0

Source: Estimates based on analysis of the 1987 National Medical Expenditures Survey.

surance, and some cover such services as prescription drugs. However, few private health insurance plans have comprehensive long-term care benefits. As a result, even those with private coverage to supplement Medicare must worry about the possibility of financial hardship if they become seriously impaired.

Health Status of Older Women

Although women live longer than men, this longevity can be a mixed blessing. Since the prevalence of chronic conditions and the risk of serious impairment increase with age, older women are especially vulnerable to illness in later life. The relatively greater rate of poverty among older women, especially among those living alone, also puts them at risk for serious illness.

Elderly men and women are about equally likely to rate their health as fair or poor (47 percent versus 48 percent) (Exhibit 3). Among poor elderly people, the numbers increase; 60 percent of poor elderly men and 64 percent of poor elderly women rate their health as fair or poor.

Elderly women are more likely to suffer from a serious chronic health condition than are elderly men. Seventy-seven percent of elderly men have chronic conditions, compared with 84 percent of elderly women (Exhibit 3). Chronic health problems are much more prevalent among the poor elderly than among higher income elderly. For example, 88 percent of poor elderly women report chronic health conditions, compared with 82 percent of elderly women with incomes of more than twice the poverty rate.

Older women are more likely to experience non–life-threatening chronic health conditions than are men. For example, 61 percent of older women, and 70 percent of poor elderly women, have arthritis, compared with 46 percent of older men (Exhibit 3). This condition, although not life-threatening, cripples and can make it extremely difficult for an older woman living alone to take care of herself and maintain her independence. Other chronic health problems that disproportionately affect poor elderly women include hypertension (62 percent), heart disease (28 percent), diabetes (21 percent), and cerebrovascular disease (8 percent).

Older men are more likely to have chronic heart disease than are older women (24 percent versus 21 percent) (Exhibit 3). However, the differences between men and women decline with age, so that in later life both men and women must be concerned about becoming victims

Exhibit 3
Health Status of Persons Aged 65 and Over, Percentage Distribution
United States
1987

	Total	Men	Women	Poor Men	Poor Women
Self-Assessed Health Status					
Excellent/Good	52.5	53.2	52.0	39.7	35.7
Fair/Poor	47.5	46.8	48.0	60.3	64.3
Percent with Chronic Conditions					
None	18.9	22.8	16.1	25.2	12.4
One	31.2	31.0	31.3	20.6	23.7
Two or More	49.9	46.2	52.6	54.2	63.9
Percent with Selected Chronic Conditions					
Arthritis	54.9	46.0	61.2	48.7	70.0
Hypertension	49.8	44.8	53.3	53.2	61.8
Heart Disease	22.1	24.0	20.8	26.4	28.2
Diabetes	14.7	15.6	14.0	24.1	20.6
Cerebrovascular Disease	7.5	9.2	6.1	15.0	8.4
Cancer	13.3	13.0	13.5	12.2	10.4

Source: Estimates based on analysis of the 1987 National Medical Expenditures Survey.

of heart attacks. Elderly women are more likely to report hypertension and be at risk for serious strokes than elderly men.

Older men are more likely than older women to have hearing impairment, perhaps as the result of occupational exposure to noise during their younger years (Exhibit 4). Hearing impairment is more common among poor elderly women. Vision problems are more common among older women. One-third of older women and one-fourth of older men have vision problems. Among poor elderly women, over two-fifths have a problem with vision. Poor vision can be an important contributing factor to falls or other injuries, and can hamper the ability of older people to take care of themselves.

Health Care of Older Women
Access to health care services is especially important for the health and well-being of older women. Living longer, more prone to chronic conditions, and most at risk for serious impairment, older women are heavy users of the health care system.

Exhibit 4
Disability among Persons Aged 65 and Over, Percentage Distribution
United States
1984

	Total	Men	Women	Poor Men	Poor Women
ADL Limitation					
Moderate	7.2	5.7	8.3	9.3	10.9
Severe	6.9	5.3	8.1	7.3	12.1
IADL Limitation					
Moderate	2.9	2.0	3.5	2.9	5.8
Severe	11.2	8.9	12.7	16.9	18.3
Percent with Selected Disabilities					
Falls	20.4	16.6	23.0	18.9	27.2
Mobility	10.1	8.0	11.6	13.6	18.8
Hearing	37.5	44.4	32.7	51.3	38.4
Vision	29.4	25.4	32.2	33.8	41.0

Source: Estimates based on analysis of the 1984 Supplement on Aging, National Health Interview Survey.

In 1987, 29 per 100 older women were hospitalized during the year (Exhibit 5). This rate increases to 37 per 100 for poor older women. For those who rate their health as fair or poor, about 42 per 100 older women were hospitalized, including 40 per 100 poor elderly women. This compares with 42 hospitalizations per 100 among elderly men who rate their health as fair or poor.

Older people also make extensive use of physician services. Ambulatory visits to physicians in 1987 averaged 8.6 per person for older women and 8.5 visits per person for poor older women (Exhibit 5). Older women in fair or poor health saw physicians 10.8 times, compared with 10.3 times for older men in fair or poor health.

Poor older women see physicians somewhat less frequently than higher income older women. Among those in fair or poor health, poor women averaged 10.5 physician visits annually, compared with 10.8 physician visits for older women with family incomes more than twice the poverty level.

Differences in use of health care services by income reflect the fact that higher income older women are more likely to have private health insurance compared to lower income women (89 percent versus 42 percent), while poor elderly women are more likely to have only Medi-

Exhibit 5
Utilization of Health Care Services, Persons Aged 65 and Over
United States
1987

	Total	Men	Women	Poor Men	Poor Women
Annual Physician Visits per Capita					
Total	8.3	7.8	8.6	6.7	8.5
People in Fair or Poor Health	10.6	10.3	10.8	10.2	10.5
Annual Hospital Admissions per 100 Population					
Total	30.1	31.9	28.9	33.1	36.7
People in Fair or Poor Health	42.0	42.0	42.0	42.7	39.9

Source: Estimates based on analysis of the 1987 National Medical Expenditures Survey.

care coverage (18 percent versus 7 percent). Studies have shown that those elderly with both Medicaid and Medicare make the same use of health care services as those with Medicare and private health insurance. However, those who rely solely on Medicare tend to use health care services at a lower rate.[12]

Older Women and Long-Term Care

Older Women and Disability

When older women need caregiving, the resources available to them are often limited. Older women are especially at risk for serious disability that limits their capacity to care for themselves. The most common measure of physical disability is whether assistance is required in performing five basic activities of daily living (ADL): eating, using the toilet, dressing, bathing, and moving from a bed or chair independently. The level of physical disability can be characterized by the number of ADL limitations and the type of assistance required. Severe physical disability is defined as the need for direct human assistance with two or more ADL. Those with more moderate physical disability require human assistance with only one ADL or can rely on special equipment or the help of another person on a stand-by basis to compensate for their ADL deficits.

Eight percent of older women living at home have severe ADL limitations, compared with 5 percent of elderly men (Exhibit 4). In addition, another 8 percent of older women and 6 percent of older men have moderate ADL limitations.

Poor elderly women are at substantially greater risk of ADL limitation than higher income older women. Twelve percent of poor older women experience severe ADL limitation, and 11 percent experience moderate ADL limitation. Together, almost one-fourth of poor elderly women living at home need some type of assistance in carrying out basic ADL, compared with 14 percent of elderly women with incomes more than twice the federal poverty level. Since poor women are much more likely to be living alone, this need for assistance represents a substantial threat to their continued independence and well-being.

Older women are also more likely than older men to be seriously limited in their ability to carry out such instrumental activities of daily living (IADL) as managing their money or keeping house (13 percent versus 9 percent) (Exhibit 4). Eighteen percent of poor elderly women report severe IADL limitation, and 6 percent report moderate IADL limitation.

Older women must also worry about a serious fall. Twenty-three percent of older women have a problem with falling, compared with 17 percent of older men (Exhibit 4). Among poor elderly women, 27 percent report problems with falls. Osteoporosis, a condition characterized by thinning of the bones, is more common among women than men, putting women at higher risk for fractures or other bone conditions. The fear that an elderly woman living alone will fall when no one is around to provide immediate assistance is a major concern of families, and often leads to institutionalization.

Frequent falling and fractures not only can cause injuries leading to hospitalization, but can lead to permanent disability. Older women are 50 percent more likely than older men to suffer from limitations in mobility. Twelve percent of older women living at home and 8 percent of older men experience mobility difficulties (Exhibit 4). Among poor elderly women, 19 percent report difficulty with mobility—more than twice the rate among older women with incomes more than twice the poverty level.

All these problems become more serious with increasing age. Women over the age of 85 are extremely vulnerable. Almost two-fifths of all women aged 85 and over living at home have moderate to severe ADL limitations, and almost half have moderate to severe IADL limitations. These rates are substantially higher than for men over age 85

(27 percent and 34 percent, respectively). Since women over age 85 are most likely to be poor and living alone, this loss of functioning can seriously undermine their well-being and places them at substantial risk of institutionalization.

Older Women and Long-Term Care

Almost 1.7 million older Americans who are limited in their ability to carry out important daily tasks live alone.[13] The great majority of these are women. Elderly people who are married or live with others usually have family members to provide assistance. Those who live alone may have family or friends nearby or pay someone to help them. Surprisingly, 73 percent of disabled elderly people living alone manage without help even though they experience difficulty with feeding, bathing, or clothing themselves.

As the disability becomes increasingly severe, however, assistance must be sought from formal paid sources or from family and friends. A quarter of a million elderly people living alone are severely disabled and receive formal or informal assistance. About 34 percent of disabled elderly people living alone who receive assistance rely solely on paid help from a personal care aide or a home care agency. Approximately 53 percent use a combination of unpaid and paid help, while 13 percent rely on unpaid help from family and friends only. (For an account of the impact of these arrangements on caregivers, see Chapter 5, "Women as Unpaid Caregivers: The Price They Pay.")

Older women living alone are major users of paid home care services. About 62 percent of all women receiving paid home care live alone; another 28 percent live with adult children or others. Only 10 percent of women receiving home care are married.

Elderly people living alone have more difficulty remaining at home when their ability to function independently is impaired, and are especially at risk of institutionalization. Fourteen percent of such people enter a nursing home within two years, compared with 8 percent of impaired people living with a spouse.[14]

Three-quarters of all nursing home residents are women. Three-fourths of these women were widowed at the time of admission; only 11 percent of women in nursing homes are married.[15]

Medicaid is a major source of financing for nursing home care. However, it is available only after a person has become impoverished. As a result, institutionalization not only robs older people of their independence, but also takes any savings that they may have accumulated over a lifetime of work. Recent legislation provides protection of some income and assets for spouses of nursing home residents living in the community. Spouses are not, however, eligible for Medicaid.

It is a tragic irony that women who have shouldered the burden of caring for others over their lifetimes all too often have no one to turn to when they need care. Twenty-five percent of elderly people living alone have no living children.[16] Another 20 percent do not have children within an hour's travel time. Although families provide an enormous amount of support to elderly parents, this care may simply not be feasible in the case of many older women.

Policy Directions

In a nation as wealthy as the United States, the plight of older women is not inevitable and should not be tolerated. Modest improvements in current programs could provide a minimum floor of economic and health security that would permit all older people to live out their lives with dignity.

Three major actions would go a long way to improving the economic, health, and social well-being of older Americans:

1. Increase the floor of income support under the SSI program to the poverty level;
2. Cover all poor and near-poor persons under Medicaid;
3. Expand Medicare to cover home care services.

SSI

The most effective approach to eliminating poverty among older people is to increase the income eligibility threshold for SSI. Raising it to 100 percent of the poverty level for everyone would reduce the poverty rate among elderly people living alone by about 29 percent, from 19 percent to 12 percent.[17] The estimated cost of this expansion is $2.3 billion for elderly people and $1.7 billion for disabled, non-elderly people (in 1987). It would raise about 600,000 persons above the poverty line, about 400,000 of them widows.

The impact of this policy change would be greater if extensive outreach efforts were made to enroll all eligible people in the SSI program. Outreach efforts to enroll eligible persons work. A demonstration of outreach for SSI conducted in three sites by the American Association of Retired Persons found that over a three-month period, applications for SSI were increased by 90 percent and awards were increased by 60 percent.[18]

Expanded Medicaid Coverage

The Medicare Catastrophic Act of 1988 contained important provisions expanding Medicaid coverage to all poor elderly and disabled Medicare beneficiaries. Although most of the act was repealed, these provisions were retained. As a result, states are now required to provide all Medicare beneficiaries whose incomes are below the federal poverty level with Medicaid "Medicare wrap around" coverage; that is, Medicaid pays for the Medicare Part B premium, deductibles, and other cost-sharing. States have the option of making all Medicaid services including prescription drugs available to poor Medicare beneficiaries. In the Omnibus Reconciliation Act of 1990 (OBRA 90) states were required to phase in the Medicare Part B premium for Medicare beneficiaries with incomes up to 120 percent of the federal poverty level.

These expansions provide important assistance to poor and near-poor elderly who would otherwise find the high cost of uncovered Medicare expenses a major financial burden. However, since the cost of prescription drugs and other uncovered expenses can easily amount to thousands of dollars, near-poor elderly with incomes between the poverty level ($6,931 in 1993) and 200 percent of the poverty level also need assistance. Medicaid should be expanded to provide coverage to the near-poor elderly, with a sliding scale premium contribution. All Medicaid services should be covered for low-income Medicare beneficiaries, not just the cost-sharing for Medicare benefits. Prescription drug coverage is especially vital for many chronically ill elderly. It is estimated that the cost of this expansion would be $4.4 billion to federal and state governments (in 1990).[19]

Medicare and Home Care

Finally, home care should be added as a covered service under Medicare for those who are seriously impaired, for example, those with two or more ADL limitations or serious cognitive impairment. Covered benefits should include in-home and adult day care services, with the number of hours of care tied to degree of impairment (for example, 15 to 25 hours of personal in-home care per week or substitution of two hours of adult day care for each hour of in-home care).

If Medicare beneficiaries contributed 20 percent of the cost, with Medicaid picking up the costs for those below the poverty level and providing sliding scale assistance to those with incomes of up to 200 percent of the poverty level, the cost in 1989 dollars would be $6.8 billion.[20]

This benefit would enable more elderly people to maintain their independence and provide relief and support to families caring for a frail elderly person. Most important, it honors the desire of the overwhelming majority of elderly people to continue to live in their own homes.

These steps are quite modest and represent an achievable public policy agenda. By the year 2000 no elderly person should continue to live in poverty. No elderly person should live in fear of the financial devastation that uncovered medical bills can inflict. And no elderly person should be robbed of her dignity in old age through avoidable institutionalization and impoverishment. These steps will in turn help provide care for the caregivers—older women who have devoted most of their lives to caring for their children and caring for their elderly parents and husbands.

Notes

1. The Commonwealth Fund Commission on the Elderly Living Alone, *Aging Alone: Profiles and Projections* (New York: The Commonwealth Fund, 1988).

2. David Wise and Michael Hurd, *Elderly People Living Alone: Aging and the Prospects of Poverty: Executive Summary*, report prepared for The Commonwealth Fund Commission on Elderly People Living Alone (National Bureau of Economic Research, 1987).

3. *Aging Alone,* 1988.

4. Ibid.

5. Wise, 1987.

6. The Commonwealth Fund Commission on Elderly People Living Alone, *Old, Alone and Poor: A Plan for Reducing Poverty among Elderly People Living Alone,* (New York: The Commonwealth Fund, 1987).

7. Ibid.

8. Louis Harris and Associates, *Problems Facing Elderly Americans Living Alone: A National Survey*, report prepared for The Commonwealth Fund Commission on Elderly People Living Alone (New York: The Commonwealth Fund, 1987).

9. Diane Rowland, "Fewer Resources, Greater Burdens: Medical Care Coverage for

Low-income Elderly People," in The Pepper Commission: U.S. Bipartisan Commission on Comprehensive Health Care, *A Call for Action: Supplement to the Final Report* (Washington, DC: U.S. Government Printing Office, 1990), 125-145.

10. Harris, 1987.

11. D. Rowland, J. Feder, B. Lyons, and A. Salganicky, *Medicaid at the Crossroads*, report prepared for the Kaiser Commission on the Future of Medicaid (Baltimore, MD: The Kaiser Foundation , 1992).

12. Rowland, 1990.

13. *Aging Alone*, 1988.

14. Ibid.

15. Ibid.

16. Harris, 1987.

17. Wise, 1987.

18. ICF, Inc., *Documentation and Assessment of the AARP-SSI Outreach Demonstration*, contract report submitted to the American Association of Retired Persons, November 20, 1988.

19. Rowland, 1990.

20. Diane Rowland and Barbara Lyons, *Medicare's Poor: A Background Report on Filling the Gaps in Medical Coverage for Low-Income Elderly Americans* (New York: The Commonwealth Fund, 1988); The Commonwealth Commission on Elderly People Living Alone, *Help at Home: Long-term Care Assistance for Impaired Elderly People* (New York: The Commonwealth Fund, 1989).

7

Women as Formal and Informal Caregivers of Children

Ruth E.K. Stein, Laurie J. Bauman, and Dorothy Jones Jessop

WOMEN PERFORM A LARGE proportion of the caregiving in our society. A major component of this caregiving is directed to the care of children, in both family and work roles. The human service delivery system, especially for children, is staffed overwhelmingly by women (e.g., social workers, teachers, and librarians). Health care professions that involve the care of children (such as nursing) are also dominated by women, and there are more women in pediatrics than in any other medical specialty. Although women's and men's roles have been somewhat redefined by the women's movement, the bulk of formal and informal child care continues to be performed by women.[1] This chapter describes the care provided by women to children as well as the ramifications and consequences of providing such care.

Nowhere is the caregiving role of women more implicit than in the role of mother. Caregiving is so much a part of the inherent and normal expectation of mothering that it is almost never referred to or discussed in treatises on caregiving. Bateson writes that "the meaning of the word 'care' is endlessly ambiguous. . . invisible care routinely given has meant that no need is ever apparent."[2] Women are socialized to take responsibility for making the family and group function and to provide support to others.[3] It is only when the caregiving reaches portions of the population for whom it is not usual to provide care (e.g., adult children, friends, parents), or involves care substantially beyond that normally expected, that the word "caregiving" is used and that the needs become at all visible.[4] Even under such extreme circumstances, it is often taken for granted that unusual caregiving is an extension of usual expectations, rather than a decision to adopt a new role or responsibility.

Our own experience with women giving care to children comes from clinical work and research with families in an inner-city environment. The majority of the women with whom we have come into contact are members of disadvantaged minority groups; many also are single parents or part of complex intergenerational living arrangements. A large segment of our experience is with families in which there is a child who has a chronic physical disorder. Thus, we have been in a unique position to see some of the most demanding situations in which women cope with child care responsibilities. We have observed tremendous strengths and resources among women. We have been intimately aware of the personal strains as well as the rewards that come from trying to fulfill the complex demands placed upon women as caregivers of children. Since so many of the issues related to women as caregivers of children are highlighted in the context of the long-term care of a child with special health needs, we will focus much of the discussion that follows on this special group of caregivers.

Health Caregiving as Part of Maternal Child Care

A woman's role in the care of children often includes responsibility for care of the children's health. Mothers are expected to provide a nutritious diet and a relatively safe and clean home, and to arrange for, implement, and supervise necessary health care, including both the provision of routine elements of health care and care during illness.[5]

In our culture, much of the utilization of health care by families is initiated and orchestrated by women, including procuring appropriate immunizations, arranging health care maintenance visits, and seeking medical attention for acute illnesses or accidents. Until relatively recently, it was quite uncommon to see young babies brought for their check-ups by fathers, and even today it is the exception to see them accompanied by male caregivers. These patterns to which men and women are socialized are reinforced by outside institutions, which often set hours of operation that are incompatible with parents' work schedules or otherwise subtly exclude other caregivers in the family. This is true traditionally for the father's work, but now increasingly for the mother's as well.

One consequence of this pattern is that, when both parents work, the mother is more often the one expected to stay home with a sick youngster. These expectations are intensified by the fact that few child care facilities (such as schools or day care centers) welcome an ill child, even when the period of contagion is past. With two-thirds of the mothers with young children working outside the home, many women experience incompatible demands from their roles as mothers and workers.[6] Needed time off to care for a child is often taken as vacation or annual leave, or through subterfuge as a personal sick day, because employers either do not allot time for family leave or look askance at the need to take time off for that reason. For many mothers, when a child becomes ill or needs to recuperate at home after a hospitalization, the need is most often short-term. But cumulatively, the amount of time lost from work due to illness of a child can be substantial; it usually is an unpredictable event and is thus disruptive. Breslau et al. have shown that caring for a child with a disability exerts a negative impact on maternal labor force participation; this is disproportionately the case in black families and among women with incomes below the median.

Caregiving for Children with Chronic and Disabling Conditions

All of these problems are exacerbated when a child has a serious ongoing condition. While all family members must make adjustments in both their outside activities and their family lives, mothers are usually defined as the appropriate ones to fill the gaps created by the increased needs for care that result from a special health condition,[7] even if it means sacrificing their own careers and other responsibilities.[8]

This is not a rare occurrence in the lives of women. It is estimated that up to 31 percent of children have a chronic condition and between 10 and 20 percent have a serious physical disorder at some point in their lives.[9] Analysis of disability trends between 1966 and 1974 shows a significant increase in the prevalence of disability among those under 17 years of age.[10] Furthermore, the rate in poor and in minority groups may be one and one-half to two times that in the general population, although more recent data suggest that this is true only for more serious conditions.[11] Approximately 4 percent of the nation's youngsters have a major limitation in activity due to chronic disorders.

Encompassed within these statistics is a range of very different types of disorders, including rare one-of-a-kind conditions and multiple conditions. Pless and Pinkerton have outlined several dimensions of illness that may color the meaning of the condition for the caregiver. For example, care demands may differ depending on the type of disorder; whether it involves locomotion, sensory impairment, or communication; the visibility and stigma associated with the disorder; the degree of disability; and the prognosis and permanence of the condition.[12] The degree to which the child acquiesces and accepts needed care regimens and the age of disease onset may significantly influence the mother's caregiving burden. As we have illustrated elsewhere,[13] the episodic nature of a condition may be important, as may be the need for hospitalizations.

The intensity of ongoing responsibility for the care of these children has deepened as a result of biotechnical advances in treatment and changing realizations and philosophies regarding optimal care for children. Such advances have enabled many children who in former times would have died to live for longer periods into adolescence and adulthood; in fact, the overwhelming majority now reach adulthood and need to be prepared to assume adult roles. This trend, combined with the realization that long-term hospitalization or institutionalization is a suboptimal condition for the child's growth and development, has led to a new issue: the care of children who have serious chronic conditions by their own family members in the community. The overall growth in the numbers of children needing intensified ongoing care at home is further magnified by changing patterns of insurance and hospitalization that have accelerated the move toward early discharge and outpatient management of even those needing life-supporting technologies (e.g., ventilators).[14] Moreover, in order to qualify for ongoing third-party payment, the reimbursement system requires that out-of-hospital care be provided at lower cost than inpatient care. These regulations mean that insufficient resources are available to pay for assistance with ongoing care in the home and may force familial caregivers into very demanding ongoing care situations. Furthermore, there is a dearth of people available to provide paid assistance to families even when the financial resources are available.

A few examples highlight these differences. In the case of a child with asthma, the situation may involve the need for daily medicines, unexpected trips in the middle of the night to an emergency room to relieve an acute attack, and avoidance of allergens known to trigger episodes of wheezing. When the asthma is severe, the child may have episodes of sleep disturbance, multiple episodes of severe wheezing, frequent visits to the doctor, and frequent use of inhaled or nebulized medications administered on a closely supervised schedule. This may necessitate intensified availability of a supervising adult who is able to be an astute observer of symptoms and who knows how to respond to the signs of increased respiratory problems. However, after a period of stabilization, the child's symptoms usually can be controlled with only minimal restrictions of daily life (e.g., the need to take medication regularly), and with only occasional disruption of the family's function and routine. The expectation is that as the child matures, he or she will begin to be responsible for his or her own health care and medications, and the parental role will return toward a more normal baseline.

In contrast, consider the life-long situation of the family that has a child with a progressive degenerative condition. The family must watch the steady deterioration of function, the increasing need for help with a myriad of daily activities, and the ultimate inability of the child to care for him- or herself. Eventually, the parent will need to provide full-time around-the-clock care—in feeding and toileting, positioning and entertaining—and may also provide several years of care to the child or young adult who is susceptible to respiratory failure. This may require that caregivers be trained in the management of a tracheostomy and ventilator, the mechanical and nursing tasks of continuous 24-hour-a-day monitoring, suctioning, and cleaning the tracheostomy. Because the child's loss of function prohibits calling for help, the caregiver must be ever-present, prepared to administer assistance day and night, including responding to and forestalling a respiratory arrest.

Still another contrast is presented by the child who is born to a mother with HIV. The parent is faced with the initial worry about whether or not the infant is infected, followed for some by the confirmation of the worst fears. After this initial uncertainty comes the decision for those who are infected about participation in experimental protocols, the need for frequent monitoring, and the wait to see how and when and in what form the symptoms will appear. The illness is more often than not punctuated by periods of extreme life-threatening infection and hospitalization—and ultimately by death—all superimposed against the backdrop of a family in which the mother who transmitted the disease and often other family members are experiencing their own spiral of deterioration.

A still different situation is experienced by the family with a child with profound mental retardation, failure to thrive, and seizures. Such a child may be only minimally responsive to the caregiver, but may show distinct signs of recognition of the familiar, and anxiety or discomfort when in unfamiliar surroundings or in the care of those the child does not recognize. There is the progressive recognition that the care needs will be lifelong, and may extend beyond the caregivers' strength and even life span. There is apt to be the need for early intervention programs, special education, and extensive physical care and vocational rehabilitation as well as various types of therapy. There is need to look long-term at who will be the caregiver when the child is 16, 26, 36, and even 56.

These illustrations provide a frame of reference for discussing the range and variation in the sources of strain that women caregivers experience. No two experiences are identical, but there are overall similarities in the types of care demands they place.[15] The demands of care impinge dramatically on caregivers' time, energy, physical stamina, and emotional reservoir. They affect the options in women's lives and the relative discretion and balance between their responsibilities and their options.[16] Additionally, all involve many aspects of care over and above those that are considered a usual part of mothering. There may be medical and nursing tasks that the caregivers must learn to perform (e.g., taking blood pressure, changing medication doses, handling seizures, reading test results, doing postural drainage, handling medical equipment, changing tracheostomies, and performing injections), some of which may be difficult logistically and emotionally for a mother. In some situations in which the necessary medical regimens may cause the child discomfort, there may be a conflict between the medical and the maternal aspects of the caregiving role,[17] which may cause mothers much emotional distress. There is, over and above all, the need for vigilance and observation—watching that goes beyond that needed as part of the parental role. Additional psychological burden is placed on the caregiver when the child's prognosis is uncertain or unfavorable.

The responsibility for the child's survival and for dealing with medical emergencies weighs heavily on caregivers. They assume great responsibility, potentially even life-and-death responsibility, which can lead to fear and anxiety as well as a sense of pride and mastery.

Care needs often eliminate or markedly limit the caregiver's ability to spend time away from the child, because of either the absence or the unwillingness of other caregivers to take on the extra responsibility.[18] Parents report that friends and neighbors are afraid to stay with their children with special needs because of the "what if" factor— "what if something happens?". . . "what if he or she gets sick?". . . "what if he or she acts up?" Thus, the need for respite may become extraordinary, with families sometimes going for years without a few hours off.

Interacting with the Health Care System
Despite the intense care mothers give to their children at home and the reliance on mothers by health professionals in the medical management of their child at home, caregivers report being ignored by health care providers when they seek medical assistance for their child. Often they report that the health care providers, especially in hospitals and clinics, assume that they have little expertise and infrequently seek their observations, input, and advice. However, although they lack the generalized expertise of the professional, family caregivers have become "experts" in the particular person they care for, with extensive in-depth knowledge based on long experience. It is difficult to develop the necessary partnership between parents and professionals and to share expertise and responsibility in a way that recognizes the contributions of each party.

This is but one of the set of challenges that lay caregivers must face in dealing with the providers of health services. As they interact with the medical doctors, nurses, social workers, therapists, and aides who assist them, they must also find providers with whom they are comfortable (though not everyone has a choice), cultivate relationships with the providers, and work their way back and forth among multiple providers, resolving the sometimes contradictory information and advice that they are given.

The demands of the patchwork "system" through which care is obtained impose additional stress. To achieve care successfully, families must interact with multiple bureaucracies, including hospitals, the educational system, health care financing agencies, and often an array of special social and community service agencies. Within each of these bureaucracies, they have to deal with multiple individuals and departments. This process is exacerbated by the turnover of staff.

A caregiver must become familiar with the complex system of eligibility and special requirements of programs in the health and education sector. The managerial aspects of caregiving also include investigating services, talking to other caregivers, pursuing media information, making call after call as one source refers the caregiver to another, securing information on eligibility, completing the forms needed for processing eligibility (multiple times if necessary), and doing what is needed to recertify at the necessary intervals. And then there is actually paying for services—through insurance, Medicaid, or self-payment—and the worry this entails. There is also the need to keep records of the medical and health status of the involved person, as well as records of services received and possible sources, and of the finances and the multiple sources of insurance reimbursement or payment.

In the midst of all this, it may be difficult to maintain a focus on the main tasks of childhood: *growth and development.* The child's caregivers must focus on development and must enrich the experience of youngsters, no matter how severe the illness or disability, so that children do not become more disabled as they grow up and have a maximal opportunity to overcome some of their own disabilities. It involves a great deal of extra care on the part of parents to make sure developmental opportunities are not missed, as well as to prevent the development of secondary morbidity, whether physical, cognitive, social, or psychological. This differs markedly from the rehabilitative features of adult or end-of-life caregiving.

In many cases, caregiving for a child with a serious ongoing condition is more than a full-time job. The push for more consumer involvement that has characterized the chronic care system is both an opportunity to make care more relevant and individualized to the needs of families, and a potential source of burden and extra work for them. There has been increased emphasis on family-centered, home-based, or community-based care because of the clear-cut developmental benefits for children. However, this puts the burden back onto the family, especially the non-paid women caregivers, without putting in place the supports that would make the job more feasible.

There are some research and service programs around the country that are addressing the special needs of children with ongoing physical health problems, for example, the Preventive Intervention Research Center for Child Health at the Albert Einstein College of Medicine in New York City. Here the goal is to minimize the psychological and social morbidity that may accompany a very serious prolonged illness in childhood. The emphasis is on reducing secondary effects in the child, the caregivers, and the families.

Impact on Caregivers

The costs to mothers of caring for children with chronic illnesses and disabilities are many. There are the concrete everyday hassles—things "being hard" as the mothers describe it.[19] There are hardships with jobs and finances. There are family problems and issues with extended family as well as marital problems. There are costs of getting and keeping the support of kin, friends, and neighbors. Finally, there are the effects on the mother herself, her mental health and well-being as well as her physical health. All of this is in addition to the responsibilities of getting care for her child.

While this discussion is framed in terms of mothers, other women are involved as well. The maternal caregivers are often supported by their own mothers, daughters, sisters, neighbors, and friends. Even among the siblings of the child with special needs, the sisters, especially the older sisters, are found to assume a disproportionate share of the care.[20] At least one study has found that in households with a chronically sick child, husbands help with the housework and with other siblings, but help less with the sick child.[21] It appears that for the most part men participate in health caregiving when a woman is not available. Husbands do care for their ailing wives, ill parents, and sick children, but if a woman is present (an adult daughter or daughter-in-law or the man's own mother, for example), men are not the ones most likely to be involved as caregivers. An exception to this has emerged with the current prominence of HIV infection among young adult homosexual men, who often receive support of male partners and friends.

There are growing numbers of female-headed households, especially among the poor and among minority groups. Particularly in the black population of the inner city, there is the tendency for a skip-generation caregiving pattern in which grandmothers often raise and care for young children.[22] This pattern has increased as a result of the AIDS and crack epidemics. Since the grandmother is also more likely to be taking care of the great grandmother, she may be caught between generations of caregiving responsibility.

Alternatively, maternal caregivers may be part of a "sandwich" generation caught between the needs of their own parents and their young children (see Chapter 6, "Women as Unpaid Caregivers: The Price They Pay"). Young grandparents may be a source of help and assistance, but many may themselves need care, regardless of age.[23] Earlier data from our research group indicate that the presence of another person in the household may be associated with additional stress as well as support.

The care of youngsters with serious ongoing health conditions has both negative and positive effects on the individual caregivers. Many describe the rich rewards and the special meaning that such caregiving has given to their lives. Yet despite these testimonials and the enormous resilience of individual caregivers, most people would not elect to experience the misfortune of having a child with intense needs for special care. Therefore, in this discussion we focus on the elements that are the source of increased stress for the family.

Romans-Clarkson et al. report that mothers' care responsibilities curtail their availability for other social roles. There is also a series of serious role conflicts for the caregiver and other members of the family, such as conflict between being mother and being spouse, or between being mother to a sick youngster and being mother to a well sibling or siblings.[24] The extra time needed for caregiving comes from several sources, including the mother's own personal time, leaving little, if any, time for leisure or relaxation. It has also been shown that time is taken from housework and caregiving responsibilities for other members of the family, including the siblings. Siblings may feel neglected or pressured to compete with their sibling with special needs and to overachieve. In sum there is role conflict, role overload, and the possible need to perform all the multiple tasks too perfectly. Role restriction of mothers appears to be directly related to the level of dependence of the ill child on the mother in activities of daily living[25] as well as to her mental health.[26]

As described above, in many families there is a polarization, with the mother being the one to take care of the youngster with the chronic condition. If there is another parent in the household, that parent and the well siblings become another subunit of the family, with the mother having a much more restricted involvement with the well youngsters.

In some situations the role of mother, especially in its caregiving dimension, may become a defining one that is most important in terms of time investment and feelings of self-worth. This may be good or bad. Some women may develop a career of taking care of a sick child and overinvest in the child in a psychologically inappropriate fashion. For other women, however, especially poor women with few job options, caregiving may provide an important role that is a source of structure and self-worth in a positive way. This "job" may be better than some other jobs available in the external labor market and have more intrinsic rewards and satisfactions. Still other caregivers who have work roles may have to balance or juggle their multiple roles.

Do mothers receive help and support as their needs increase? In general a child's ongoing condition restricts the social life of the caregiver and is associated with isolation. Some studies have shown that the helping network of those with children with handicaps is smaller, more dense, and more concentrated than the network of those without such children.[27] Bauman and Adair have found that women report in ethnographic interviews that they get help principally from trusted individuals to whom they make their needs known. This help is made available by those in their network who understand their situation and offer to help without needing to be asked. In a second type of situation, the mother has an exchange relationship with someone she is close to and trusts. Each person feels free to tell the other what type of help is needed because the nature of their relationship is reciprocal. ("It's never a matter of asking, we just plan and talk about it ahead of time, what she has to do and what I have to do.")

A woman's ability to work outside the home is compromised when she is caring for an ill child.[28] The cumulative loss of educational, vocational, and occupational experience will have a lifelong effect even if the child ultimately becomes self-sufficient and the caregiving demands wane in later years. Additionally, many parents who do work cannot afford to switch jobs because of the lapse of insurance through which their youngsters with chronic conditions are covered, and because the child's condition would become a pre-existing condition in terms of a new insurance policy in a new employment situation. Also, many parents are discouraged from working because the income would disqualify them from public assistance programs that provide medical insurance for their child. This problem is accentuated by experience-rated self-insurance policies of corporations or small businesses. In these circumstances, family members who have a youngster with a chronic illness are often dissuaded from joining an employment group, because doing so would change the group's experience rating and hence the cost of the entire group's insurance. While denial of employment on this basis is an illegal form of job discrimination, it is not uncommon.

Finally, there is the economic issue of Social Security benefits. Many women who care for children with chronic illness never become eligible for Social Security themselves or have reduced benefits in their old age. Breslau has documented marked differences in maternal benefits as women become elderly, as a result of their caregiving devotion and lowered earnings.[29]

The data tend to portray mothers of children with physical illnesses as experiencing emotional distress. For example, Klein reports that "the emotional impact of the child's [kidney] disease is greater for the parents than the children, and greatest for the mother."[30] Klein and Simmons report that mothers of ill children were more anxious and less happy than mothers of control populations.[31] Breslau and colleagues found that mothers of children with disabilities had significantly higher scores on two indexes of psychological distress and had more depressive symptoms than mothers in a control group.[32] Although these mothers had only somewhat higher rates of diagnosable depressive disorders,[33] they had more depressive symptoms.

Studies by the Preventive Intervention Research Center for Child Health at the Albert Einstein College of Medicine consistently demonstrate that psychological morbidity among mothers of ill children is quite high. Specific characteristics of the child's illness (for example, the child's functional status[34] and length of illness[35]) may put mothers at increased risk. Among mothers of newborns, low birthweight is a greater risk factor for psychological morbidity than even serious illness of a full-term infant.[36]

A mother's mental health, in turn, is an important factor in predicting the psychological development and adjustment of her children.[37] Thus, the difficult emotional toll of the child's health care needs on the mother and the effects of the other components of the burden have an impact on the ill child's mental health as well as on that of the other children in the family.

Policy Implications

The presence of a child with a serious physical health problem or disability is associated with major consequences for the child's mother. This in turn compromises our ability to keep children who have serious health care and caretaking needs in the community, because the single most powerful predictor of whether a youngster or an elderly person is kept at home is the ability of the caregiver to sustain the burden of giving care.[38] Society ultimately pays for its lack of support to caregivers when some of them are forced to give up the caregiving at an earlier point than they would freely choose. This has detrimental effects for the youngster, as well as for the entire family. Additionally, the need to abandon the care of their children or to sustain it without help may create in many families a lasting sense of failure, burnout, and depression.

There are some plausible schemes for ameliorating the burden on caregivers. All involve recognizing the contribution that women make to the care of seriously ill and disabled children and providing support for the very important job they do. Several other nations have adopted strategies to provide such recognition and support. For example, in England and Wales a weekly tax-free cash attendance allowance is available for families of children over two years old who have special health care needs. This allowance is supplemented by additional allowances if the child needs around-the-clock care (invalid child allowance) or is unable to walk by the age of five years (mobility allowance). Other forms of family assistance are available without a means test, such as home visitors. Similar services exist in other countries in Europe.[39] Although formal evaluations are lacking, anecdotal evidence suggests that they at least partially improve the situation.

One policy approach that has been adopted recently is the provision for extended leave of absence from work for serious illness of a family member ("family leave").[40] While this is not a total solution, it has the potential to be an enormous help to some families who experience a health care crisis involving the care of an ill child. Additionally, there is a need for protection from job discrimination on the basis of the high medical insurance costs paid for a chronically ill child or family member, and guarantees of insurability when employment changes.

However, many caregivers are not part of the formal work force, sometimes because of the financial disincentive due to loss of benefits for the child. Clearly, this regressive policy should be reversed. It is important to consider that for some caregivers, employment activities outside of child care may be a necessary ingredient that allows them to tolerate the intensely burdensome task of providing the care for their own child during other hours. Alternative child care arrangements in special day care or at home should be available, and funding for such care should be provided. These choices should not be dictated, as they currently are, only by short-term cost savings inherent in schemes that depend on full-time parental care. Additionally, for both employed and non-employed caregivers, there should be adequate and affordable respite care.

Another possibility is the creation of mechanisms for subsidizing the care provided by family members and considering it a form of employment. At the very least, there should be serious consideration of ways to compensate for the inability of women caregivers to accumulate their own Social Security retirement benefits.

Finally, eligibility procedures and forms for application and recertification should be simplified, and a system of services and care that is user-friendly should be developed. Services should be centralized, or at least coordinated, so that there is "one-stop shopping" for entitlements and eligibility. The potential benefits of properly executed case management are also significant. Unfortunately, in its current configuration, case management sometimes becomes merely another layer of bureaucracy and red tape, with little tangible benefit and no real coordination.

In conclusion, there are many women silently providing care to children with serious ongoing health conditions. Most of this care is rendered without appearing on the ledgers of the nation's economy. Much of it is done quietly, without fanfare or even passive recognition, and in some cases with very little appreciation. For most of these women there is the assumption that this is what is expected of them, and there is little consideration of the possibility of an alternative. In our experience, most of these women rarely, if ever, express a sense of resentment, and many do not consider the care they provide a burden, despite the increasing data documenting the ways in which it affects their own health and life options. It is an open question whether this silent contribution will continue in the face of the growing economic constraints on families, the increasing expectations for women to enter the work force, and the widening horizons of women in the twenty-first century.

Notes

1. D. Belle, "The Stress of Caring: Women as Providers of Social Support," in L. Goldberger and S. Breznitz, eds., *Handbook of Stress: Theoretical and Clinical Aspects* (New York: The Free Press, 1982); D. Belle, *Lives in Stress: Women and Depression* (Beverly Hills: Sage, 1982).

2. M.C. Bateson, *Composing a Life* (New York: Penguin Books, 1989), 142.

3. Belle, 1982.

4. R.W. Toseland, C.M. Rossiter, and M.S. Labrecque, "The Effectiveness of Three Group Intervention Strategies to Support Family Caregivers," *American Journal of Orthopsychiatry* 59(1989): 420-429.

5. N. Breslau, K.S. Staruch, and E.A. Mortimer, "Psychological Distress in Mothers of Disabled Children" *American Journal of Diseases of Children* 136(1982): 682; S.E. Romans-Clarkson, J.E. Clarkson, I.D. Dittmer, R. Flett, C. Linsell, P.E. Mullen, and B. Mullen, "Impact of a Handicapped Child on Mental Health of Parents," *British Medical Journal* 293(1986):1395-1397.

6. N. Breslau, D. Salkever, K.S. Staruch, "Women's Labor Force Activity and Responsibilities for Disabled Dependents: A Study of Families with Disabled Children," *Journal of Health and Social Behavior* 23(1982):169-183.

7. W.R. Avison, S. Noh, and K.N. Speechly, "Parents as Caregivers: Caring for Children with Health Problems," *Advances in Medical Sociology* 2(1991): 65-93.

8. Breslau et al., "Women's Labor Force Activity"; N. Holmes and J. Carr, "The Pattern of Care in Families of Adults with a Mental Handicap: A Comparison between Families of Autistic Adults and Down Syndrome Adults," *Journal of Autism and Developmental Disorders* 21(2)(1991):159-176.

9. E.g., S. Gortmaker and W. Sappenfield, "Chronic Childhood Disorders: Prevalence and Impact," *Pediatric Clinics of North America* 31(1984):3-18; P. Newacheck and W.R. Taylor, "Childhood Chronic Illness: Prevalence, Severity, and Impact," *Journal of Public Health* 82(3)(1992):364-371.

10. A. Colvez and M. Blanchet, "Disability Trends in the United States Population 1966-76: Analysis of Reported Causes," *American Journal of Public Health* 71(1981):464-471; P. Newacheck, P. Budetti, and P. McManus, "Trends in Childhood Disability," *American Journal of Public Health* 74(1984):232-236; P.W. Newacheck, J.J. Stoddard, and M. McManus, "Ethnocultural Variations in the Prevalence and Impact of Childhood Chronic Conditions," *Pediatrics* 91(5)(1993):1031-1039.

11. L. Egbuono and B. Starfield, "Child Health and Social Status," *Pediatrics* 69(1982):550-557; J. Gliedman and W. Roth, *The Unexpected Minority: Handicapped Children in America: A Report of the Carnegie Council on Children* (New York: Harcourt, Brace and Jovanovich, 1980); P.W. Newacheck, J.J. Stoddard, and M. McManus, 1993.

12. Avison et al., 1991.

13. Jessop and Stein.

14. L.A. Aday, M.J. Aitkin, and D.H. Wegener, *Pediatric Home Care: Results of a National Evaluation of Home Care Programs for Ventilator Assisted Children* (Chicago: Pluribus and Center for Health Administration Studies, 1988).

15. E.g., S. Klein and R. Simmons, "Chronic Disease and Childhood Development: Kidney Disease and Transplantation," in R. Simmons, ed., *Research in Community and Mental Health*, vol. 1 (Greenwich, CT: JAI Press, 1979).

16. Ibid.

17. Cf. D.A. Allen and S.S. Hudd, "Are We Professionalizing Parents? Weighing the Benefits and Pitfalls," *Mental Retardation* 25(1987):133-139.

18. Cf. Romans-Clarkson et al., 1986.

19. L.J. Bauman and E. Adair, "The Use of Ethnographic Interviewing to Inform Questionnaire Construction," *Health Education Quarterly* 19(1992):9-23.

20. Klein and Simmons, 1979.

21. Ibid.

22. M.N. Wilson, "The Extended Family: An Analytical Consideration," *Developmental Psychology* 22(1991).

23. E.g., D.J. Jessop, C.K. Riessman, and R.E.K. Stein, "Chronic Childhood Illness and Maternal Mental Health," *Journal of Developmental and Behavioral Pediatrics* 9(1988)1476-156.

24. Bauman, 1991.

25. Breslau et al., "Psychological Distress in Mothers," 1982.

26. Avison et al., 1991; Jessop et al., 1988.

27. E.g., A.E. Kazak, "Professional Helpers and Families with Disabled Children: A Social Network Perspective," in M. Ferrari and M.B. Susman, eds., *Childhood Disability and Family Systems* (New York: Haworth Press, 1987).

28. Breslau et al., "Women's Labor Force Activity," 1982.

29. Ibid.

30. S. Klein, "Chronic Kidney Disease: Impact on the Child and Family and Strategies for Coping," unpublished doctoral dissertation, University of Minnesota, 1975, p. 190.

31. Klein and Simmons, 1979.

32. Breslau et al., "Psychological Distress of Mothers," 1982.

33. N. Breslau and G.C. Davis, "Chronic Stress and Major Depression," *Archives of General Psychiatry* 43(1986):309-314.

34. Jessop et al., 1988.

35. J. Lauby, L. Bauman, H. Ireys, D.J. Jessop, and R.E.K. Stein, "Effects of a Child's Chronic Illness on Mother's Mental Health," abstract submitted to *Ambulatory Pediatric Association*.

36. E.J. Silver, L.J. Bauman, C. Fontana, and A. Fleischman, "Neonatal Illness and Maternal Mental Health," *Pediatric Research* 23(1988):213A.

37. P.S. Jensen, L. Bloedau, T. Degroot, T. Ussery, and H. Davis, "Children at Risk: Risk Factors and Child Symptomology," *Journal of the American Academy of Child and Adolescent Psychiatry* 29(1990):51-59; Walker et al.

38. Cf., D.A. Cole, "Out-of-Home Child Placement and Family Adaptation: A Theoretical Framework," *American Journal of Mental Deficiency* 91(1986):226-236; B.R. Sherman, "Predictors of the Decision to Place Developmentally Disabled Family Members in Residential Care," *American Journal of Mental Retardation* 92(1988):344.

39. S. Goodwin, "Children with Special Needs in England and Wales: The Care of Hearing Impairment, Myelomeningocele, and Adolescent Pregnancy," *Pediatrics* 86(1990):1112-1116; J. Perrin, "Children with Special Health Needs: A United States Perspective," *Pediatrics* 86(1990):1120-1123.

40. Family and Medical Leave Act of 1993, Federal Register, June 4, 1993, Vol. 58, No. 106, pp. 31794-31839.

III

WOMEN AS HEALTH CARE PROVIDERS

Health care, like other areas of American society, is often given to stereotype. When reporters seek expertise on a health care issue, the person interviewed is likely to be a male physician wearing a white coat. The health care leaders and lobbyists seen in the thick of policy debates are also usually white men.

Yet in health care, more than in any other field of American endeavor, the work is done mainly by women. More than three-quarters of all health care workers are female, including 97 percent of nurses and the majority of home health aides, nurse's aides, medical librarians, and laboratory technicians. Just as women dominate the nursing home patient population, they dominate the nursing home work force. Some fields, such as home health care, are disproportionately dependent on women of color; yet often these workers are underpaid and lack the protection of health insurance or other benefits.

But the picture is changing. Nearly one in every five physicians now is a woman, as are nearly two in five medical students. Nursing, once condemned as handmaiden's work, has become a powerful force in health care and promises to become even stronger as the health care system is reshaped by reform. It can be hoped that women in the allied health professions may look forward to similar gains. This revolution was long in coming, but it seems that a field that has been rooted in the work of women since the beginning is now recognizing their contributions.

8

Women in Medicine

Phyllis Kopriva

OVER 100,000 STRONG and still growing . . . that is the picture of women in medicine today. The number of female doctors in the United States has more than quadrupled since 1970. Women now represent a significant part of the medical work force, making up 18 percent of all physicians and nearly 42 percent of all enrolling medical students.

Opportunities for women in medicine in the United States have improved since 1848, when Elizabeth Blackwell became the first American woman to receive a medical degree. During the late 1800s, a small number of women began to find limited acceptance in medical training and either enrolled in a few traditionally male schools or started their own medical schools. However, as late as the first half of this century, more than 50 percent of the medical schools in the United States still did not accept women, and many others had strict quotas limiting female enrollment.

Growth in Numbers

But women persevered, and today the picture for women in medicine is much brighter. The biggest growth came in the 1970s, when the percent of female physicians grew from 9 percent in 1969 to 28 percent in 1979. Since then there has been a slower but steady rise in the numbers, and the American Medical Association (AMA) projects that by the year 2010, women will represent one-third of all physicians (Exhibit 1).

In 1970, there were slightly more than 25,000 female physicians in the United States (7.6 percent of all physicians). By 1980, that number had more than doubled, to 54,284 (11.6 percent). Between 1980 and 1990, the number of physicians grew by 31.6 percent, while the num-

Exhibit 1
Physicians by Gender (Excludes Students)
United States
1970-2010

	1970		1980		1990		1992		2010*	
	Number	%	Number	%	Number	%	Number	%	Number	%
Male	308,627	92.4	413,395	88.4	511,227	83.1	534,543	81.9	477,800	70.6
Female	25,401	7.6	54,284	11.6	104,194	16.9	118,519	18.1	198,900	29.4
Total	334,028	100.0	467,679	100.0	615,421	100.0	653,062	100.0	676,700	100.0

* Projection from *Physicians Supply Utilization in the U.S.*, 1988 ed.

Source: Physician Characteristics and Distribution in the U.S., 1993 ed., and prior editions.

ber of women physicians increased nearly 91.9 percent. This increase was pushed by the growing number of women in medical training, as the number of male applicants to medical schools decreased and the number of female applicants increased. In the 1969-70 class, 9.2 percent of those enrolled were female. By 1979-80, that number had risen to 28.3 percent and by 1989-90, to 39.2 percent.

Medical Specialty
Almost 60 percent of all women physicians in 1992 were in one of seven specialties: internal medicine, pediatrics, general or family practice, psychiatry, anesthesiology, obstetrics/gynecology, or pathology (Exhibit 2). While the number of women physicians has increased in each of these specialties, the rank order has remained the same since 1980. (Prior to 1980, pediatrics was the top specialty choice of women, followed by internal medicine; otherwise, the ranking was the same.)

Women are about three times as likely as men to be pediatricians, making up 40 percent of the total specialty (almost 20 percent of all women physicians versus 5 percent of all men physicians); they are less than half as likely to be in general surgery or a surgical subspecialty. In 1970, only seven specialties had more than 1,000 women physicians. By 1992, 15 specialties had more than 1,000 women physicians, representing almost 68 percent of all women physicians. From 1985 to 1990, 19 specialties exhibited growth of 35 percent or more in number of women physicians (Exhibit 3).

Medical residents constituted 21.5 percent of women physicians in 1970 and 30.1 percent in 1992. Specialty preferences have remained

Exhibit 2
Specialties with Highest Numbers of Women Physicians
United States
1970, 1980, and 1992

	1970	1980	1992
Internal Medicine	2,383	8,130	23,043
Pediatrics	3,816	8,117	18,147
General or Family Practice	2,486	4,677	12,036
Psychiatry	2,459	4,361	9,028
Anesthesiology	1,516	N/A	5,170
Obstetrics/Gynecology	1,337	3,243	8,721
Pathology	1,273	N/A	4,156
Total	**25,401**	**54,284**	**118,519**

Source: Physician Characteristics and Distribution in the U.S., 1993 ed., and prior editions.

consistent in residency training also. According to the 1993 medical education report of the *Journal of the American Medical Association,*[1] almost 28,000 female resident physicians were on duty as of September 1992. More than one-third of women residents were training in internal medicine or pediatrics. Another 26 percent were in obstetrics/gynecology, family practice, or psychiatry.

Are these specialty choices based solely on preference or are exclusionary attitudes or policies a factor? There is no simple answer, but clearly, the profession must work to increase gender diversity and eliminate any specialty selection barriers that exist. Women may be deterred from surgery and some subspecialties because of the rigid training requirements and the lack of female role models in those fields. In a recent AMA newsletter opinion poll, about 45 percent of respondents said they were discouraged from choosing their preferred specialty, primarily because of "discouragement from advisors," "lifestyle incompatibility," and "gender bias."[2]

Professional Activity

Between 1970 and 1990, the number of women physicians in patient care increased by more than 100 percent, in large part because of the increasing number of women physicians in office-based practice—51 percent in 1992 compared to 61 percent of men (Exhibit 4). While the *number* of women in each activity category has increased, the *percent-*

Exhibit 3
Specialties with Fastest Growing Number of Women Physicians
United States
1985–1990

	Percent Growth 1985–1990
Allergy/Immunology	266.7
Colon and Rectal Surgery	106.7
Forensic Pathology	73.6
Gastroenterology	69.5
Emergency Medicine	52.7
Neurological Surgery	52.7
Dermatology	51.7
Otolaryngology	48.4
Orthopedic Surgery	43.7
Pulmonary Diseases	42.3
Plastic Surgery	41.1
Cardiovascular Diseases	40.3
Occupational Medicine	38.6
Ophthalmology	38.4
Radiation Oncology	38.3
Neurology	38.1
Urological Surgery	36.7
Pediatric Cardiology	36.3
Diagnostic Radiology	35.8

Source: Association of American Medical Colleges.

ages have decreased in each except *physicians in office-based practice* and *residents.*

The percentage of medical school graduates joining medical school faculties is higher for women than for men. And the proportion of faculty that is female has been growing steadily. However, the "glass ceiling" still exists in academia. In 1992, although 22 percent of full-time faculty were women, less than 10 percent were full professors. There are currently only three female medical school deans and two female acting deans.

Age

Female physicians are younger, on average, than male physicians (Exhibit 5). Because women began entering the profession in large numbers relatively recently, the age gap has widened over the years. In 1970, 51 percent of men physicians and 58 percent of women physi-

Exhibit 4
Women Physicians by Professional Activity
United States
1970, 1980, and 1992

	1970	1980	1992
Patient Care	18,362	39,969	100,024
Office-Based Physicians	9,217	20,609	60,695
Hospital-Based Physicians	9,145	19,360	39,329
Residents	5,464	13,322	26,580
Full-Time Staff	3,681	6,038	11,120
Clinical Fellows	N/A	N/A	1,629
Other Professional Activity	2,956	4,737	6,960
Medical Activity	N/A	1,090	1,583
Administration	N/A	1,178	1,919
Research	N/A	2,077	2,788
Other	N/A	392	671
Total	**25,401**	**54,284**	**118,519***

* 11,534 women physicians are inactive, not classified, or have no known address.
Source: Physician Characteristics and Distribution in the U.S., 1993 ed. and prior editions.

cians were under the age of 45; in 1980, the percentages were 51 percent and 69 percent, respectively; and in 1992, 46 percent and 72 percent.

Practice Characteristics
The practice characteristics of men and women physicians are more alike than not; however, some key differences remain. Women physicians are twice as likely as men physicians to be employees and less likely to be self-employed. They work about 10 percent fewer hours per year than male physicians, and spend about five to six fewer hours per week on practice activities (Exhibit 6). Their average number of total weekly patient visits also is consistently lower; in 1992, male physicians saw about 20 more patients per week (Exhibit 7).

Income
Female physicians continue to earn less than male physicians. Their lower income levels (Exhibit 8) can be attributed largely to their overrepresentation in the lower paid primary care specialties, generally younger age and lower level of experience, and lower number of

Exhibit 5
Federal and Non-Federal Physicians by Age and Sex
United States
1992

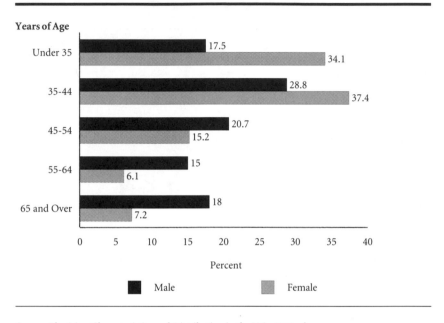

Source: Physician Characteristics and Distribution in the U.S., 1993 ed.

Exhibit 6
Average Hours per Week Spent by Physicians in Different Settings
United States
1990

	Office	Hospital	Other	Total	Percent Change 1982-1990
Male	27.1	8.9	24.7	59.8	4.4
Female	25.0	7.5	22.6	54.3	1.1

Note: Excludes residents.

Source: AMA Center for Health Policy Research, Socioeconomic Monitoring System, Core Surveys for 1982–1992.

Exhibit 7
Average Patient Visits per Physician per Week
United States
1990

	Office	Hospital	Other	Total	Percent Change 1982-1990
Male	80.8	24.5	15.4	120.9	−7.8
Female	67.7	17.2	16.3	100.5	−3.6

Note: Excludes residents.

Source: AMA Center for Health Policy Research, Socioeconomic Monitoring System, Core Surveys for 1982–1992.

Exhibit 8
Average Unadjusted Net Income for Physicians
United States
1992

Years in Practice	Males	Females
1–4	$147,100	$100,100
5–9	220,500	131,000
10–19	211,400	125,200
20 and Over	173,000	125,300

Source: AMA Center for Health Policy Research, Socioeconomic Monitoring System Core Surveys for 1982-1993.

patient visits and work hours. When these factors are controlled for, the income gap shrinks; nevertheless, disparities remain, indicating some level of gender bias in professional pay. There is also some evidence that women may undervalue their services when negotiating for salaries.

However, disparities in the economic practice characteristics of male and female physicians have begun to shrink. Over the past decade, female physicians have earned from 59 to 63 percent of the male mean annual net income, and women physicians' number of visits, particularly inpatient visits, and income per visit have crept closer to those of males. With the expected growth in managed care practices, these gender differences may disappear. In addition, there is a movement among young physicians, both male and female, to reduce the traditionally long and rigorous training and practice schedules and to find ways to maintain a more healthy and humane balance among their professional, family, and medical leadership responsibilities.

Concerns of Women in Medicine

There is no disputing the considerable gains that women have made in the medical field. Women physicians are represented in a variety of practice settings. They hold increasingly more of the top posts in government, management, public health, and organized medicine. Women physicians have become a marketable commodity as well, especially among women patients, as a result of the common perception that they are especially sensitive, compassionate caregivers. The success of women-only health centers—there are now more than 200 nationwide—reflects that preference.

However, women continue to face medical training and practice obstacles as a result of their additional responsibilities as childbearers and family caregivers and as a result of a remaining element of gender bias in the profession. The AMA Council on Ethical and Judicial Affairs, in its 1993 report "Gender Discrimination in the Medical Profession,"[3] documented the enormous progress of women physicians but pointed out that, despite their success, "women in medicine are generally not advancing to the highest levels of the profession and are continuing to encounter subtle and overt forms of discrimination in their training and careers." Gender-based economic and professional discrimination, sexual harassment, and a wide range of more subtle acts of discouragement continue to impede the professional progress of many women physicians.

Sexual Discrimination and Harassment

Women in medicine continue to report instances of sexual discrimination and harassment and gender-based stereotyping, particularly in medical school and residency training. Eighty-one percent of females responding to a 1988 AMA survey of a third-year medical school class on medical school abuse reported that they had been subjected to sexist slurs. Other respondents reported sexual advances, denied opportunities, and varied forms of sexual discrimination.[4] Of 2,500 women responding to a more recent AMA opinion poll of women physicians and students, almost 75 percent said they had experienced sexual harassment at some point in their careers.[5] Also alarming was their stated reluctance to report such incidents due to their fear of a negative impact or feelings that no action would be taken. Other studies of sexual harassment have produced similar results. While the number of medical institutions dealing with this issue is increasing, sexual harassment is inherently an abuse of power, and until women have equal access to positions of power, it will continue to be an area of concern.

Balancing Family and Professional Responsibilities

Gender role stress remains a problem for women in medicine, many of whom must try to "fit in" the bearing and raising of children while conforming to traditionally rigid medical training requirements. Family demands are frequently cited as a significant factor in the continuation of the "glass ceiling," particularly in academia, where the imperative to "publish or perish" works against women who have chosen to publish less in order to accommodate family obligations.[6] Negative attitudes, unconscious or otherwise, about women and pregnancy may also decrease a woman's likelihood of success, and pregnancy leave may be resented by colleagues who feel the burden of work has been shifted to them. With the growing number of women in training, most of them in their prime reproductive years, new and more flexible plans must be explored, including developing comprehensive maternity and paternity policies that are fair to the parent and her or his colleagues, lengthening tenure track requirements, establishing modular or other flexible program options, offering child care services in hospitals and other medical care settings, and encouraging the development of nontraditional practice options for women physicians with family obligations who wish to limit their practice hours. The development by some institutions of two tenure tracks, with differing requirements, is an attempt to deal with this issue. However, such efforts run the risk that the "alternative" track becomes devalued as a "mommy track." The best solution may lie in creating greater system flexibility for all who enter medicine.

Mentoring

There are many reasons why women continue to be concentrated in the primary care fields, not the least of which is the lack of female mentors in other specialties. The importance of mentors cannot be overestimated. Female and male mentors can be instrumental in bringing more women into the specialties where they have been traditionally underrepresented. Women still represent a minority in medicine, with many of the same issues as other minorities: professional isolation or loneliness, lack of role models, and exclusion from peer networks. In many cases, it is both necessary and helpful for men physicians to take the lead mentorship role. However, women mentors can be of special help as both career and personal role models, as women continue to struggle with combining their professional and family responsibilities. In medical education in particular, where few women hold department chairs or other senior positions, young women may receive a discouraging message about the career prospects in academia.

Leadership in Organized Medicine
Women physicians have traditionally joined organized medicine in proportionately lower numbers than have male physicians. During the years that men often begin their leadership involvement in organized medicine, women may be otherwise occupied with their dual roles as professionals and family caregivers. However, this situation is changing. Women have been elected president of more than one-third of all medical societies.[7] Women serve on the board of the AMA and all its councils, and the percentage of women in the AMA House of Delegates has risen to 8 percent from 2 percent a decade ago. However, while women remain underrepresented in the membership and leadership of organized medicine, the doors are open. Women must make the commitment to support and participate in their professional societies.

Conclusion
While women have made significant progress in medicine in terms of both numbers and influence, many inequities remain that appear impervious to the changing demographics of medicine. Women's career progress continues to be hindered by inflexibility in training programs, a lack of sensitivity to accommodations needed for family responsibilities, pay inequities, and underrepresentation in leadership or senior positions. Many studies have documented these needs and have made corresponding recommendations for change. Most recently, the AMA Council on Ethical and Judicial Affairs recommended the following actions to improve the professional environment for women in medicine:

Increased leadership roles for women physicians in medical schools.

Changes in academic tenure and mentoring programs to promote fairness and equity for women physicians.

Blind peer review to avoid gender bias.

Studies of sexual harassment to improve professional relations.

Strict anti–sexual-harassment policies and grievance committees.

Help for physicians with children, on-site day care, flexible hours, and job security for those on leave but not covered by the Family and Medical Leave Act.

Equal pay for women physicians who have the same specialty and experience, and who do the same work, as male colleagues.

Educational programs to prevent gender discrimination for medical staff, physicians in training, and students in academic and institutional settings.[8]

"Medicine needs talented and committed physicians and researchers and cannot afford to discourage valuable members," the report concludes.[9] Medicine's future will be greatly influenced by women, and its future may depend on its ability to include and accommodate both genders in the medical workplace.

Notes

1. Medical education report, *Journal of the American Medical Association*, 1993.

2. AMA Member Matters Newsletter, March 1993.

3. AMA Council on Ethical and Judicial Affairs, "Gender Discrimination in the Medical Profession."

4. K.H. Sheehan et al., "A Pilot Study of Medical Student Abuse: Student Perceptions of Mistreatment and Misconduct in Medical School," *Journal of the American Medical Association* 263(1990):533-537.

5. Survey of AMA members/nonmembers, October 1992, AMA Member Matters Newsletter.

6. W. Levinson, S.W. Tolle, and C. Lewis, "Women in Academic Medicine," *New England Journal of Medicine* 321(1989):1511-1517.

7. AMA Federation Survey, 1990.

8. AMA Council on Ethical and Judicial Affairs.

9. Ibid.

9

The Woman Physician

Eli Ginzberg

A Look Back

In 1969, I published an analysis of "the woman physician." At that time, women accounted for about 8 percent of the total physician supply in the United States, up from 5 percent some years earlier. This increase occurred despite the fact that the preparatory cycle for medical practice had been elongated and the costs of preparation had risen substantially. It occurred even though women were marrying at a younger age, with the result that those in medical school, with outstanding loans, would be in debt when they married. This was a deterrent to women's entering medical school, especially in light of the new openings for women in other professions.

In my 1969 analysis, I also considered a miscellany of other forces that would contribute to and determine the lifestyles of women physicians. I predicted that they would not work full time because many would be married to men who were relatively high earners. I pointed out that many women would probably prefer to be treated by women physicians, but that the opposite was true for many men. I noted that the high earnings in medicine made men disinclined to welcome more women members; that many facets of medical practice were highly entrepreneurial, not the long suit of most women physicians; and that many of the new medical schools were being opened in sections of the country where women represented a smaller proportion of admissions.

I also noted the rigidity of most residency programs, which did not allow adjustments for pregnant women who needed to take time off for the birth and care of their infants. I concluded by observing that culture—in terms of young people's expectations, institutional behavior, and consumer preferences—plays a determining role in career choices and that in the United States medicine was seen as a male preserve. Although I concluded with a plea for making it easier for women to choose medicine as their life's work, I did not have even an inkling of the transformations that were already under way and that would accelerate to a point where women currently account for more than 40 percent of all admissions to medical school.

The Forces of Change

Between the end of the 1960s and the beginning of the 1990s, several forces led to the spectacular increase in the number of women physicians beyond the boost provided by the Civil Rights Act of 1964 and its subsequent implementations.

Among the new and potent factors that altered the gender distribution in U.S. medicine, which were still hidden in the late 1960s, first and foremost was the doubling of the capacity of U.S. medical schools; most of the expansion took place in the 1970s. Since the federal government tied funding to increased enrollments, almost every school succumbed to the bait.

By the end of the Vietnam War in the early 1970s, however, the large number of male applicants seeking admission to medical school to avoid being drafted declined, a decline that continued uninterruptedly until 1988. The decline in male applicants was encouraged by the rising costs of a medical education; the opportunities that were opening up in other fields, professional and managerial; and the uncertainties about the future of medical practice in an environment of evergreater governmental and other third-party involvement in clinical decision making.

In this environment, there was no way for U.S. medical schools to fill their expanded capacity with qualified students except by opening their doors wide to women applicants. And that is what they did.

At the same time, the number of qualified women applicants for medical schools grew, aided and abetted by the following: the women's revolution, which stressed full equality and full participation of women in all sectors of American life; the concomitant change in women's participation in the labor force, with more women opting for full-time employment; and the change in the timing of marriage and childbearing. No longer were early marriage and early childbirth the preferred patterns. Both were delayed.

The fact that women came to account for over 53 percent of all college graduates, up from 40 percent in the late 1960s, also contributed to the large pool of well-prepared applicants. The pre-existing barriers against women in the higher earning occupations began to tumble in response to the powerful forces of demography, civil rights, and economic expansion. These changes made medicine a much friendlier environment than it had been in the days when the dominant male establishment treated women as second-class citizens.

This is not to say that all discrimination and bias against women in medicine has evaporated either within the medical establishment or among the public at large. But in light of the depth of prejudice and discrimination that existed only a generation ago, the transformation has indeed been striking.

The Current Status of Women Physicians

An article in the *New England Journal of Medicine* by Francis D. Moore and Cedric Priebe provides a wealth of illuminating data about women physicians.[1] The first point worthy of note is that, although women in 1991 accounted for just under two of every five admissions to the first-year class in medical schools, they accounted for only 15 percent of all active physicians in 1986, and only several percentage points higher in 1991.

As in other areas where large numbers of a formerly discriminated-against group have entered the labor force, it is difficult to assess whether the low proportion of women physicians who are deans, department chairpersons, and holders of named professorships reflects continuing discrimination or whether the disproportion can be explained by the fact that insufficient time has elapsed to enable more women to rise to the top, or some combination of these two and still other factors. My preferred explanation is that multiple factors are at work and that time will see many more women rise to top positions as those who have broken the ice prove themselves, as the earliest resistant males retire, and as more women raise their sights and succeed.

In 1967 women accounted for 8.4 percent of all physicians below the age of 35 and 7.4 percent of those over 65. The comparable data for 1986 were 25 percent and 7.5 percent, respectively, figures that reinforce the contention that time must pass before the full effects of the sizable increases in the number of women in U.S. medicine are fully reflected in their career achievements.

The Moore–Priebe article illuminates critical differences in specialty choices: women account for 19.9 percent of all physicians in medicine but only 8.2 percent of all surgeons. The conventional explanations for these differences are probably sound, reflecting on the one hand the gender prejudice of surgeons and on the other the career choices of women applying for residency training. Equally striking is the fact that women are underrepresented by about 2.3 percentage points in primary care. A look at the distribution of women currently in residency training by field of specialization reveals an above-average number of women in pediatrics, psychiatry, obstetrics and gynecology, pathology, and family practice. Women are conspicuously underrepresented in all surgical specialties except gynecology and are particularly underrepresented in orthopedics and urology (5.2 and 4.2 percent, respectively).

The overrepresentation of women in low-paying specialties like pediatrics, psychiatry, and family practice and their underrepresentation in all but one of the surgical specialties where average earnings are above the median for the profession mean that women will be among the lower, not the higher, earners in the profession. This pattern is likely to continue unless efforts to adjust the current fee schedules away from procedures toward evaluation succeed to a much greater extent than appears likely. But women physicians' choice of specialty is only one of several reasons that their earnings are likely to be, on average, considerably lower than men's. The other income-determining factors affecting women physicians' earnings result from their working fewer hours and seeing fewer patients per hour.

What Lies Ahead

The present still has the quality of a transitional era that has not yet run its course. Whether the proportion of women entering medical school will increase from just below the present 40 percent mark to 50 percent or even higher will largely depend on how men assess a medical career in the years ahead. In the years since 1989, after a steep 15-year decline in male and total applicants to medical schools, the trend began to reverse substantially. No one has a satisfactory explanation for this reversal other than the fact that the earnings of physicians have remained high, and after the stock market decline in 1987, medicine's attractiveness compared to a career on Wall Street appears to have improved substantially.

But the outlook for medical practice in the decades ahead appears, at least to me, to be considerably less favorable than in the last several decades, because of more stringent fee controls, the expansion of managed care arrangements, and the more intensive intrusion of government in health care delivery. This leads me to conclude that medicine will be a less attractive choice for well-educated men, who continue to have the greatest career options. I would not be surprised therefore to see women account for about half of all newly licensed physicians some years down the road.

What would be the effect of a further increase in the proportion of women physicians on the future of medicine in the United States? Will the growing proportion of women in medicine have a significant impact on biomedical research? My tentative answer is, probably not, because biomedical researchers are more likely to be drawn from among the ranks of Ph.D. scientists than from physicians, and women have long accounted for a high proportion of all Ph.D.s in the biological sciences. Further, more recent evidence indicates that women scientists who become mothers do not suffer any significant retardation in their career productivity.[2]

The research arena aside, what are the other possible consequences of a growing proportion of women physicians, a proportion that is almost certain to grow even if we remain unsure as to whether women will eventually account for more than half of the profession? As noted earlier, current data reveal that on average, women physicians work fewer hours per week, about 15 percent less, than their male colleagues. But there is some reason to believe that male physicians are reducing their average hours of work, among other reasons because of higher non-practice income, reflecting the contributions of their wives to total family earnings. In short, the current gender differences in hours of work are more likely to narrow than to widen in the years ahead. So long as women physicians continue to work fewer hours than men, that pattern will help to mitigate the impact of the extraordinary increase in the physician/population ratio in the United States, which has experienced a more than 70 percent increase since 1960, an increase that will approximate a doubling by the end of this decade.

There is considerable evidence that women physicians are more attracted to less entrepreneurial forms of practice arrangements and more willing to accept salaried positions that provide benefits in the form of fewer hours of work. If such a trade-off were to continue, it would mean that it would be easier to recruit physicians for new forms of organized practice arrangements involving managed care, which in turn would enhance the rapid growth of these new modes of service delivery.

The striking underrepresentation of women in surgery, except in gynecology, invites attention and correction unless chemotherapeutic and other nonsurgical forms of treatment experience breakthroughs greater than currently appear likely. Even if one can appreciate the reasons that few women practice urology and project that this trend is likely to continue, the same cannot be said for orthopedics. Hence, early and substantial correction appears to be indicated.

The steep increases that have taken place in the numbers and proportion of women physicians in obstetrics and gynecology, internal medicine, and pediatrics help to explain the explosive growth in the 1980s in the number of hospitals and out-of-hospital settings that have established and expanded specialized services under the rubric of "women's health care," which often include the care of children as well. There is no question that many health industry marketers have found gold in such promotions, for they continue apace. Clearly, the growth of these women's health care centers points to their meeting a strong consumer demand. Just what attracts the clients/patients is not altogether clear, but the presumption is that clients believe that women physicians—and male physicians oriented to treating women's conditions—provide them with better and more responsive care.

It was noted earlier that women physicians, on average, treat fewer patients per hour than their male counterparts. This reflects the presumption that they devote more time and effort to talking with their patients and responding to their questions and concerns. Since we know that a high percentage of patients report that their physicians fail to communicate adequately with them, the fact that many women physicians engage in a less harried form of practice must be viewed as a gain in terms of patient satisfaction, disregarding the cost of this added attention. Although I know of no definitive studies that have critically assessed the cost/benefit ratios of more leisurely versus more harried patient visits, I am inclined to believe that the extra time that many women physicians spend with their patients is likely to yield a positive outcome, even after covering the additional costs.

The United States is at the threshold of a demographic revolution with many dimensions, not the least important of which is a potential 50 percent extension in the productive years of life. Until now, the conventional work span of a man was roughly 40 years; most men retired in their early sixties. But the span of life, or more correctly, the number of persons who live into their eighties and nineties in good mental and physical condition, is increasing rapidly, with the result that the productive life span is increasing from 40 to 60 years. Moreover, women who live into their mid-eighties tend to have a three- to four-year longer life than their long-lived male counterparts.

Accordingly, one of the almost certain consequences of the increasing number of women physicians will be the considerable number of them who will have an elongated productive life span. I am not arguing that women physicians will remain in full-time practice until they are 85—although I suspect that a minority is likely to do so—but only that many men and women physicians, like all other professionals and nonprofessionals, will remain active and productive over a longer life span than they do today.

I will conclude with one final observation about the impact of the growing numbers and proportions of women physicians. Many observers expect that the U.S. health care system will undergo radical changes in the near future after enactment of national health insurance or some variant thereof. I do not anticipate such a radical change or its imminent arrival. On the other hand, I do expect that the extant system will undergo smaller and larger changes not only in the years immediately ahead but throughout the decades to come, as the American people belatedly respond to the growing problems of the uninsured, the ever-higher expenditures for health care, and the need to sort out important from marginal technological improvements in care.

The leaders of the medical establishment are predominantly male physicians, and they understandably are and will continue to be unsettled by, if not hostile and actively opposed to, many of the changes that are occurring and the more radical changes that lie over the horizon. The male leaders of the profession, now in their fifties and sixties, have practiced medicine only during the profession's heyday of expansion when they were subjected to few, if any, constraints. The recent and continuing pressures on their clinical autonomy and earnings, and harassment by payers have deeply disturbed many of the older male cohort.

Women physicians are in a more advantageous position. Only a small minority of present women practitioners were part of the golden age of American medicine (1965–1985). Most of those currently in practice are not hindered by memories of a past when their decisions went unchallenged. Further, many have values and preferences that are more congruent with the shape of the new health care system that is evolving. Many prefer salaried employment; many are attracted to primary care specialties; many prefer the flexibility that medicine offers them to extend or contract their hours of work.

Now that the worst discriminations against women in medicine have been lowered or removed, women physicians are likely to be better attuned to what lies ahead than their male colleagues, many of whom are prisoners of a time that is past and will not return. Economists have long observed the advantage of being second.

Notes

1. Francis D. Moore and Cedric Priebe, "Board-certified Physicians in the United States, 1971-1986," *New England Journal of Medicine* 324(8)(February 21, 1991):536-543.

2. Harriet Zuckerman, Jonathan R. Cole, and John T. Bruer, eds., *The Outer Circle* (New York: W.W. Norton & Co., 1991).

10

Women and Nursing: A Historical Perspective

Joan Lynaugh

JUST AS IT IS IMPOSSIBLE to examine women and health care without discussing nursing, so is it impossible to discuss nursing without considering its femaleness. This special link between women and nursing—its origins, influences, benefits, and costs—affects every aspect of nursing work and service, and underlies a wide array of issues related to health care access, health administration, and the caregiving values we all share.

In the United States today there are more than 2.2 million registered (licensed) nurses; nearly 90,000 more nurses graduated in 1993 from the nation's nursing schools. At any given time about 80 percent of these nurses are practicing their profession; of these, 7 out of 10 care for acutely ill patients in hospitals. Another 10 to 12 percent work in community settings like schools, home care agencies, industries, and public health services, while 10 percent work in the nation's nursing homes. The rest teach, do research, consult, and practice in offices, health maintenance organizations, or clinics. The descriptor for American nurses is ubiquitous.

About 96 percent of American nurses are women. Throughout its history as an organized, countable occupation, nursing has been women's work. And public demand for this form of women's work has proven relentless. Although the number of nurses per capita has risen steadily since 1910, including a very sharp increase since 1960, complaints of shortage have recurred two to three times every decade since before World War I.

The value of nursing, evidenced by this constant demand, derives from the content of its work. Nurses care for those who cannot care for themselves; their promised compassion and availability offer visible reassurance that Americans have constructed a civilized society. The very existence of nursing testifies to America's nineteenth century social contract with dependent citizens, which promised that, notwithstanding our culture's traditional preference for rugged individualism, we would not abandon the sick and injured, our children, or the elderly. Whether this contract with the sick and dependent is fulfilled by the public sector or, as is much more common, by the private sector, there is continuing consensus that care should be given when needed.

But a consensus about how to pay for that care has never emerged. Much of nursing's history as a poorly remunerated occupation is linked to our society's unwillingness to face the true cost of its preference for readily available nursing services.

Now, even as we become increasingly dependent on nurses to help fill the caring needs of an industrialized and aging society, we question whether we can continue to attract talented, capable people to the field in numbers sufficient to meet the demand. Today women have a wide array of occupational choices competing with nursing. And so, as demand continues to rise, we may again, as we did in the 1980s, face a falling supply of candidates to do the work.

Nursing proved an appealing and fulfilling discipline for millions of women during the first 100 years of its history as a distinct occupation. At the same time that these women realized the benefits of nursing, however, they also suffered inequitable treatment from the society they served. As the century draws to a close, the dualism "nursing and women" haunts the health care future of the United States. A brief history of this occupation so closely identified with women's work will clarify our present situation by casting today's concerns in the perspective of the last 125 years.

A Historical Overview

In 1903, my aunt Mary chose nursing as a way to make an independent living. As the oldest daughter in a farm family of 13, it was vital for her and for her family that she find paid work. Her choices included teaching, factory work, shopkeeping, domestic service, library work, and nursing. Nursing was a novel, perhaps daring, choice in 1903; she left the protection of home and family for a large city and unfamiliar work. As it turned out, she not only supported herself, she contributed to the education of her brothers and sisters, traveled, became a specialist in the social and health problems of abandoned children, and practiced nursing for 35 years until her death.

For roughly four generations, American women who chose nursing were choosing, as my aunt Mary did, from a limited menu. Of course, in their eyes the menu was much more varied than it had been for their mothers before 1890; *their* choices ranged from marriage, to dependence on fathers and brothers, to domestic service or sewing, to factory work. The women of my aunt's generation sought and found a way to live through the work of nursing. Their release from domesticity was both a newfound freedom and a plunge from the family into the harsh American economic system. Although nursing was hard and uncertain work, it was a salvation for many women, who through it could not only support themselves but find their way to the middle-class ideal of respectable individual productivity.

The new field of nursing was also enticing, interesting, even romantic—immersed as it was, and is, in fundamental life-and-death experiences. Further, nursing merged easily with a wide range of turn-of-the-century moral and progressive philosophies that stressed the "usefulness" of women's work as a proper modern substitute for earlier standards of womanly piety and family commitment.

The societal assignment that these women accepted when they became nurses was to substitute for the caregiving function of the family. Prior to the 1880s, care of the sick and dependent was the exclusive domain and problem of the family. Where possible, families hired servants to help do this work, and some men and women took up hired nursing for pay. Social and economic changes strained the traditional family-based arrangement, however, and, in response, new institutions began to appear in American communities.

American Hospitals and Nursing

The local general hospital spread quickly across America in the late 1880s and early 1890s. In 1875, about 172 hospitals dotted the landscape; by 1914, there were 4,000, with more being added every week. This widespread enthusiasm for hospitals was driven by several social forces. Importantly, employment was relocating from home and farm to more centralized offices or factories. If a family member became ill, there might be no one who would be able to stay home and give care. Moreover, the loss of income from both the sick person and the caregiver could threaten family economic stability. And as American families migrated to the cities, they left behind the relatives and friends who normally might have cared for them in times of illness. Foreign immigrants, of course, had even less access to assistance if they or a family member fell ill. Irish Catholic, German, Jewish, and other ethnic or religiously based hospitals often solicited funds with stories of the worthy but needy new immigrants they served. All in all a consensus emerged in America that recognized the hospital's importance to each town's image as a progressive, modern community.

These new hospitals were owned by church groups or other voluntary, philanthropic groups, physicians, railroads or industries, or local government. Most were small and simple, with 50 beds or so. One or sometimes two trained nurses were in charge of both the care of hospital patients and the nurses' training school. Once a system of nursing was in place, the hospital could become a substitute home in times of injury or illness. Without nurses, hospitals could not be made safe, much less attractive to the sick. But together, and with amazing speed, the institution of the general hospital and the system of nursing care based on nurse training schools captured a place in the social fabric of every community.

The hospital patients were cared for by women recruited to the training school who learned their new work by doing it. At first the "training" period lasted only one year, but by the 1900s, most schools kept their pupils for three years. The new trained nurse graduated with a diploma in nursing from the hospital; her work in the hospital was taken over by a new pupil.

The graduate was then free to make her living by practicing as a private duty nurse. Her cases came from physicians by referral or through registries set up by her school, the local drug store, or medical groups. Practically no graduates were employed by hospitals, since the essential point of the training school was to save money by using pupils to give patient care.

The trained nursing that grew up during this period of initial hospital development comprised an amalgam of carefully executed domestic work, detailed personal care of the sick, dispensation of medication and treatment following physicians' prescriptions, and institutional management. For patients and their families, trained nurses embodied safety and order in the face of illness and relief from caretaking responsibility. For physicians, nurses embodied a caretaker who would share and respect the physicians' ideas about treatment of disease. For the nurse herself, trained nursing meant an interesting, respected, and often reasonably paid occupation, which provided some measure of security and freedom at a time when choices for women were severely limited. And for the community hospital, trained nursing meant its very existence.

These inventions of the late nineteenth and early twentieth centuries—trained nursing and community hospitals—were of course energized and given direction by exciting new scientific gifts from the emerging fields of microbiology and chemistry. A dawning ability to comprehend and control infection, the result of the germ theory and subsequent identification of the pathogens causing deadly contagious diseases, made hospitals much safer. Even more important were advances in anesthesia and pain control, which made surgery endurable. As a result of these advances, physicians became more effective and grew in prestige. As nurses found ways to keep patients from infecting one another in the hospital wards and as surgery became safer and free of intolerable pain, physicians and their patients found hospitals more and more appropriate places for people who were sick or needed surgical treatment.

But at the same time, in spite of advances in medical knowledge and surgical treatments, other forms of treatment for illnesses were slow to develop. Caregivers, whether family members, nurses, or physicians, continued to rely on careful instruction about rest, exercise and diet, and watchful waiting. To a considerable extent, the best that anyone could do was to follow Florence Nightingale's 1861 injunction to "put the patient in the best condition for nature to act upon him."[1] And in these early hospitals, nurses assisted physicians while retaining a domestic form of moral, personal control over the daily lives of the patients and workers. The nurse superintendent was appointed by the hospital board of trustees and reported to it. Unless the hospital was owned by physicians, affiliated with a medical school, or directed by a physician, it was the superintendent nurse and the trustees who controlled patient admissions and thus the mission and income of the hospital.

During the last quarter of the nineteenth century and the first few years of the twentieth century, a period I have elsewhere dubbed the "domestic era" of nursing and hospital reform, the "hospital as home" metaphor prevailed in community hospitals.[2] The nurse superintendent acted as mother and the board of trustees as father, responsible for hospital finances and overall decision making. Physicians, especially those with hospital staff appointments, received respectful attention but were in no position to control internal hospital events. The familiar triangular relationship among trustees, nurses, and physicians was invented in the domestic era of hospital history, when hospital trustee and nurse received the knowledgeable physician as a visitor in their "home."

But after the turn of the century, change and conflict began to overwhelm the earlier domestic arrangement as hospitals became more and more important in laboratory-based, interventive medical practice. Surgeons, in particular, found that access to hospital beds for their patients was essential to successful practice. Both competition among doctors and reforms in medical standards made physicians eager to control membership on medical staffs of hospitals. In hospital after hospital, physicians insisted on more control over both patient admissions and the appointment of physicians to hospital staffs. To gain these privileges, they promised hospital trustees that they would exclusively admit their patients to the particular hospital, thus keeping its beds full. As hospital boards began to concede these powers to physicians during the first two decades of this century, control over hospital affairs shifted away from nurses.

From the beginning nurses relied on physicians to support nursing authority in patient care. Now, as their domestic authority within the hospital was undermined, they lost control over events in the setting in which they worked. Moreover, they confronted serious problems realigning their loyalties among hospital boards, physicians, and patients. Differences arose over which patients should be admitted, how long each should stay, and what resources should be committed to their care. Hospital boards, having given physicians power over the financial welfare of the hospital by allowing them to control patient admissions, were less able to effectively mediate disputes about these matters between physicians and nurses.

By 1920, there were 7,000 hospitals in the United States and almost 105,000 trained registered nurses at work. Women still managed a significant proportion of the smaller hospitals but exerted little control over the total nurse training system or the number of nurses entering the work force. About 80 percent of the graduates of the hospital schools did private duty work; of these nurses, close to half cared for patients in hospitals; the rest cared for patients in the patients' own homes. Private duty nurses contracted directly with patients for their fees.

As the number of graduates of the hospital schools continued to soar, competition for patient referrals grew. By 1930, nearly 215,000 trained nurses were competing for cases, and chronic unemployment was a reality for many of them. Moreover, hospitals competed with their nurse alumnae, admitting patients who formerly would have been cared for by nurses at home. This competition was especially apparent as hospitals opened maternity units and urged women to use hospitals for childbirth. One irony of this situation was that women nurses seeking work were competing, in many cases, with the women superintendents of hospitals who had trained them.

Nursing at the Midpoint of Its History

Thus, by 1940 nursing presented something of a paradox as women's work. It was flourishing in the sense that the numbers of nurses and nursing schools had grown phenomenally since nursing emerged as a formal occupation in the 1880s. It supported large national organizations: the American Nurses Association (ANA), the National League for Nursing Education, and the National Organization of Public Health Nursing, and it sustained a viable press in the form of journals and books, whose publishers had discovered the large nursing market. It attracted many truly competent and innovative twentieth century women to its ranks, women who led important social changes, such as Margaret Sanger, pioneer of family planning; Lillian Wald, public health reformer and founder of New York City's Henry Street Settlement; and Mabel Staupers, crusader for the rights of African-American nurses. And although the public image of nurses always was complicated by American prudishness about intimacy and sex, nurses enjoyed a positive image in movies and magazines and a certain measure of public support, especially during the depression and as World War II loomed.

But nursing was also a deeply troubled occupation. It could control neither its numbers nor its access to the consumers of nursing services. The number of nursing schools had multiplied 75-fold between 1880 and 1910; only the Great Depression finally succeeded in reducing expansion in hospital schools. Nonprofit hospitals were exempt from collective bargaining, so even when hospitals began to hire graduate staff nurses in the late 1930s, nurses could not materially influence their economic situation via the union movement. Perhaps as many as 10,000 nurses belonged to unions in 1939, but effective bargaining for nurses did not occur until well after World War II.

World War II, however, was to prove a turning point for nursing, as it was for American women in general. Demand for nurses for military service created an instant crisis and nursing shortage. Nursing leadership responded by speeding up the production of nurses through the hospital school system, but simultaneously, they successfully agitated for financial support for nursing students. In 1943, the Cadet Nurse Corps, a federal program that underwrote nursing education, set in motion the ongoing federal subsidy of the education of women in certain professions. And, like other American women who found work barriers dropped during the war emergency, nurses who went to war found joy and satisfaction in their expanded responsibility and new opportunities for practice.

Signs of Change in Nursing

The careful division of labor between physicians and nurses that became entrenched when physicians moved into hospitals in the early twentieth century depended on the principle that the physician prescribed and controlled virtually every clinical detail regarding patient care while the nurse reliably executed the physician's orders. The war emergency challenged that level of medical dominance because nurses were able to provide safe care inexpensively and efficiently.

Fundamentally, of course, nurses' work was care of the sick person throughout the duration of his or her illness or dependency. However, the hierarchy of authority put physicians in a position of total responsibility for both their own diagnostic and therapeutic work and the nurses' work. Physicians were, of course, not trained in nursing, nor were they present at the bedside to oversee the nurse's work. This awkward and illogical nineteenth century arrangement probably was adopted because nurses were women and believed incapable of sufficient knowledge and coping ability to carry such responsibility without direction from physicians, most of them male. At the same time, physicians relied on nurses' loyalty and dependability in carrying out the medical regimen.

Thus, early in the century physicians succeeded in parlaying their "special knowledge" and social authority into control over another occupation. Limits on nurses' education and scientific knowledge were thereby justified and necessary. Justified, because as long as the physician was in charge of everything, the nurse did not have to know much. Necessary, because if the nurse learned too much, she would not accept her subservient role. Such an arrangement could be expected to last no longer than the social assumptions about gender relationships and privilege upon which it was based.

And so the upheavals associated with World War II and its aftermath shook this dysfunctional, jerryrigged work relationship until it began to slowly crumble. Other more intransigent barriers also started to break down. Throughout its history, nursing served as an imperfect vehicle for social mobility. Easy access to the profession via the hospital training schools and recognition as a respected, distinct occupation with high geographic mobility helped working-class women find a way up. It is important, however, not to exaggerate nursing's social mobility function, because racial barriers, class barriers, and a wasteful employment system put limits on real movement from one stratum to another. In America successful social mobility requires both money and education.

Nevertheless, a significant episode during World War II signaled changes in and outside nursing. Mabel Staupers, head of the National Association of Colored Graduate Nurses, led an effort to force the integration of black nurses into the military nursing services during the war. An effective coalition builder and negotiator, Staupers was able to turn the wartime nursing shortage and a brilliant information campaign into a 1944 presidential decision to admit black women into the formerly all-white military nursing service. The campaign used radio, news articles, and posters to point out the irony that black nurses were available and pleading for admission to military service while the war department was demanding that white nurses be drafted to fill depleted nursing ranks.

Staupers and her colleagues charted an undeviating course toward integration in reaction to their experiences of the debilitating limitations of a segregated nurse education and practice system. The limits placed on the practice opportunities of African-American women were particularly problematic because black nurse graduates found few black patients who were sufficiently affluent to employ them as private duty nurses. Although some found practice opportunities in public health work and hospital administration, racism compounded the inequities encountered by their white counterparts. The creation and survival of viable nursing services for African Americans before the civil rights reforms of the 1960s are a testament to the tenacity and discipline of black nursing leaders, such as Staupers, and their supporters.[3]

Out of the war crisis and the postwar decision to rebuild and expand America's hospital system came the impetus for educational and practice changes for nursing. Collaborating groups included nursing leaders, the surgeon general and federal government, philanthropists, the American Hospital Association, physicians, and insurers. The postwar situation posed some complicated realities: (1) 90 percent of nurses were still being educated in hospital schools, many of which were small, underfinanced, and peripheral to the American educational system, (2) demand for specialized care was rising—for the mentally ill, children, and the acutely ill in hospitals, as well as for public health services, and (3) a generally rising standard of living and the mind-expanding experiences of World War II accelerated nurses' intense dissatisfaction with their low pay, long hours, and lack of control over their work.

Most planners assumed that improved community hospitals would become the arbitrators, centers, and guarantors of the postwar health care system. In this context the first question that had to be addressed was how best to care for patients in hospitals.

The introduction of fully trained graduate nurses to hospitals in the 1930s had been a long, hotly debated, and incomplete process. After the war many hospitals continued to rely on students to care for their expanding patient population. Hospital head nurses, in charge of wards accommodating 40 to 60 patients, and hospital nursing supervisors, directing large medical, surgical, pediatric, or obstetric services, usually learned what they knew about management on the job. Chiefs of nursing services in hospitals were often promoted from within, up through the ranks. In hospital after hospital, these nurses now confronted the task of coping with a rapidly expanding demand for patient care services using a work force of a few graduate nurses, students, and untrained assistants.

In this climate influenced by demand for nursing services and informed by wartime experience with the federally supported Cadet Nurse Corps, new educational opportunities developed for women who were or aspired to become nurses. Nurse veterans took advantage of the postwar GI Bill to earn baccalaureate and master's degrees; later legislation created funding for training nurses who were willing to work in psychiatry. And in 1963, the first federal nurse "traineeship" programs gave direct aid to individuals, while other federal and state programs assisted nursing schools. These initiatives subsidized women from the middle and working classes who aspired to higher education. It was by these means that women nurses joined the postwar pilgrimage of America's middle class to college.

Early in the 1950s a new and successful avenue for nursing education opened as the community college movement added nursing to its offerings. These associate degree nursing programs, as they were called, helped make nursing education part of the publicly funded educational mainstream. At the same time, tenacious and imaginative nursing deans and faculty in American universities created new schools and expanded existing programs to produce baccalaureate- and master's-prepared nurses. Thus, the education of nurses finally became separated from nurses' hospital employers and was more effectively controlled by professional and educational standard setters.

During this era the nursing organizations, particularly the ANA, began to assume responsibility for the economic security of nurses. Bargaining units and collective action—strategies long shunned because of nurses' feelings of loyalty to patients, lack of acceptance in the labor movement, and general atomization—began to make inroads in nursing's discouragingly low salaries and poor work conditions. Although nurses were slow and reluctant to unionize, the economic agenda pursued by the ANA played an important role in clarifying relationships between nurses and their hospital employers. It was not until 1974, however, that nonprofit hospitals lost their exemption from national laws mandating participation in collective bargaining.

Nursing Practice Expands and Specializes

Public demand for health care services in the 1960s and 1970s helped create and sustain financial support for more and better-prepared nurses from the federal government, foundations, and others. A growing public assumption of a "right" to health care, epitomized by the passage of the 1965 Medicare and Medicaid legislation, created opportunities for advancement for some nurses—and they responded. Health care planners, political leaders, and professionals agreed that meeting the public's expectations for more services required a broader array of health care providers. New ways of thinking about how to deliver patient care services led to the development of alternatives to the medical dominance over direct patient care so characteristic of the first half of the century. Interdisciplinary neighborhood clinics, midwifery services, and new school health and mental health facilities led thousands of nurses to expand their career horizons and change their practices.

These specialists—psychiatric mental health nurses, midwives, and nurse practitioners—found their new roles mostly outside the hospital bureaucracy. They often started out in collaborative practice with like-minded physicians. These new nurses, with intensive training and broad experience, demonstrated a level of therapeutic effectiveness and a personal practice style that attracted public support. Public approval seems to have been driven by four factors: (1) the desire for easy access to friendly services; (2) demographic changes that increased demand, especially for child care, women's health care, and care for the chronically ill; (3) the women's movement and the civil rights movement, both of which tended to undermine the cultural authority of physicians; and (4) the prospect of lower-cost services from nurses, who did not command the same price as physicians.

Inside the hospital another scenario was playing out in intensive care units, where patients considered physiologically unstable were gathered together for special care. Here, since the 1970s, nurses have assumed control over an arena of new knowledge, especially in cardiology and respiratory support, and its associated technology. Critical care nurses began to band together in the late 1960s to learn from one another and from physicians. By the 1980s, they were setting standards for nursing practice in the hospital. Through certification, special training, and position statements via their national organization, they began to standardize the level of knowledge required to practice in intensive care units. As a group, critical care nurses take great pride in their expertise and have a strong esprit de corps. Their pride in practice, process of specialization, standard setting, and nurse determination of events have come to characterize many areas of practice.

Conclusion

Nursing lends itself poorly to generalizations because as an occupation it encompasses so broad a range of skills and activities, from the mundane to the highly complex. At the same time, the size and heterogeneity of nursing make it a mirror of women's experience in American life over the last 125 years.

As women's work, nursing has had the advantages of free mobility for individuals inside the profession, so that women were able to rise to the top of large nursing care and nursing education institutions. Access to the occupation was easy and, as has been noted, nursing was of some social mobility value to working-class women. Women related freely, often vociferously, with one another inside American nursing and dominated virtually all arenas of decision making. As at women's colleges, individual freedom of movement in a women's world was possible.

But the nature of nursing as women's work has some disturbing implications, for both the profession and the public. Historian Susan Reverby offers the most thoughtful analysis of the implications of assigning caring work, like nursing, solely to women. In her words, "ordering [women] to care" without attaching social value to personal caregiving leaves nursing in a dilemma.[4] Nursing fell under the dominance of medicine largely because of prevailing ideas about the appropriate sexual division of labor between women and men in the nineteenth century. It is really only during the last four decades that the public has begun to pay heed to nursing's arguments for committing resources to safer, more humane care in hospitals, home care, and nursing homes. The continuing underdevelopment of home care and nursing home care verifies the extreme difficulty of diverting resources toward caregiving.

In addition, nursing and the public it serves have not benefited from the contributions of the many men with caregiving skills who, except for social disfavor, would have joined nursing's ranks. American men enter nursing in small numbers both because they fear their career choice may impugn their masculinity and because nursing has a history of poor pay and working conditions. Now that nursing careers are more attractive, it may be possible to attract more men, but our cultural ideas about what is appropriate work for men and women will need to change.

Nurses, physicians, and the public have struggled to conceptualize a better, more equitable, and more functional system. It is difficult because changing our system means changing how we value and dedicate resources to the different parts of the health care system. For much of the twentieth century we valued and rewarded the physician above all others because we hoped that medicine could relieve our pain and delay our inevitable mortality. The success of our tertiary acute care system is, in some measure, our reward for that investment. But an unbalanced over-focus on diagnosis and therapy has led to lack of attention and poor facilities for the chronically ill, the aged, well children, and others whose problems fall outside the twentieth century sphere of medicine. As Claire Fagin points out elsewhere in this book, Americans are only gradually and painfully coming to grips with the complex and monumental task of addressing these late twentieth century health and caregiving issues.

Early nursing leaders have been criticized in recent years for their obsession with raising standards of education for nurses and their seeming lack of compassion for the laboring masses of nurses.[5] It is true that from 1900 to the present nursing leaders shared the idea that better education was the key to "lifting all boats." Experience showed early nurses that the education strategy, as a means of creating access to expert status and control over work, was successful for physicians, social workers, engineers, and others. Nursing leaders assumed it would work for nurses too; maybe if they were here today they would declare they were right. They might say that access to college and freedom from hospital schools explain the more equitable position nursing is now beginning to enjoy. They would surely agree that the generally improved status of women in the workplace is a boon to nursing.

But events of the last 50 years indicate that another explanation may be a better fit. Public demand for nursing services of higher quality and greater variety both in and outside of hospitals seems to be the biggest lever prying nursing free from its bondage to medicine and hospitals. Americans want nurses to help them feel safe in hospitals, they want access to mental health services, they want primary care for themselves and their children, and they want midwives to deliver their babies. To the extent that nursing responded to these demands for service, the public could be persuaded to invest in more nurses and higher standards of education. In 1990 we saw that salaries rose dramatically when access to nursing services seemed to be threatened by shortage.

Of course, the story of nursing would be different if it was not "women's work." Founders of modern nursing, in both Great Britain and the United States, often reminded their colleagues that the future of women and the future of nursing were the same. Societal values associated with giving care were, and still are, largely identified with women. The real question for the future is whether we will ever so desire a civil, sympathetic society that we attach higher value to this "women's work." Will we come to see one another as valuable human beings to the point where we all, whether men or women, will feel both free and obliged to take care?

Notes

1. Florence Nightingale, *Notes on Nursing: What It Is, And What It Is Not* (London: Harrison, 1859), 76.

2. Joan Lynaugh, "From Respectable Domesticity to Medical Efficiency: The Changing Kansas City Hospital, 1875-1920," in Diana Long and Janet Golden, eds., *The American General Hospital—Communities and Social Contexts* (Ithaca: Cornell University Press, 1989), 21-39.

3. See Darlene Clark Hine, *Black Women in White—Racial Conflict and Cooperation in the Nursing Profession, 1890 -1950,* (Bloomington, IN: Indiana University Press, 1989) for the best discussion of this little-known saga.

4. Susan M. Reverby, *Ordered to Care: The Dilemma of American Nursing, 1850-1945* (Cambridge: Cambridge University Press, 1987).

5. Barbara Melosh, *The Physician's Hand* (Philadelphia: Temple University Press, 1982); Reverby, *Ordered to Care*, 1987.

11

Women and Nursing, Today and Tomorrow

Claire Fagin

IN THE LAST DECADE NURSING has been revolutionized. Nurses have more, and more complex, skills and provide primary care as well as expert technical care in an increasingly technological medical universe. They also provide the emotional and physical care essential to the broader needs of a public currently experiencing such devastating health and social problems as AIDS and homelessness, as well as the effects of aging and chronic and fatal illnesses. Nurses are treating the poor, teenage mothers, infants and children, minorities, and rural Americans. They are clinicians, researchers, politicians, policy analysts, administrators, and teachers.

The decade ahead promises to be no less revolutionary. Although prospects for national health care reform legislation have dimmed, most reform proposals envisioned a large role for registered nurses (RNs) in delivering health care services. Under most health reform proposals, advanced practice nurses—nurse practitioners, certified nurse midwives, and clinical nurse specialists prepared at the master's level—would be able to provide a full range of health care services to patients, diagnosing, treating, and prescribing medications for everyday health care needs. This recognition of nurses' potential contribution to the health care system is without precedent.

Who are the nurses who will provide these services? The RN population today consists of more than 2 million people. Ninety-seven percent of them are women; of the 8.3 percent who are minorities, 3.6 percent are black (non-Hispanic), 2.3 percent are Asian/Pacific Islander, 0.4 percent are American Indian/Alaskan Native, and 1.3 percent are Hispanic.[1] Thirty percent hold the baccalaureate degree in nursing, and 8 percent hold the master's degree or doctorate degree.

Approximately two-thirds have an associate degree (AD) or diploma in nursing.[2]

The Nursing Shortage

Joan Lynaugh has described the nursing "yo-yo,"[3] society's oscillating relationship with nursing. From nursing's beginning, repeated and episodic shortages have been one part of the yo-yo. Although 83 percent of the more than 2 million nurses in the United States are in the nursing labor force—a greater proportion than in most other professions—shortages are likely to recur: the U.S. Bureau of Labor Statistics predicts that nursing occupations will grow at more than twice the rate of other fields by the year 2005.[4]

Unlike earlier nursing shortages, the most recent "shortage" brought economic adjustments. In hospitals, salary increases have been significant, for both experienced clinical nurses and entry-level nurses. Although the crisis in hospitals appears to have subsided, it is unclear whether there has been a real change in the ratio of nurses to patients, or whether with higher salaries there are fewer positions to fill. In some parts of the country, layoffs are occurring and new graduates are finding interview doors closed and no positions available.

What remains clear is that shortages do exist and will continue to exist among baccalaureate-educated nurses, nursing school faculty at colleges and universities, and specialists with master's degrees. The Seventh Report to Congress of the U.S. Department of Health and Human Services indicates that the demand for master's- and doctoral-level nurses will be twice the supply in the year 2000.[5] The demand will be further fueled by the expanded role envisioned for advanced practice nurses in a reformed health care system.

These predictions of future shortages do not take into account current experiences in nursing education, however. Enrollment in master's programs is declining, vacancy levels among full-time faculty have increased—perhaps because faculty salaries in nursing have not kept pace with other parts of the nursing marketplace (see "Nursing Salaries," below)—and the use of part-time faculty has increased concomitantly. Furthermore, advanced educational programs are extremely expensive in terms of both actual layout of money and foregone income, a consideration some reform plans recognized by proposing to double the training funds for advanced practice programs. Some such adjustment would be necessary in order to reach the ambitious goal of doubling the supply of advanced practice nurses by the year 2000.

Enrollment in Nursing Schools and Student Interest in Nursing

During the 1980s academic institutions were reeling from the sharp reductions in the number of applicants to nursing programs. Some programs had trouble staying alive; others had difficulty retaining faculty, a problem that had secondary effects more recently as faculty numbers became insufficient for the expansion in enrollments.

During the 1980s the Cooperative Institutional Research Program presented cautionary data about interest in nursing among college freshmen.[6] From 1983 to 1988 the number of students enrolled in nursing schools declined from a peak of 250,000 to 184,000. Baccalaureate programs suffered a decline of 32 percent in enrollment of first-time nursing students during this period. In the 1980s more women college freshmen indicated an interest in medicine than in nursing, by a ratio of 10 to 8, as compared with a previous ratio of 3 to 1 in favor of nursing.

Current information about student numbers shows a reversal in the downward trend. Enrollment of entry-level bachelor's degree nursing students in the nation's universities and colleges rose by 12.4 percent in September 1992. This surpassed an 11.1 percent increase in the 1990-91 year. The number of current nursing students is the highest in 20 years.

Even if one recognizes that the major problem in the most recent nursing shortage was not on the supply side, the marked reduction in student enrollment creates a real threat to a constant future supply. The reduction in interest in nursing was inextricably linked to the demand side problems in nursing accurately perceived by young people considering careers. The next few years will be important indicators of whether we are viewing a long-term upward trend or a brief blip caused by the recent recession.

On the positive side, nursing educators have been impressed by recent changes in the applicant pool. There appears to be a sharp increase in interest among men and older women in nursing. Most of these applicants are career changers who have degrees in other areas. They come from fields as diverse as law, veterinary medicine, biology, and finance. Some had thought of nursing earlier in their lives, others had not. Many have had a personal experience in a hospital or at home with an ill relative or friend, or have been ill themselves. These applicants have made a considered decision about nursing, and they often know exactly where they want to practice.

Freshmen applicants have also increased in quality since the gloomy days of the mid-1980s, when concern was expressed not only about numbers but about academic ability. Even more interesting to admissions counselors is the knowledge that these freshmen applicants have about nursing, and the questions many ask about nursing research and the nursing researchers they will work with at a particular institution. While not a scientific conclusion at this time, impressions nationwide suggest a marked change in the applicant pool in terms of numbers, academic ability, age, and career interests.

Can nursing continue to attract women in a greatly changed female labor market? Current information would indicate that the answer to that question must be affirmative. However, over time, nursing has been very sensitive to media reports of shortage, oversupply, lack of salary progression, and poor working conditions. Therefore, one could imagine a scenario in which newspaper articles cited the end of the nursing shortage, new graduates' difficulties in finding jobs, and lay-offs among nursing personnel, based, perhaps, on regional realities. Judging by past experiences, it is possible to predict the rapid results such a report would have on nursing: the very parents who today are proud that their children are choosing nursing might be discouraged, while the career changer confident about making a living in the new field might be deterred from making this career choice.

Men in Nursing

Early in the 1980s, when asked what the nursing population would look like at the end of the decade, I predicted that fewer women would choose nursing as a career because of the apparent opening of many other opportunities for women. I also indicated my belief that the number of men choosing nursing would increase markedly as all fields became more androgynous. I was wrong. The most recent Sample Survey of the Registered Nurse Population shows that only 3.3 percent of the RN population is male.[7] However, recent enrollment figures show a doubling of men in RN programs, from 5.7 percent in 1981 to 11.1 percent in 1992.[8] There was a significant increase in male graduates in that period, from 5.8 percent to 9.9 percent, with most of the growth occurring in the last four years of that period.

These increases show a positive change with respect to men and nursing; still, greater attention must be paid to the recruitment of men (and minorities, as I will discuss below) to the nursing profession. To widen choices for women in our society, there must be an analogous widening of opportunities for men in a more androgynous occupational society. Women should not and do not have a corner on caring for others. Changing relationships between men and children, and men and parents, are receiving considerable attention. As the caring role becomes more acceptable to men, we should see even greater changes in the nursing applicant pool. There is certainly no shortage of opportunities for men in the enormously varied roles of professional nursing.

Minorities in Nursing
Recent data indicate that members of ethnic and racial minorities make up 17 percent of first-year baccalaureate nursing students. First-year enrollments in all RN nursing programs in 1992 indicate that 15.4 percent were members of minority groups. In that same year, close to 13.3 percent of graduates from all RN programs were from minority groups. Contrary to popular perceptions, baccalaureate programs in nursing enroll more members of minority groups than do AD programs. In fact, "Representation of Hispanics is almost identical among the different program types,"[9] while larger proportions of black and Asian students are enrolled in baccalaureate programs.

Licensed practical nurse (LPN) and licensed vocational nurse (LVN) programs have significantly greater minority enrollment than do RN programs. Almost 16 percent of the graduates from these programs are black, compared to 7.2 percent from RN programs. Similarly, Hispanics and American Indians are more heavily represented in LPN and LVN programs.

Although minority groups are better represented in nursing than in many other disciplines, the increasingly complex nature of our diverse society, nursing's historic mission, the large expected growth curve of Hispanic and Asian populations, and the modest growth trend anticipated among African Americans speak to the need both to recruit more members of minority groups to nursing and to support programs that will enhance retention of students once they are admitted.

However, like all institutions of higher education, nursing schools have problems recruiting and retaining African Americans and Hispanics. Recruitment is "handicapped by the fact that many inner-city youth—those who have earned a high school diploma to say nothing of those who have not—cannot cope with the nursing curriculum because of deficiencies in language, mathematics, or science."[10] Ginzberg points out that success in recruiting minority students and in developing successful programs for upward mobility requires adaptations and innovations in curriculum and financial support for students. Clearly, financial support is also essential for junior high school and high school programs to enable them to address one of the major problems facing American society today.

I look back on more than 20 years of activism with regard to this issue. My interest in the area is two-fold. First, for as long as I can remember, I have been involved in the struggle for civil rights. Second, during my leadership of a graduate program in psychiatric nursing, I became aware of the difficulties of recruiting African Americans. Almost without exception, those I interviewed had been advised into LPN programs during high school. Then, with considerable struggle, some few managed to achieve the baccalaureate degree, sometimes after a hospital or diploma school RN program. Finally, these extraordinary women were applying to a master's program. Concerned about their difficult and indirect route and the poor guidance they had received, I developed a proposal to recruit and retain minority group students in baccalaureate nursing. After several rejections I took the proposal with me to a new position at the City University of New York (CUNY). There, in 1971, with some revision, it became one of the first two federally funded programs for minority recruitment in nursing in the United States. (The other was in Texas and addressed a different population.) Ironically, the funding of the program coincided with "open admissions" at CUNY, so recruitment was not a problem. Rather, methods of retention—including financial support, tutoring, and counseling during high school and college—became the focus.

Lives were changed dramatically as a result of this program and others, but there have been all too few sufficiently funded programs over the past two decades to create systemic, nationwide change. Furthermore, during the 1980s, those upwardly mobile minority students whose educational preparation was on a par with that of majority group members experienced the same disaffection with nursing careers, no matter what the described opportunities. With the exception of a few major foundations, funders have generally received proposals focusing on the upward-bound minority student and nursing with lukewarm interest, at best.

Nonetheless, opportunities in nursing for men and minority group members abound. Judging by the number of African Americans and men in leadership positions in the field, one could say that given equivalent preparation, there are no glass ceilings in nursing. However, the pool of minority nurses is small, requiring efforts at a variety of levels in order to change the picture in the coming decade. Programs in junior high and high schools, programs for guidance counselors, upward bound programs for LPNs and LVNs, and recruitment programs for nursing in black colleges must all be implemented on a nationwide scale. These programs must include financial support for students, short- and long-term mentoring, and other supports.

Nursing Salaries

The wage rate of RNs came to the public's attention during the last nursing shortage. The public learned that RNs had had relatively low wages for the three decades preceding the current shortage and were not keeping up even with other female-dominated professions. Hospital nurses received only modest wage increases from 1982 to 1985, despite cries of vacancy rates. In 1985, the average salary for teachers was 19 percent higher than that for nurses.[11]

From April 1989 to April 1990, the Hospital Compensation Service reported an increase of 14.7 percent in the average salary for all hospital-based RNs. In October 1993 the University of Texas survey of a group of teaching hospitals, medical centers, and medical schools found an average salary of $35,960 for staff nurses.[12] Other data report raises for nurse specialists outpacing those for staff nurses, and certified RN anesthetists averaging 33 percent more than other specialists.[13] An *American Journal of Nursing* survey reported a spread of 20 percent to 40 percent from minimum to maximum salary among staff nurses. Hewitt Associates consultants on nursing salaries predict a 100 percent spread by the year 2000.

Nursing's Image

Nurses still suffer from leftover stereotypes and negative images. Some of these images are the result of the way nursing has been viewed historically; others are the result of crosscurrents in the feminist movement.

Correcting Stereotypes

Several major foundations have supported efforts to improve the image of the profession. Major campaigns during the 1980s dealt with nursing's image by stressing the necessity of improving the working environment in hospitals and of enhancing training and funding for nurse researchers.[14] Raising the level of discussion of nurses and nursing emphasized the significance of the profession.

Several prestigious groups commissioned studies during the shortage crisis period, including the Institute of Medicine, the U.S. Department of Health and Human Services, and The Kellogg Foundation.[15] In 1987, The Pew Charitable Trusts sponsored a national conference to discuss "Nurses for the Future," and followed that with a grant to the Tri-Council on Nursing Organizations[16] to fund a media education program, which attempted to alter the negative, stereotypical images prevailing in the press, on the radio, and, in particular, on television. As part of the Pew project, the Peter Hart Organization conducted a nationwide survey of attitudes on health care and nurses.[17] In addition, another study examined health news coverage in the United States, analyzing the content of 423 articles about health care that appeared in the *New York Times, Washington Post,* and *Los Angeles Times* during the first quarter of 1990.[18]

The Hart survey results refuted some commonly held beliefs about the public image of nurses and indicated that *"Nurses are far and away the health care provider the public most respects and supports. By an overwhelming percentage, nurses are perceived much more positively than the other health care institutions and groups tested in the survey."*[19] The institutions and groups with which nurses were compared were doctors, hospitals, nursing homes, hospital administrators, the federal government, and insurance companies. In line with this respect, the respondents indicated their belief that nurses held at least the baccalaureate degree, and that they were willing to see the role of nurses expanded in the interest of cost savings.

What makes these results even more interesting are the findings of the newspaper survey. Here the authors found that out of 423 articles about health care, government officials (some of whom were physicians) were the main source for 28 percent, business people for 7 percent, physicians for 7 percent, and nurses for only one article. Physicians were the group most quoted; nurses were quoted only 10 times out of 908 quotes. In general the doctors quoted were male.

Following this study an article appeared in the *Washington Post* that offered an egregious example of the problem. It referred to the work of J.M. Eland, a nurse.[20] While the article mentions Eland's work, it does not name her; instead, she is referred to as an "unlikely catalyst." Like most articles about health care, the article is cast in such a way that the nurse is invisible and doctors are credited with whatever we know about the subject—even the outcomes of studies initiated by nurses.

However, the Hart survey suggests that despite the unfavorable portrayals of nurses on television and the lack of attention to nurses and nursing in the press, the public has a strong belief in the worth of the group. The only negative part of the image is that nurses are underpaid and somewhat beleaguered. Pretty accurate!

The New Feminism and Nursing

Has the term "feminism" come to mean that women do what men do? Ellen Baer describes the paradox of feminism, "which glorifies women who emulate masculine behavior while virtually ignoring women who choose traditionally female roles and careers."[21] She and others have commented that some American feminists avoid the subject of caring, defend women against the obligation to care, and focus almost exclusively on helping women move into the male marketplace. Gordon acknowledges that women in "women's work" often feel that mainstream feminism is hostile to their interests.[22]

Interestingly, at the height of the women's movement, in the late 1960s and 1970s, nursing, despite public derogation by leading feminist speakers, attracted growing interest from a wide spectrum of college-educated and college-aspiring women and men.[23] Students believed that the field offered opportunities for the political activist equal to or better than those achievable in law (the most frequent comparison). In the 1980s, on the other hand, nursing became almost a pariah field as women and families placed restrictions on what intelligent people ought to do. Smart, achieving women have always had a hard time selecting nursing as a career. Active battles with families, guidance counselors, and teachers had to be fought and won in order for many young women to matriculate at university schools of nursing, particularly in the private sector. Yet as indicated above, there appears to be a resurgence of interest in nursing among highly qualified applicants, and acceptance among families that their daughters (and a few sons) are making the right choice.

Gordon differentiates between adaptive feminism and transformative feminism. Adaptive, or equal-opportunity, feminists define success as being a man's equal in a man's world. They reject the caring professions as duplicating the imprisonment of women in the home. Transformative feminists see "women's experiences and concerns as the source of a . . . needed transformative vision."[24] This vision would change the values of the marketplace, creating a more humane society with a commitment to caring.

The tension between these opposing views of feminism seems, in recent years, to be decreasing. Women in the traditional professions are more assertive about their rights, and many women who are "making it" according to the adaptive view are publicly stating their unhappiness about conforming to the male value system. All these social phenomena will have an effect on nursing and other predominantly female fields during the coming decade.

Nursing's Leadership

There are many ways to approach the topic of nursing's leadership. One might be to determine who really speaks for nursing and how effective these spokespersons have been on a national level with regard to health and nursing policy. A look at the credentials of nurse administrators and educators is another way. Yet another is to examine current nursing research. Finally, we might wish to examine what nursing's leadership has to do with its followership.

Who Speaks for Nursing?

The two million nurses in the United States are an extremely diverse group educationally and socially. They have been extremely resistant to "groupthink" and have, until recent years, been difficult to unite around specific causes. However, the increased awareness among women in general to the commonalities of their experiences has had a major effect on the nursing group and on its ability to unite behind its leaders for positive action.

Over the past decade nursing has made extraordinary strides in developing a critical mass of individual nurses and nursing organizations able to speak for large segments of the nursing population. In the past, nursing has been open to criticism because of the perceived distance between its spokespersons and the masses of nurses, and because of infighting among its professional associations. However, with few exceptions (most notably, the issue of the profession's entry-level credential), the coalescence of nurses around issues important to the strength of the profession, the health of the public, and the image of the group has been striking. Most recently, nurses successfully united behind their leaders to convince the Clinton administration and others of the role nurses are qualified to play in a reorganized health care system. This example of leadership and unity shows that there is a large group of nursing leaders, in and outside organizations, who can obtain support from the masses of nurses on a variety of issues.

As the number of nurses with baccalaureate degrees grows, it can be expected that even more unity in political action will be achieved, since nursing's most divisive issue—the educational requirement for entry into the profession—will have less hold on its population. It is here that leadership has had a less than dramatic effect.

The issue of the entry-level credential for professional practice has plagued nursing and nursing leaders for most of the century. The question appears at times to reach resolution, or agreement about resolution, but then these plans are hindered by strong opposition both in and outside the profession, and thwarted by the reappearance of episodic nursing shortages.

Leaders in nursing administration speak about the need for baccalaureate-prepared practitioners, and, when possible, recruit predominantly these nurses. Worried about the minimal preparation of less educationally prepared RNs and the cost of upgrading their education and credentials, nursing administrators are nonetheless forced by the pool available in their geographic area to employ a mixed group. Further, they have not been successful in offering sharply differentiated pay schedules for staff nurses with different educational levels. Experimentation with pay scales and other issues is ongoing, but the question of entry-level credential keeps nursing and nurses divided in a very basic sense.

The profession does not require legislation to institute quality regulations or indicators; thus, national certification of professionals can emanate from the professional organizations. However, even here, leadership efforts to require the master's degree for specialists, or even the baccalaureate, are impeded by the nature of the nursing population and a view of egalitarianism, influenced, in my view, by feminist values.

It is somewhat ironic that some nursing leaders, in their frustration about this issue, have almost abandoned the quest for baccalaureate entry to the nursing profession and are recommending the master's degree. In my opinion this is a wrong-minded approach that essentially declares that AD or diploma preparation is acceptable for the basic caregiver, while some 10 percent of the nursing population (given optimistic forecasts) will be prepared at the new professional level. Such an approach would certainly complicate the question of the profession's leadership. In discussions of leadership, representativeness is always a crucial dimension. The small population of master's-prepared nurses will certainly not be representative of the critical masses, prepared at the AD level. To believe that the master's-prepared nurse will be the basic caregiver refutes economics, numbers, marketplace concerns, individual interests of people prepared at this level, and the work and schedule requirements of staff nursing practice.

While a small group of nursing leaders is thus far indicating its advocacy of graduate entry, the convergence of this view with the real interests of AD educators and graduates will provide an interesting scenario in the coming decade. On the one hand, the leaders have a lofty reason for their proposal: quality health care requiring longer and more complex educational preparation. On the other hand, they will be joined by a group only too happy to inherit the turf being abdicated. Nursing, like politics, makes strange bedfellows.

Despite this issue, the presence of nurse leaders at the "table" of decision making in many important governmental and private groups, at local and national levels, is striking. In political office, in major interdisciplinary organizations, on decision-making committees, and on corporate boards, nurses exercise considerable power on behalf of women, health, and the nursing profession. The number of nursing leaders is growing, and if personal experience and discussions with peers are any indication, they are a group about whom nurses at large speak with pride. There seems to be a sense that, for the most part, these leaders speak for the group and support, sustain, make sense of, and further the work of practicing nurses.[25]

Credentials of Educators and Administrators

In 1992, 88 percent of directors of baccalaureate and higher degree programs reporting to the American Association of Colleges of Nursing held the doctoral degree. Forty-one percent of faculty in these programs held the doctorate, an increase of almost 300 percent since 1978, when the proportion was 15 percent; 58 percent held the master's degree in 1992. In the educational setting, the pressure on faculty and administrators to hold terminal degrees has been intense. Survival of schools has sometimes rested on the qualifications of faculty. Therefore, the upgrading of faculty credentials was essential and has progressed steadily for half of the twentieth century.

The difference in educational credentials among practicing nurses is even more dramatic than among educators. As the 1980s began, only about 25 percent of directors of nursing held advanced degrees. As of 1991, 41 percent held advanced degrees. The changes among nursing administrators in practice settings occurred much later and have been particularly concentrated in the last decade. Changes in practice are inevitable given the increased preparation of nursing administrators and the concomitant increases in education among second and third tier leaders in these settings.

Nursing Research

Various groups, including the National Academy of Sciences, have tied the future of nursing to the quality and quantity of doctorally prepared nurses capable of conducting sophisticated research on nursing phenomena. The escalation in numbers of such nurses in the past 15 years has had a major effect on the research literature. Although funding has become increasingly available, the competition for these funds has increased disproportionately.

Nursing research examines phenomena of care and cure from the nursing perspective; nursing policy issues dealing with the nursing shortage, staffing, and organization; and health policy issues dealing with cost and access to health care. With grants from the National Institute of Nursing Research, established in 1993, and from other sources, nurses are examining issues ranging from managing the side effects of radiation therapy to how specially designed units for care of patients with Alzheimer's disease can reduce their rate of deterioration.[26]

Nursing research promotes collaborative relationships with physicians and others by linking professionals of equal preparation in the solution of major problems. Increasing the appreciation of nursing phenomena is a secondary gain as members of other disciplines acquire an understanding of nursing's focus and priorities. This kind of collaboration has been enhanced by major private foundation programs, including two Robert Wood Johnson national programs: the

Primary Care Faculty Fellowship Program and the Clinical Nurse Scholars Program.

As noted above, it is interesting and ironic that nursing can celebrate its accomplishments in research at the highest level of achievement and governmental status at the same time that it refuses to come to terms with the issue of its entry-level credential.

What Lies Ahead for Nursing?

A combination of factors leads me to believe that nursing will not only survive into the next century, but that its values will prevail in the health care system of the future. There are many reasons for this view; I will outline seven.

1. The public's interest in cost, care, and quality mandates its support of nursing. This is already evident in consumer pressure for access to nurse midwives and the public's expressed willingness to use nurse practitioners.[27]

2. The future health care delivery scene will shift some of its primary focus from cure to care. This shift accentuates the need for nurses, whose knowledge, interests, and skills in the caring mode have formed the basis for nursing as long as nursing has been known.

3. There is now a critical mass of nurse leaders in positions of influence and visibility.

4. The acknowledgment of women's rights facilitates nursing's claims for its legitimate roles, and more and more women are supporting nursing's claims.

5. The longer work life of women and nurses provides greater incentive for appropriate career behaviors, including establishing job security, than was evident in the past when the bulk of nurses worked only episodically.

6. The quest for independence on the part of nurses, and control on the part of physicians, will decline markedly by the year 2000, as a result of the growth of managed care options, with salaried positions for both physicians and nurses, and the decline in fee-for-service practice. As physicians' work environment, roles, and autonomy alter, they will recognize the convergence of issues affecting nurses and doctors and will be more open to collaboration.

7. The nursing group will have a different mix of educational preparation by the year 2000, with a majority prepared at the baccalaureate level. In the mainstream of our educational system, and with better communication and management skills, these nurses will serve both the profession and the public well.[28] This prediction, so often wrong before, may be right this time.

That nursing will attract new entrants to the occupation can be answered confidently and affirmatively. Many parts of the nursing career are attractive to vast segments of the population. With better differentiation of roles and education, it would be quite possible to have an affordable AD in a less than RN program and prepare effectively for many parts of the health care world.

Can nursing attract new entrants to the *profession* rather than to the *occupation*? Nursing's success at any of its missions can be seen only in the context of the entire health care field. Nursing, like other fields, is dependent on the complex conditions of its work world. Should nursing continue to advance and receive the positive attention now prevailing, should the conditions of nursing's work continue to improve, and should the current pendulum shift of interest in service professions continue, the answer must be "yes."

Many women interested in health fields will choose medicine, of course, and it is hoped that the choice will be for the right reasons. Recognizing the parts of the cure–care continuum that interest the individual most and choosing medicine or nursing based on this recognition serves the individual careerist and our society best. There are already many unhappy nurses and physicians who chose their field thinking it was interchangeable with the other but for status, and who have found that the parts of their field that they like best are not those that are rewarded. Women and men interested in medicine, and visualizing themselves correctly in medical roles, do not belong in nursing. By the same token, women and men visualizing nursing roles correctly, and believing that their satisfaction lies in these peer-consumer relationships, do not belong in medicine.

An unfortunate outcome of the increased number of women in medicine would be an increase in distancing behavior between the two professions. Current surveys support the view that women physicians do not relate to nurses "any better" than do men physicians. Indeed, articles written by women physicians in the lay press indicate that the problem may be worse when both professionals are women, because women physicians must declare their differences from women nurses behavioristically, thus increasing their status while lowering nurses'. Greater clarity about these ambiguously separated disciplines will be the most helpful strategy for the continuing strength of both fields. The trends outlined above—in nursing research, clinical specialization, and linkages between university faculties and nursing practitioners in hospitals and health agencies—all serve to increase this clarity of role.

Conclusion

The future of nursing, like its present and past, can be understood only within the context of the determinants of its practice. The continued development of the nursing profession is tied to the present and future of health care and its payment structure in the United States, nursing's fit with the needs of the American public, and nursing's ability to project accurately its potential for problem solving.

We are blessed in the United States with the best health care providers in the world because of our excellent educational systems in medicine and nursing (and in other health disciplines). But we have never examined the health care problems we face as a nation in a way that would capitalize on this broad array of educational preparation for the health professions. Rather, we have challenged medicine to assume responsibility for the entire realm of health and medicine, thus aggrandizing and ultimately threatening one profession, while we denigrate or deny other professions. Viewing the health care world through this medical prism has not met past needs, does not meet current needs, and will not prepare us for a different future.

We need to take a new look at the health care paradigm and explore collaborative solutions to the access, quality, and cost problems we face. The professions of nursing and medicine have developed vertically, with little horizontal crossover in education and practice. We are only beginning to examine health care problems from an interdisciplinary perspective.

As we look at the viability of nursing and women's interest in this profession in the coming decades, it is well to view nursing in the context of reform of the health care system in the United States. A broad look at who does what well, cost effectively, and how and with whom could lead to more lasting solutions to professional and service delivery problems. Nursing is a major player in these solutions now, and will be more so in the future.

It is clear to most observers that the coming years will not allow business as usual to continue in the delivery of health care. Concerns have been expressed about perceived and real threats on the horizon that will impact on all health professions. These include profound changes in the way we pay doctors and hospitals; a reported surplus of hospital beds with a concomitant growth in competition among hospitals; a perceived surplus of physicians and concerns about the effects of this growing surplus on the costs of health care generated by these physicians; a perceived and long-lasting shortage of nurses; concerns about reduced interest of students in health professions; new technologies in and outside hospitals; rapid growth of ambulatory care services, often in competition with hospitals; the growing problems in financing care for vulnerable populations (the working and nonworking poor, people with AIDS, the homeless, the chronically mentally ill, and the health-impaired elderly needing long-term care); and the changing patterns of disease created by changing demographics and social trends (e.g., the drug epidemic, adolescent pregnancy, deaths from violence).

Nursing's stance and visibility in examining the implications of these external forces, and in developing solutions that serve the American public, will allow us to measure in the next decade the degree to which the nursing body politic has reached the maturity of a profession—and whether or not it can survive through its ability to attract intelligent and active men and women.

Notes

1. U.S. Department of Health and Human Services, *The Registered Nurse Population, Findings from the National Sample Survey of Registered Nurses* (Washington, DC: Government Printing Office, 1992).

2. Ibid.

3. J. Lynaugh, "The Yo-Yo Ride," *American Journal of Nursing* (December 1987):1606-1610.

4. Bureau of Labor Statistics, "A Look at Occupational Employment Trends to the Year 2000," in *Monthly Labor Review* (U.S. Department of Labor, November 1989).

5. U.S. Department of Health and Human Services, *Health Personnel in the United States, Seventh Report to Congress* (Washington, DC: Government Printing Office, 1990).

6. K.C. Green, "What the Freshmen Tell Us," *American Journal of Nursing* (December 1987):1610-1615.

7. *The Registered Nurse Population*, 1992.

8. National League for Nursing, Division of Research, *Nursing Datasource 1990, A Research Report. Volume III: The Silent Few: Men and Minorities in Nursing Education* (New York: National League for Nursing Press, 1991).

9. Ibid.

10. E. Ginzberg, "Health Personnel: The Challenges Ahead," *Frontiers of Health Services Management* 7(2)(1990):3-21.

11. L. Aiken and C. Mullinex, "The Nurse Shortage: Myth or Reality?" *New England Journal of Medicine* 317(10)(1987):641-646.

12. *National Survey of Hospital and Medical School Salaries*, University of Texas Medical Branch at Galveston, 1993.

13. P. Brider, "Solid Gains Behind, Leaner Times Ahead," *American Journal of Nursing* (February 1991):28-36.

14. These efforts include The Robert Wood Johnson-Pew Foundation initiative to restructure hospital care, and the collaboration between The Robert Wood Johnson Foundation and the National Center of Nursing Research.

15. The Kellogg Foundation supported the work of the National Commission on Nursing (NCNIP) and subsequent to that report supported a program to implement the recommendations of the Commission. In addition to other work done by NCNIP, a television campaign was launched to stress the many and varied personal components necessary for a career in nursing. Their slogan "If caring were enough, anyone could be a nurse" was accompanied by compelling portraits of nurses in action.

16. The Tri-Council on Nursing Organizations includes the American Nurses Association, the American Association of Colleges of Nursing, the American Organization of Nurse Executives, and the National League for Nursing.

17. P. Hart, *A Nationwide Survey of Attitudes on Health Care and Nurses* (Washington, DC: 1990).

18. S. Gordon, B. Buresh, and N. Bell, "Who Counts in News Coverage of Health Care?" *Nursing Outlook* 39(5)(1991):204-208.

19. Hart, p. 10.

20. Patricia McGrath, *Pain and Children* (New York: Guilford Press, 1990).

21. E. Baer, "The Feminist Disdain for Nursing," *New York Times*, February 19, 1991.

22. S. Gordon, *Prisoners of Men's Dreams: Striking Out for a New Feminine Future* (Boston: Little Brown, 1991).

23. *New York Times*, October 10, 1972.

24. Gordon, p. 7.

25. J. Lynaugh and C. Fagin, "Nursing Comes of Age," *Image* 20(4):184-189.

26. Nurses of America Media Project, National League for Nursing, 1990.

27. Hart, 1990.

28. C. Fagin, "The Visible Problems of an 'Invisible' Profession: The Crisis and Challenge for Nursing," *Inquiry* (Fall 1986).

12

Women in Allied Health Professions

Charlotte Muller

THIS CHAPTER IS CONCERNED with non-nursing health care personnel, specifically with various types of technicians, technologists, and therapists, as well as dietitians, physician assistants, and home health care workers—all of whom have essential roles in the delivery of care in the hospital, ambulatory practice, school system, and elsewhere.

Allied health occupations comprise those in which personnel assist, facilitate, or complement the work of physicians and other health care specialists with more advanced training.[1] This is definition by inclusion within somewhat fluid boundaries. Allied health professions are also defined by exclusion, again rather fluidly, since groups that do not choose to be identified as allied health personnel—doctorate-holders such as psychologists as well as others with various levels of training—are omitted from the allied health cluster. Tabulations and analyses in Labor Department publications vary as to just which occupations are included within the allied health category. As has been pointed out by the Institute of Medicine, exact definitions are useless because of the constant obsolescence of existing job titles and the emergence of new ones.

Women make up a large proportion of the labor force in many of these fields. This pattern is likely to continue even if increasing proportions of women enter those health professions requiring substantial postcollege training, because the number of jobs to be filled in allied health and the number of young women entering health careers are far greater than the number of places in medicine and dentistry that women would occupy, given full gender equality. Hence, from the standpoint of health care adequacy and efficiency, and from the standpoint of women's status, allied health deserves serious attention.

In particular, the public has a stake in the sufficiency of supply in the face of expected need and demand for those services that draw on the diagnostic, treatment, health maintenance, and rehabilitative skills of allied health practitioners—in other words, most health care services.

Demand for Allied Health Personnel

Various reports have noted the factors that sustain and expand demand for health services.[2] The growth of the elderly population, especially those aged 85 and over, implies a need for allied health professionals who specialize in rehabilitation or operate diagnostic and monitoring equipment. Similarly, the spread of AIDS and HIV-related conditions has generated heavy needs for chronic disease services.[3] Changes in technology affect the mix of occupations required; some innovations substitute machines for human labor (as in automated laboratory processes), and others replace hospitalization with outpatient drugs (e.g., prophylaxis for pneumonia occurring as a complication of AIDS). These changes are continual and may rapidly increase or decrease the demand for specific types of personnel.

Innovation is sometimes believed to spell progress in employment opportunities as well as in diagnostic and treatment possibilities. This is not necessarily so. True, workers with skills to handle the new technology are needed, trainees can and will be recruited, and money is found to do so. To offset this, such jobs may displace other workers, either when capital is substituted for labor directly or when a new surgical or other treatment procedure avoids or reduces use of hospital inpatient services, as mentioned earlier. Moreover, high-technology medical care is often expensive and the indications for treatment notoriously expandable because of the enthusiasm of innovators and others. The resultant cost pressure on the system may lead to curbing of outlays. This can be done by screening claims for past service and authorizations of future service for medical justification, simple quantity rationing, or exclusion of a procedure from coverage. Thus, both private third-party and governmental regulations become variables in the prediction of employment. If limitations are imposed on utilization or benefits, then the labor-expansive impact of technical change is dampened.

The impact of changes in health care financing is equally ambiguous. Some changes may shift the setting of care rather than expand— or contract—the volume of services; examples are incentives under the prospective payment system for hospitals to discharge patients so quickly that a new demand for home care is created, and insurance benefits supporting oxygen therapy or artificial feeding in the home. But a freeze on benefit expansion or actual curtailment of benefits by employers or government has an overall negative effect on the demand for allied health personnel. For example, certain nursing home reimbursement rules may severely limit rehabilitation possibilities and admission of cases likely to need considerable rehabilitation therapy.[4] In addition, if ceilings are placed on physician charges or earnings, physicians may stop delegating some functions to ancillary personnel; that is, in order to maintain their net earnings at the previous level, physicians may prefer to do certain tasks themselves rather than turn them over to allied health workers. Ceilings of this kind may be associated with cost-containment policies in public or private programs.

Supply Issues
The growth in the supply of allied health personnel in recent years reflects, to a large extent, the increase in women's labor force participation. By the year 2000 women are expected to make up almost half of the civilian work force and 63 percent of the added workers filling new jobs. However, the increase in the labor force participation of women will eventually taper off and in the meantime cannot be counted on to assure an adequate supply of new entrants into specific allied health occupations[5] or in geographical areas with rapidly increasing demand. Attention must be given to the job choices of those in, or about to enter, the labor force.

Educational qualifications of women have improved more rapidly than those of men. Between 1975 and 1988 the number of men in the labor force with one to three years of college education rose 58 percent and with four or more years, 74 percent. For women in the labor force, comparable increases were 147 percent and 265 percent, respectively. Furthermore, the labor force participation rate of men fell slightly, from 93.3 percent to 91.3 percent for those with one to three years of college, and from 95.7 percent to 94.4 percent for those with four or more years, whereas for women, there was an increase from 57.3 percent to 74.7 percent for those with one to three years of college, and from 62.7 percent to 80.8 percent for those with four or more years.[6] Health occupations attracted a larger proportion of female college graduates over time—under 5 percent chose them in

1970, 11 percent in 1986. However, with the withdrawal of federal aid to allied health educational programs after 1974, enrollment of both sexes fell. And since training programs depend on clinical facilities, cuts in federal health care programs further affected training opportunities. In short, the supply-increasing effects of women's growing commitment to paid work, plus federal subsidy (direct and indirect) to training, tended to dry up.

In addition, fewer young women will be coming to maturity and thus be available for training: the number of women aged 18 to 24 was 13.1 million in 1989, but is projected to be 12.0 million in 1995 and 12.5 million in 2000.[7]

These developments underscore the merits of making jobs more attractive and creating alternative pathways for both youthful first-job seekers and returners to the labor force. Reduction of attrition is likewise an issue insofar as difficult cases and workloads, limited current rewards, and low-ceiling career outlooks discourage incumbents as well as potential applicants.

Occupational Groups and Earnings

Exhibit 1, from Bureau of Labor Statistics (BLS) data, shows the number of full-time workers of each sex in major allied health occupations in 1990.[8] Median weekly earnings are also shown, but only when the base is 50,000 or more workers; the ratio of female to male earnings is therefore available only for clinical laboratory technical personnel. This occupation, the largest among those listed, has total employment of close to a quarter of a million workers, 75 percent of them female. In this group, women's median earnings are 89 percent of men's, which could reflect men's higher levels of responsibility rather than unequal pay for the same work. In three of the listed occupations (dietitians, health record personnel, and dental assistants), 90 percent or more of full-time workers are female; 99 percent of dental assistants are female, the highest proportion among these professions. Dental hygienists are not shown in Exhibit 1, but according to other information from BLS for full-time and part-time employees combined, they are over 99 percent female.[9] These two dental-supportive occupations are the most classically sex-typed fields in allied health and, in fact, in health care professions generally. (Podiatry, a holdout as late as 1977-1978 with less than 5 percent of the degrees awarded to women, had 24 percent female enrollees in the first year of training in 1987-

Exhibit 1
**Employment and Median Weekly Earnings of Full-Time Workers
in Allied Health Occupations, by Sex
United States
1990**

	Both Sexes		Men		Women			
	Workers (000)	Median Weekly Earnings	Workers (000)	Median Weekly Earnings	Workers (000)	Median Weekly Earnings	Percent Female	Female/Male Earnings Ratio
Dietitians	71	$454	7	*	64	$457	90.1	NA
Inhalation Therapists	50	518	21	*	29	*	58.0	NA
Physical Therapists	56	525	16	*	41	*	73.2	NA
Therapists, n.e.c.	58	477	17	*	39	*	67.2	NA
Physician Assistants	60	510	41	*	19	*	31.7	NA
Clinical Laboratory Technologists and Technicians	238	445	61	$482	178	431	74.8	89.4%
Health Record Technologists and Technicians	70	342	5	*	65	334	92.9	NA
Radiological Technicians	97	481	24	*	73	468	75.3	NA
Dental Assistants	107	300	1	*	106	300	99.1	NA

*Base too small; data not shown.

Source: BLS Table 56.

1988.[10]) Among the other allied health fields in Exhibit 1, three-quarters of the physical therapists and radiologic technicians and three-fifths of the inhalation therapists are female.

The median wage for dental assistants, $300 weekly, is well below the $445 earned by laboratory personnel of either sex. The health record workers, 93 percent of them female, earning $342 weekly, are also well below the wage level for all the other listed occupations except dental assistants. Even a fairly well paid group, the dietitians, 90 percent female, earn less than inhalation or physical therapists or physician assistants (32 percent female).

Further information on earnings and employment is available for employees of private hospitals as of March 1989 (Exhibit 2).[11] Although not broken down by gender, the statistics bear on the status of women in allied health. First, they show the extent of part-time employment. Among 373,000 workers in 16 occupational groups (if "medical machine operating technicians" are counted as one group), 20 percent (74,000) worked part-time. If their hourly wages are annualized for comparison with full-time employees (using 2,080 hours, or a 40-hour week[12] for 52 weeks, and converting the weekly figures for full-time workers into earnings for a 52-week year), the part-time workers earned at a lower rate than full-time workers (a difference of $1,000 or more) in five fields plus one subfield (EEG technicians) of the medical machine operating group, at a higher rate in two fields (occupational and physical therapists), and about the same in the rest. The evidence suggests that wage rates for women (or men) who work part-time might be more or less similar to the rates for those who work full-time. (In 1987, of married couples with earnings, 21.6 million wives worked at full-time and 10 million at part-time jobs. The proportion of husbands working part-time was much less.[13]) Some of the employees covered in the survey might be putting together a full-time work week by having multiple employers.

Both immediate earnings after qualifying for an entry-level position and the prospects of improved earnings with further experience—an important feature of the available career ladder—vary by occupation and by level of responsibility within an occupation in the allied health field. Exhibit 2 sheds light on this by showing median earnings by level within occupation, and by occupation. For four subgroups of workers within the medical machine operating technician group, the distribution of persons among several levels with progressively higher earnings is shown. Level 3 workers account for over two-fifths of all employees in this group, but the distribution varies by subgroup, with 70 percent of sonographers at level 3, a similar percent of EEG technicians at level 2 (there is no level 4), 64 percent of EKG technicians at level 1, and 50 percent of respiratory therapists at level 3. The salary difference from the lowest to the highest level is 84 percent overall, 62 percent for sonographers, 66 percent for EEG technicians, and 72 percent for respiratory therapists. Women (or men) who count on a current job choice to achieve a long-term income goal need to consider both the modal level (the one with the most workers) and the percent of personnel who attain a higher level.

Variation in earnings among allied health occupations for full-time workers in private hospitals is also shown in Exhibit 2. Most employed individuals are in occupations with average earnings between $18,000 and $29,500. Six occupations with earnings of $29,500 or more employ 14,952 workers, or 6.7 percent of the total; five occupations with earnings under $18,000 employ 24,553 persons, or 10.9 percent of the total.

Allied health earnings can be compared with mean earnings in 1987 for men and women with different educational attainment levels.

Mean Earnings by Sex and Education[14]

	High school (4 years)	College (1–3 years)	College (4 years)
Men	$24,745	$29,253	$38,117
Women	16,223	19,336	23,506

Although a high school diploma and on-the-job training may suffice for entry into several of the low-paid allied health categories, some college education or completion of accredited postsecondary programs is necessary for higher paid upper-level and supervisory titles.[15]

For women with some postsecondary education, average earnings in allied health pursuits compare favorably with the overall mean of $19,336. For men, the allied health earnings are rarely as high as the

Exhibit 2
Average Earnings for Health Care Occupations in Private Hospitals
United States
1989

	Full-time				Part-time				
Occupation and Level	Percent	Number of Workers	Average Weekly Earnings	Annualized Earnings (X52) (000)	Number of Workers	Average Hourly Earnings	Annualized Earnings (X2080) (000)	Total Employment	Part-time as Percent of Total Employment
Dietitians		5,673	$507.00	$26.4	1,798	$12.67	$26.4	7,471	1.3
Medical Laboratory Technicians		12,675	409.50	21.3	5,451	10.26	21.3	18,126	30.1
Medical Machine Operating Technicians		(39,724)	431.00	22.4	14,638	10.62	22.1	54,362	26.9
Level 1	17.4	6,923	316.50	16.5					
Level 2	38.9	15,446	413.00	21.5					
Level 3	41.6	16,506	492.50	25.6					
Level 4	0.1	250	582.50	30.3					
a. Diagnostic Medical Sonographers		(3,971)	501.50	26.1					
Level 1	2.1	82	375.00	19.5					
Level 2	22.8	904	453.50	23.6					
Level 3	70.4	2,796	516.50	26.9					
Level 4	2.8	112	606.50	31.5					
b. EEG Technicians		(2,001)	387.00	20.1	729	8.90	18.5	2,730	26.7
Level 1	24.9	499	306.50	15.9					
Level 2	68.8	1,370	406.50	21.1					
Level 3	5.5	111	509.50	26.5					
c. EKG Technicians		(5,626)	337.50	17.6	2,745	8.09	16.8	8,371	32.8
Level 1	64.5	3,629	313.00	16.3					
Level 2	29.1	1,635	374.50	19.5					
Level 3	3.6	201	483.50	25.1					
Level 4	0.1	38	550.50	26.6					

d. Respiratory Therapists		(24,404)	$446.50	23.2	9,072	$11.24	$23.4	33,476	
Level 1	7.4	1,795	328.50	17.1					
Level 2	40.9	9,987	416.00	21.6					
Level 3	50.4	12,309	486.00	25.3					
Level 4		61	566.50	29.5					
Medical Records Administrators		2,770	615.00	32.0	130	11.49	23.9	2,900	4.5
Medical Records Technicians		11,707	343.50	17.9	2,207	8.16	17.0	13,914	15.9
Medical Social Workers		10,338	523.50	27.2	2,775	13.70	28.5	13,113	21.2
Medical Technologists		36,878	517.50	26.9	14,148	13.11	27.3	51,026	27.7
Nuclear Medicine Technologists		4,337	512.50	26.7	853	12.37	25.7	5,190	16.4
Occupational Therapists		5,326	549.00	28.5	1,255	14.51	30.2	6,581	19.1
Physical Therapists' Supervisors		1,913	747.50	38.9	182	18.08	37.6	2,095	8.7
Physical Therapists		8,983	583.50	30.3	2,763	16.18	33.7	11,746	23.5
Radiation Therapy Technologists		2,774	502.00	26.1	463	11.33	23.6	3,237	14.3
Radiographers' Supervisors (X-ray)		3,633	592.50	30.8	178	13.57	28.2	3,811	4.7
Radiographers (X-ray)		24,882	441.00	22.9	10,171	11.08	23.0	35,053	29.0
Speech Pathologists		1,997	556.50	28.9	962	14.71	30.6	2,959	24.3
Surgical Technologists		15,043	365.50	19.0	3,270	9.15	19.0	18,313	17.9
Total		**224,655**			**73,790**			**373,099**	**19.8**

Source: BLS Bull. 2364, pp. 9-10, 35-36.

mean earnings for men with either one to three years of college or a baccalaureate degree.

Actual allied health earnings are understated in these figures because premium pay for overtime, weekends, holidays, and late shifts is omitted. Systematic information about these payments is lacking, but these types of work are not uncommon in inpatient facilities, especially those rendering acute care. However, since such work activity is difficult for individuals to sustain, the standard wage is a better representation of what employees can count on. Their ability to meet personal obligations while responding to regular and extra needs of providers may depend on the employer's benefit design. Hospitals employing 14 percent of nurses and 13 percent of other workers sponsor day care centers in or near the hospital; the cost is usually shared with employees. Only 6 percent of nurses and 5 percent of other employees are covered by employer plans providing benefits such as "paying for babysitting expenses when employees work overtime."[16]

Much more information is needed to assess the adequacy of day care and related provisions. In those organizations that offer such benefits, waiting periods for eligibility, number of places, financial limits on benefits, and, where direct service is involved, program quality are among the features that would interest allied health workers with responsibilities for child care. In the majority of organizations, it is clear that benefit needs of individuals with such obligations are not yet incorporated into the standard benefits package. Such benefits are particularly important for low-income families, whether with one or two earners, who are interested in leaving poverty behind them through careers in allied health.

Specific Occupations
The next sections discuss briefly the situations in several allied health fields that are predominantly occupied by women today.

Laboratory Workers
Laboratory technical workers are the largest non-nursing allied health group in hospitals. Pathology emerged as a medical specialty after World War I, but it was not until after World War II that many hospitals established clinical pathology laboratories where technicians were employed to assist pathologists. The latter retained control over the training of the technicians for some time. What is now the American

Society for Medical Technology (ASMT) split off from the physician organization, the American College of Clinical Pathologists (ACCP), in 1977.[17] The ACCP continues to oversee certification, but ASMT presents members' views about certification, laboratory standards, and supply issues in the public forum and maintains a data base on the composition of the work force, wages, and vacancies.[18] In the last decade the number of accredited training programs for medical technologists has declined by 21 percent. The lack of government funding and a drop in the number of applicants, attributed to the perception of poor salaries and working conditions,[19] are believed to have helped cause the closing of programs. Fear of infection (antedating the AIDS epidemic, but magnified by it) may also be a deterrent to choosing a laboratory career.

Between 1989 and 1991 both vacancy rates and the number of hospitals reporting shortages substantially increased. The vacancy rate was highest for cytotechnologists (27.3 percent).[20]

According to a 1990 survey of laboratory technical personnel registering with the ACCP Board of Registry, 77 percent are white women and another 7.5 percent, women of other races.[21] However, the proportion of females in training programs was only 74 percent in 1989-90, presaging a drop in their proportion in future employment.[22]

The growing interest of health policymakers in the wider use of Pap-smear testing has made laboratory quality a public issue. New regulations affect out-of-hospital sites as well as in-hospital testing. While proficiency assessment is directed at the facility's performance, both individual competence and adequate staffing will be critical in meeting standards. Thus the stabilization of the supply of qualified personnel (such as cytotechnologists) is important in order to maintain the quality of preventive services. At the same time, automated techniques and new equipment will demand new learning. With proper planning and financing, workers' and providers' concerns can be harmonized with those of consumers (in this case, women) and of government, acting on their behalf. This planning includes providing opportunities for refresher courses and additional training for both currently employed personnel and for re-entrants (chiefly women), and supportive arrangements that make participation feasible for persons with dual role responsibilities. Planning should also include measures to protect laboratory personnel against health risks.

Physician Assistants (PAs)

Entering allied health in an era of public interest in equal opportunity in health care, women now constitute the majority of PAs in training. Enrollment of females in 1989–1990 was 1,762 out of a total of 2,966, according to the profile of accredited educational programs.[23]

The PA field came into existence to answer a presumed shortage of physicians[24] but retained its foothold even after the expansion of medical schools with federal help. Federal funding was provided for training PAs in 1971. The market was strengthened by the restriction on the entry of foreign medical graduates into graduate medical education, which caused hospitals to seek PAs to substitute for physician house staff, and by the growth of large corporate organizations in health care, which meant that a PA would not need a single doctor as sponsor. PAs were originally expected to do primary care (treatment of common ailments, plus prevention) but have increasingly specialized. Completion of an accredited program is required in almost all states; the programs tend to require two years of college, and generally are two years in length. Today about half the applicants have a bachelor's or master's degree.[25]

The field will continue to have utility owing to the growth of the elderly population and concern with chronic disease management, and the possibility of a fairly rapid supply response to increased demand. It is a relatively good occupation for persons with a science background who can devote the requisite time to acquire further training.

Speech Therapy and Audiology

Information on practitioners of speech therapy and audiology is provided by their joint professional organization, which conducted a membership survey in 1990.[26] Of speech-language specialists, 91 percent are women; 70 percent of audiologists are women; and the overall percentage is 89 percent female. The men have an average age of 44, compared to 36 for women, and are more likely than women to have a doctorate (38 percent versus 3 percent). Three-fourths of the members work full-time. Among these, the majority of both sexes have vacation and sick leave, plus life insurance. The men are more likely to have disability insurance and vacation leave, but the women are more likely to have sick leave and parental (in this case, maternity) leave and health insurance. Many speech therapists, who make up three-quarters of the membership, work in schools, which may explain why 45 percent of the total group have a nine- to ten-month work year. The mean number of hours per week spent taking care of family members was 24.7, or 3.5 hours a day. Although this applies to both sexes, the figure largely reflects female activities of home maintenance and child care, since most practitioners are women. Most members are married, and more than half are parents. The group is 95 percent white, and 91 percent have a master's degree. The two professions are almost equal in earnings, the median as of January 31, 1990, being $30,000 for speech-language therapy and $32,000 for audiology; earnings for the noncertified, a small percent, are $25,000.

Reports of shortages may reflect some growth in demand by hospitals (possibly related to the increase in elderly patients with communication difficulties) and the pull of better salaries in other pursuits. However, most current members report that they are satisfied with their careers. Because of the length of training, advance planning is desirable to assure adequate supply. More training and career opportunities for nonwhite women would promote a more balanced ethnic mix. In the general population, 82.5 percent of the labor force is Caucasian—the percentages being very similar for men and women—7.1 percent Hispanic, and 10.4 percent black and "other."

Physical and Occupational Therapy
Two other occupations that are largely female—physical therapists (PTs), 74 percent female, and occupational therapists (OTs), 94 percent female, both estimates based on member surveys of the respective professional associations—are more than 90 percent Caucasian.[27] (With response rates of 50 percent for the American Occupational Therapy Association and 45 percent for the American Physical Therapy Association, the statistics in this section should be taken as suggestive only.) Here, too, more opportunities for nonwhites would appear to be indicated.

According to the member survey of the American Occupational Therapy Association (AOTA),[28] registered OTs are generally college graduates: more than four-fifths of those at the entry level have a bachelor's degree and another 6 percent, a master's degree. More than three-fourths of those currently employed work full-time, and one-third of the active OTs are in private practice. The earnings of those in private practice average more than $44,000, the highest of any of the work settings. Mean earnings for all OTs rise from $29,000 to $39,000, or 35 percent, with 15 years of experience. Those in administration also earn about $44,000, but these practitioners may be the same individuals as those in private practice. Almost half (46 percent) of the reimbursement comes from federal programs, and another 26 percent from state and local programs. Hence, financing changes could affect employment.

PTs, according to a survey by the American Physical Therapy Association (APTA),[29] have tended to move from hospital settings to private practice, but most PTs practice in more than one setting. According to the APTA survey, the proportion of females (about three-quarters) has changed little since 1978. Male PTs are almost four years older than female PTs, and they have higher gross earnings than women in each category of employment.

Gross Earned Income by Gender and Employment Status[31]

| | Full-time | | Part-time | |
	Salaried	Self-employed	Salaried	Self-employed
Female	$38,211	$ 73,396	$21,032	$26,317
Male	50,721	122,671	28,229	76,565

These figures must be adjusted for practice expenses in interpreting returns to self-employment. Men work slightly more hours than women.[31] Career interruption was far more common among women than among men (39 percent versus 9 percent), and women were more likely to have more than one interruption. Men interrupted their career to go to school or change fields; women, to raise children. (This may also enter into the difference in hours worked.) Men were also more likely to have postbaccalaureate training; for both sexes there has been an increase in such training since 1987.

Projections to 2000
The BLS report on the occupational outlook for the year 2000 presents detailed projections for health care occupations with 25,000 or more workers in 1988.[32] Exhibit 3 shows actual employment for 1988 and projected employment for 2000 based on a moderate-growth scenario.

The moderate-growth projection assumes that the gross national product growth rate will be slower than in the previous 12 years. A main reason will be less labor force growth: fewer youths will enter the labor force—a consequence of the end of the baby boom in 1965—and net immigration will decline somewhat. In this scenario, men will remain a majority of the labor force, but their projected growth rate between 1988 and 2000 is 11 percent compared to 22 percent for women in the labor force.[33]

Nineteen allied health fields qualify by size for inclusion in the projections (Exhibit 3). Nine of these 19 are among the 20 occupations, drawn from all occupations of 25,000 or more, with the highest projected growth rates. But because they are individually small (compared to such large categories as salespersons and secretaries), they do not figure among the top 20 in terms of largest future job growth. Their overall expected growth, about 700,000 jobs, amounts to an increase of 41 percent.

None of the allied health occupations are expected to have a decrease in employment. However, the proportion of jobs in the higher-level occupations is expected to decline slightly and the proportion in the lower-level ones to increase. This is largely attributable to the sharp increase projected for medical assistant and home health aide jobs. Employment in the latter field will outnumber that in the clinical laboratory personnel category, a reversal of the 1988 ranking.

The five entry-level fields are expected to grow from 660,000 in 1988 to 1 million in 2000, a 50 percent increase. The 14 fields above the entry level (physician assistant, despite the "assistant" label, is a credentialed occupation included in the upper 14) are expected to grow from about 1 million workers in 1988 to more than 1.3 million in 2000. The future employment in the 19 fields combined, of 2.3 million, represents a substantial labor market for women workers at various skill levels. Thus the expansion of employment is a favorable prospect for women.

As an offset to the optimism this projection may produce, one should keep in mind that home health jobs are included, and their growth means expansion of a field in which pay, benefits, and job security are minimal, yet where workers bear substantial responsibility for the chronically ill, making these workers good candidates for stress. The labor supply for these jobs has overwhelmingly been drawn from women of color, who typically have many current burdens and limited alternative opportunities.

For those with limited skills who do not plan a long-term career in home health, flexible hours and short-term engagements may be an attraction. For many others, however, growth of these jobs may amount to perpetuation of inferior status (reminiscent of domestic service) unless it is accompanied by improvement in the terms of employment and initiation of career ladders. Such a limited future would continue the no-opportunity horizon of the domestic worker of former days.

The entrenchment of the present unsatisfactory arrangement for the delivery of care in the home is largely due to the permissiveness of government and other major payers and the fragmentation of responsibility for worker conditions and deployment of personnel. A local government may contract with private agencies for service delivery without setting a standard for agency employee compensation, and the client is sometimes expected to assume the role of employer in taking care of Social Security payments, while the worker is expected to bargain successfully to obtain the client's compliance in this regard.[34]

Home care has received very little of the total expenditure for health care services or even of the long-term care budget (the bulk goes to nursing home care); it has been financially and socially marginalized while remaining shielded from public scrutiny. The isolation and low status of the work have been a breeding ground for exploitation of both worker and patient.

Place of Care
Many issues determine whether an occupation holds promise for women: overall employment growth, opportunity to benefit personally from one's productivity, length of training required, adjustability of training and work schedules to family needs and goals, and freedom from oppressive harassment of all kinds.

The setting of allied health work affects the economics of the job. According to detail presented in an earlier version of its *Projection to 2000*, the BLS predicts that the hospital will be the major place of employment for more than 80 percent of nuclear medicine technologists and respiratory therapists and for more than half (54 percent) of radiologic technologists and technicians. Dietitians, emergency medical technicians, OTs, and PTs do not find most of their employment in hospitals (emergency medical technicians, for instance, tend to be em-

Civilian Employment in Health Care Occupations
with 25,000 or More Workers, Moderate Growth Scenario
United States
1988 (Actual) and 2000 (Projected)

	Employment (000)		Change		Percent of Employment	
	1988	2000	Number	Percent	1988	2000
1. Dietitians and Nutritionists	40	51	11	28.0	2.4	2.2
2. Physician Assistants	48	62	14	28.0	2.9	2.6
Therapists	(236)	(367)	(111)	(43.0)	(14.3)	
3. Occupational	33	48	16	49.0*	2.0	2.1
4. Physical	68	107	39	57.0*	4.1	4.6
5. Recreational	26	35	10	37.0	1.6	1.5
6. Respiratory	56	79	23	41.0*	3.4	3.4
7. Speech Language and Audiologists	53	68	15	28.0	3.2	2.9
Health Technicians and Technologists	(672)	(2,211)	(566)	(34.0)	(40.6)	
8. Clinical Lab Technologists and Technicians	242	288	46	19.0	14.6	12.3
9. Dental Hygienists	91	107	16	18.0	5.5	4.6
10. Emergency Medical Technicians	76	86	10	13.0	4.6	3.7
11. Medical Records Technicians	47	75	28	60.0*	2.8	3.2
12. Opticians, Dispensing and Measuring	49	65	16	31.0	3.0	2.8
13. Radiologic Technologists and Technicians	132	218	87	66.0*	8.0	9.3
14. Surgical Technologists	35	55	20	56.0*	2.1	2.4
15. Dental Assistants	166	197	31	19.0	10.0	8.4
16. Medical Assistants	149	253	104	70.0*	9.0	10.8
17. Pharmacy Assistants	70	89	19	27.0	4.2	3.8
18. Physical and Corrective Therapy Assistants and Aides	39	60	21	52.0*	2.4	2.6
19. Home Health Aides	236	397	160	67.9*	14.2	17.0
Total Lines 1–14 (Higher level)	996	1,344	351	35.2	60.1	57.4
Total Lines 15–19 (Lower level)	660	996	335	50.8	39.9	42.6
Grand Total	**1,656**	**2,340**	**686**	**41.4**	**100.0**	

* Among the 20 detailed occupations with the highest growth rate.

Source: BLS Bull. 2352, pp. 51, 54.

ployed by transit systems (37 percent) and state and local governments (40 percent)).

Until recently, working for hospitals has meant that wage levels are
affected by the rates paid to nurses and by the weakness of unionism
in hospitals. Allied health workers could not derive advantage in wage
determination from a strong market for their services. But this may
change owing to the 1991 U.S. Supreme Court ruling permitting
workers to form up to eight separate bargaining units in a private hospital. This affects especially the laboratory workers, who make up the
majority of the non-physician, non-nurse health care professionals in
hospitals.[35]

Linkage of wages to those of nurses may also occur in "offices" of
practitioners as large organizations replace solo practice. However,
employment in a large medical "firm," nonprofit or otherwise, may
increase the probability of substitution of other internally available
health care workers if employers wish to avoid labor cost increases, so
long as Medicare regulations and other rules are not violated.

Another channel whereby the economic status of allied health
workers may be affected by future place of work is productivity in different settings. For example, if services for the elderly at home are financed by third parties, demand for allied health workers may be increased more than if the services are rendered in large institutions,
because care at home requires more time.[36] This could affect fields
like physical therapy (because of travel time, a smaller inventory of
equipment, and a different organization of work). Compared to an inpatient facility, an outpatient facility may have higher productivity
(fewer workers for the same output, or more output without an increased number of workers, as would occur if a skilled worker with an
essential role is kept fully occupied, or if division of labor and delegation of some duties to less skilled personnel are possible in a setting
with many clients). If the elderly are transported from their residence
to an outpatient facility for services, demand for the skilled personnel
might be less. However, the lower price that might result from enhanced productivity could lead to an increase in the volume of services used and in employment.

Perspectives of Parties in the Market
Each of the parties in the health care market place has a special perspective on the allied health occupations.

Providers

Providers are concerned with shortages (inability to fill vacancies) in non-nursing roles.[37] They are interested in attracting the new entrants to the labor force, designing alternative pathways, retaining personnel, and assuring basic literacy and numeracy of job seekers. They sometimes oppose the addition of advanced training requirements for certification and licensure, which they do not view as functionally essential.

Providers are also motivated to redesign processes so as to reduce the utilization of scarce types of personnel, to contract out when doing so is compatible with patient processing efficiency and quality, and to substitute equipment for labor (thereby presenting a market for equipment designers and manufacturers), if filling slots and retaining workers become chronically difficult. Training programs affiliated with hospitals have declined in number in some allied health fields, thus making recruitment more difficult for many hospital employers. Refresher programs may be useful for those returning to the labor force or shifting back to health care from other industries, and, from the provider's perspective, facilitate recruitment of currently qualified personnel.

Workers

Individuals—men and women alike—who plan to work in an allied health field for a substantial period of time are attracted to a career that does not demand prohibitively long or expensive formal training or educational qualifications or skills beyond their reach. They will consider the entry wage and the earnings to be expected with some experience (factoring in the probability of attaining a supervisory level), and compare these with alternative opportunities. They will also consider fringe benefits. These are the major pecuniary features of a potential career. The nonpecuniary features include the respect or prestige attached to the work, the more pleasant (or unpleasant) details, the absence of risk of illness or injury,[38] the opportunity to organize one's own work, and the quality of relationships with patients or others. Not only will the match of the tasks to the tastes and strengths of the worker produce different occupational choices, but the other job features just mentioned will also vary in their meaning to different individuals. For some, take-home pay is what counts; for others, health benefits are critical. However, at the end of the choice process is the question of whether the pecuniary return overall compensates for any perceived disadvantages of the job.[39]

Absent from the preceding discussion is the issue of the durability of skills. It used to be suggested that employability following an extended absence from the labor force was a major factor in women's career choices. Today this generalization is questionable, owing to women's more permanent attachment to the labor force. In any case, rapid technical change means that women who reenter the labor market after an absence may have to adapt by seeking additional training unless an employer or other party sponsors retraining by paying a wage equivalent as well as tuition.

The pecuniary and nonpecuniary elements of the job, for women as well as for men, must survive a comparison with alternative occupations to draw applicants. However, portability of one's credentials and standing across state lines may still be valuable to women who are married or expect to be and who may be prompted to move by a spouse's job change. And occupations that offer part-time options may attract women who wish to limit their working hours as well as those who wish to piece together a full-time schedule from several part-time situations, possibly with self-employment and entrepreneurial status as a goal.

Ideally, an occupation is good for women if it offers equitable treatment in terms of pay and promotion, and protection against gender or sexual harassment, and is not pressed into the historic mold of dominant/subordinate role pairing with an exclusively male profession. One of the proposed remedies for sex-typing is recruitment of males for formerly female occupations, which may run up against men's cultural reluctance to be in a "women's" field. However, men may respond to the appeal of higher salaries, even without formal recruitment efforts.

Increasing opportunities for women in formerly male health occupations should mean that more women who enter allied health fields do so as an act of choice. If they do, the prospects for permanent satisfaction should be greater, and the quality of service may be benefited by a good fit of the person to the job.

Another long-range remedy for dominant/subordinate pairing is the expansion of the scope of practice and authority of non-physician occupations when consistent with the public welfare; in the same spirit, and perhaps more accessible, is the acceptance of a sociomedical model of healing, which would generate more respect for the contributions of others besides physicians.

Evidence that gender issues have not been put to rest comes from dental service occupations. Dentistry has remained largely male, and dental hygienists are almost exclusively female. Flexibility of schedules and part-time work attract many women to dental hygiene, but full-time wages are low relative to other fields. Rather than work at recruiting men as dental hygienists, it may be more important for women (and thus for equity) if terms of employment are improved and if upward career paths are encouraged. Dental assistants are almost all female also, and theirs is an entry-level job, with lower wages than those of the dental hygienists. Many have only informal on-the-job training, and for those with some formal training in a program for dental assistants, credits may not be transferable to training programs for dental hygienists. Whether job restructuring and different training are feasible may depend on scientific developments affecting the services offered in dental practices, for example, prevention of decay in early life leading to less need for highly specialized restoration procedures. (Expanded financing of preventive services is also a prerequisite for shifts in service mix.) Having more women dentists would break up the male/female, master/servant dyad, but would not necessarily change task distribution, productivity, and relative rewards. Such a change might occur in a future reorganization of health care, which would have on its agenda the most effective and equitable deployment of allied health personnel.

Consumers and Providers
The interests of health care consumers and those of allied health workers in general and women in particular derive from different goals—but are they capable of being harmonized?

Consumers can be expected to be interested in having their care processes performed with competence and promptly so that their chances of a good health outcome are maximized. They are also better served if those involved in their care are satisfied with the terms of their employment and have high morale. Consumers seem to rely on the implied guarantee of competence associated with employment by a credentialed provider (a physician or dentist) or accredited facility, and have shown little concern with the details of training or licensure of allied health personnel. But this indifference may disappear as understanding and appreciation of the contribution and critical role of allied health services develop. (Concern with qualifications would also be heightened if the incidence of health problems traceable to insufficient competence should increase.)

Generally, the interest of the public in receiving good and sufficient health care is in accord with both providers' interest in assuring supply and workers' interest in job quality and security. Policies advancing the welfare of women workers are not inconsistent with those protecting workers in general. If the health care system is reorganized to improve efficiency and performance, jobs filling a valid function should be protected. This will call for public discussion and negotiation in the legislative process.

Most of the licensure and certification of allied health professions occurs at the state level, but the federal government has complemented the regulation of professions by the states; for example, conditions of participation in Medicare and Medicaid oblige providers to use certified technical personnel in their laboratories.

Examinations given by national organizations and programs accredited by the American Medical Association are often specified as ways of meeting requirements. The image of licensure as a disinterested action on behalf of the public has been blurred by turf battles and allegations that excessive training has been required in order to qualify.[40] Yet doing without some regulation of this kind could entail a risk of damage to health and waste of consumer dollars because of the many individuals who would obtain allied health employment or, as entrepreneurs, hold themselves forth as health experts without specific training. An example is the poor nutrition advice that is often marketed to frail elderly persons who do not have the capability to conduct a proper market search, but who are at risk of serious consequences.[41]

There have been modest experiments in cross-training and cross-employment around the country, usually involving a "correction" to narrow specialization.[42] New York State has allowed rate adjustments in payments to hospitals for such demonstrations.[43]

Concerns of Women in Allied Health

How do occupational regulation and conventional pathways concern women in allied health work? Women who have completed the requirements, often against real obstacles, and have established themselves in an occupation may not be motivated to entertain easier access for potentially competitive entrants. But if moves to widen access to training are a response to a predicted excess of demand over supply, job loss and lower prevailing wages are not likely. However, unusually high wages dictated by persistent vacancies may vanish. Moreover, the increased supply produced by more open training opportunities means that wages for incumbents would not rise as much as they would otherwise, given an expansion of demand. But providers wishing to retain both new entrants and senior staff would not worsen terms of employment; meanwhile, the more senior workers may be eligible for increased compensation based on experience. Older workers may also benefit from day care and other inducements deemed to be valuable to new entrants.

It is not rational to expect that tight control of entry conditions to favor established personnel that does not take account of consumers' interest in adequate supply will survive. Yet the protection of women who have provided for families alone or with a spouse, or simply been self-supporting, through their work in allied health fields should not be overlooked. Since sex-typing of occupations and sex differentials in wages have not been eliminated from the economy, older women may face fewer job choices than younger ones, especially if their education is limited. Furthermore, the initial inducements mentioned above may not be sustained if federal or state laws restrict the revenue available to health care employers for labor compensation.

Those women who can enter allied health fields without alternative pathways could continue to do so if access conditions were liberalized; they might, in fact, obtain more flexibility to combine work with training, or change the pace of preparation in order to meet family needs with less pressure. The women who have the most to gain from alternative pathways are those whose wage sights and career expectations are really raised by allied health opportunities. However, in view of the ebb and flow of changes in hospital and health care markets and reimbursement policies, the degree to which such aspirations are realized should be monitored. In particular, care should be taken that curricula are not too narrowly tied to the tasks of a specific job without a foundation for future career needs of the individual.

Conclusion

The various features of a job naturally affect labor force members of both sexes; however, they often impact differently on women because of double role obligations and socioeconomic status. The importance of particular features will vary for individual women, depending on their age, resources, prior education, current situation or plans regarding marriage and fertility, and tastes for work requiring interaction with patients or other social dynamics found in health care. It is a mistake to assume homogeneity of women in circumstances or preferences and to generalize too freely.

For women as well as men, the general determining elements and trends of the markets in various allied health occupations are essential knowledge for career planning. Objective information at the national level is provided by the BLS in its occupational outlook publications.

At the same time as common rights, interests, and aspirations of all workers and potential workers regardless of gender are recognized, it is relevant to policy determination that women in contemporary society are more affected than men by certain considerations. These include:

> *Getting out of poverty.* Women need training, child care during training, entry jobs with career possibilities, and adequate wages.
>
> *Solving the dual-role problem.* Women need employer support of regular and emergency caregiving obligations, and family insurance for health care costs.
>
> *Breaking through restrictive traditions.* On the personal level, women need opportunities to receive advanced training for higher-level jobs without occupational sex-typing, and equal consideration for promotion and skill development. On the social level, women allied health workers need a long-range commitment to task and job restructuring to avoid subordination as a class.

Much of the foregoing discussion points out the difficulties of exact predictions. As an economic sector, health care, although not alone in its sensitivity to technological change, has certainly exhibited dramatic innovations that affect the occupational structure, while continuing to encompass new and different needs based on disease patterns, life expectancy, and changing personal aspirations. Women in allied health face challenges in fitting into these developments. Their outlook can be optimized by appropriate policies that give support to desirable and cost-effective health programs, protect wage standards, and prevent waste of health care funds. Retraining as well as training needs should be anticipated. Enlightened planning can improve the economy's infrastructure of health care services and its structure for dealing effectively with economic risks of labor market changes at the social level.

Notes

1. U.S. Department of Health and Human Services, Health Resources and Services Administration, *Seventh Report to the President and Congress on the Status of Health Personnel in the United States*, DHHS Pub. No. HRS-P-OD-90-1 (March 1990), chapter 10, "Allied Health."

2. Institute of Medicine, Committee to Study the Role of Allied Health Personnel, *Allied Health Services: Avoiding Crisis* (Washington, DC: National Academy Press, 1989), chapter 3.

3. Richard Alba, "Factors Influencing the Demand for and Supply of Health Care Workers" (prepared for the New York State Department of Health, October 1987).

4. C.M. Murtaugh, L.M. Cooney, R.R. Der Simonian, H.L. Smits, and R.B. Fetter, "Nursing Home Reimbursement and the Allocation of Rehabilitation Therapy Resources," *Health Services Research* 23(4):467-493 (October 1988).

5. Alba, 1987.

6. U.S. Department of Commerce, Bureau of the Census, *Statistical Abstract of the United States: 1990*, 110th ed. (Washington, DC: 1990), Table 627.

7. *Statistical Abstract of the United States*, 1991, Tables 12 and 18.

8. U.S. Bureau of Labor Statistics, *Median Weekly Earnings of Full-time Wage and Salary Workers by Detail Occupation and Sex*, Table 56.

9. *Statistical Abstract of the United States*, 1991, Table 652.

10. U.S. Department of Health and Human Services, Health Resources and Services Administration, *Minorities and Women in the Health Fields*, HRSA-P-DV-90-3 (1990), 102, 103, 143.

11. U.S. Bureau of Labor Statistics, *Industry Wage Survey: Hospitals, March 1989*, Bulletin 2364 (Washington, DC: 1990), 9-10.

12. The work week for 86 percent of hospital personnel. Ibid.

13. *Statistical Abstract of the United States*, 1990, Table 735.

14. Ibid., Table 737.

15. U.S. Bureau of Labor Statistics, *Health Diagnosing Occupations and Assistants*, Bulletin 2350-7 (Washington, DC: 1990); U.S. Department of Labor, Bureau of Labor Statistics, *Dietetics, Nursing, Pharmacy, and Therapy Occupations*, Bulletin 2350-8 (Washington, DC: 1990).

16. U.S. Bureau of Labor Statistics, Bulletin 2364, 4.

17. Virginia Kotlarz, "History of Medical Technology in the United States," *Clinical*

Laboratory Science 4(4):233-236 (July/August 1991).

18. Barbara M. Castleberry, "Medical Laboratory Personnel Data Collection Activities of the American Society of Clinical Pathologists," 1990.

19. New York State Department of Health, *Final Report*, p. 59.

20. Barbara M. Castleberry, Alma M. Kuby, and Lisa Nielsen, "Wage and Vacancy Survey of Medical Laboratory Positions in 1990: Part II," *Laboratory Medicine* 22(4)(April 1991):253-257.

21. Castleberry, 1990.

22. Gupta.

23. Ibid.

24. Harold C. Sox, "Quality of Patient Care by Nurse Practitioners and Physician's Assistants: A Ten-year Perspective," *Annals of Internal Medicine* 91(1979):459-468.

25. U.S. Bureau of Labor Statistics, Bulletin 2350-7, 11.

26. American Speech-Language-Hearing Association, *1990 Omnibus Survey Results*, (Rockville, MD) Karin Malm, Research Coordinator; American Speech-Language-Hearing Association, *1990 Omnibus Survey Results*, Committee on Equality of the Sexes (Addendum).

27. *Statistical Abstract of the United States, 1990*, Table 625.

28. American Occupational Therapy Association, *1990 Member Data Survey* (Rockville, MD: 1991).

29. American Physical Therapy Association, *1990 Active Membership Profile Report* (Alexandria, VA: 1991).

30. Ibid.

31. The difference was 4-1/2 hours per week for full-time self-employed, and 2-1/2 hours for full-time salaried PTs. American Physical Therapy Association.

32. U.S. Bureau of Labor Statistics, *Outlook 2000*, Bulletin 2352 (Washington, DC: April 1990).

33. Ibid.

34. Doris R. Fine, "Women Caregivers and Home Health Workers: Prejudice and Inequity in Home Health Care," *Research in the Sociology of Health Care* 7:105-117 (1988).

35. Anne Paxton, "NLRB's Rule's Effect on Labs Uncertain," *CAP Today*: 5, 9 (July 1991).

36. U.S. Department of Health and Human Services, *Seventh Report*, 1990.

37. New York State Department of Health, *Final Report*, 1989.

38. Today's risks in health care jobs include chemicals, such as the sterilizing agent, ethylene oxide; musculoskeletal injuries; and infection (HIV and hepatitis). Linda Hawes Clever and Gilbert S. Omenn, "Hazards for Health Care Workers," *Annual Review of Public Health* 273-303 (1988-89). Careful work practices may be difficult to observe if equipment is not well maintained and if there is a heavy workload. Despite the many skin and eye irritants, carcinogens, mutagens, and teratogens in hospitals, under one-half of 174 hospitals surveyed had health and safety services for employees. Gilbert Omenn and Sharon L. Morris, "Occupational Hazards to Health Care Workers: Report of a Conference," *American Journal of Industrial Medicine* 6(1984):129-137.

39. Bruce E. Kaufman, *The Economics of Labor Markets and Labor Relations* (Chicago: Dryden Press, 1985), chapter 8.

40. New York State Department of Health, *Final Report*, 1989.

41. Denise Webb, "Eating Well," *New York Times*: C4 (August 14, 1991).

42. New York State Department of Health, *An Action Plan to Improve the Utilization of Health Personnel in New York State, A Report to the Commissioner of Health from the Health Personnel Utilization and Productivity Committee*, December 1990.

43. Edward S. Salsberg, *Hospital Workforce Demonstration Program*, Interoffice Memorandum, New York State Department of Health, May 28, 1991.

13

Contributions of Women of Color to the Health Care of America

Elaine Hart-Brothers

Ironically, women of color, who as a group have one of the poorest health statuses, have labored for centuries, directly and indirectly, to improve the health of others. This group, the most underrepresented at the top of the pay scale (surgeons and administrators), is the most overrepresented at the bottom (nurses aides, hospital housekeepers) of the complex pyramid called the health care labor force (Exhibit 1). This chapter describes the contributions of minority women in the medical field, who have struggled to gain respect and a decent income. As photographic essayist Brian Lanker has written, "Women of color had to survive as wholly and healthily as possible in an infectious and sick climate. Their hands have brought children through blood to life, nursed the sick, and folded the winding cloths."[1]

History
When blacks were brought from Africa in the 1600s, they carried with them an ancient heritage of medical care with special remedies, medical professional science, and rituals.[2] Indeed, black women have been successful midwives in western Africa for centuries. During slavery, medical attention was often provided by slaves to one another, while traditional medicine was offered to slaves on an irregular acute basis. The form of medicine that was practiced in Africa established itself more strongly in the West Indies than in North America. Plants and roots were used to cure illness but could also be used as poisons. Laws were passed in 1748 and 1792 to permit slaves to administer medicines with good intention, provided there was no harm caused by the

Exhibit 1
**Employed Civilians in Selected Health Occupations and
Percent Women, Black, and Hispanic
United States
1989**

Occupation	Total Employed	Percent of Total		
		Women	Black	Hispanic
Health Diagnosing Occupations	854,000	16.5	3.2	4.4
Physicians	548,000	17.9	3.3	5.4
Dentists	170,000	8.6	4.3	2.9
Health Assessment and Treating Occupations	2,240,000	84.8	7.3	3.1
Registered Nurses*	1,599,000	94.2	7.2	3.0
Pharmacists	174,000	32.3	4.7	2.2
Dietitians	83,000	90.8	17.1	5.3
Therapists	324,000	76.3	6.4	3.0
Inhalation Therapists	63,000	52.2	12.5	2.7
Physical Therapists	90,000	77.3	4.8	6.1
Speech Therapists	63,000	88.6	3.3	0.9
Health Technologists and Technicians	1,276,000	82.3	14.6	4.6
Clinical Lab Technologists and Technicians	308,000	74.4	14.7	4.1
Dental Hygienists	80,000	99.2	1.7	0.9
Radiologic Technicians	124,000	75.8	10.1	4.3
Licensed Practical Nurses	414,000	96.1	19.0	4.4
Health Service Occupations	2,042,000	90.0	26.4	6.5
Dental Assistants	187,000	98.9	7.4	9.0
Health Aides, except Nursing	416,000	84.5	17.7	7.0
Nursing Aides, Orderlies, and Attendants	1,439,000	90.4	31.4	6.0

* Estimates from the 1988 Sample Survey of Registered Nurses sponsored by the Bureau of Health Professions indicate that the percentages of employed registered nurses who are women, black, and Hispanic are 96.3, 4.0, and 1.4 percent, respectively.

Source: Health Personnel in the United States, Eighth Report to Congress, 1991, 213.

"roots." In 1823, a slave woman "practitioner" was found guilty of administering medicine outside of the established guidelines and was transported out of Virginia. Also around this time, selected slaves were allowed to administer "white remedies" in their own treatment to others on the plantation. Black nurses, the majority of them women, acquired some respect for their skills in the medical field. These "black plantation nurses" are described in the literature by name; for example, Aunt Amy Green, Aunt Amy, and Aunt Judy are remembered for their nursing skills. Jensey Snow was praised by Benjamin Harrison in 1825 for her patience and extraordinary skills in practical nursing; she was later freed and opened a hospital in Petersburg, Virginia.

Hospitals: Off Limits for Care, Practice, and Education

In the early 1900s, blacks who wished to become physicians or nurses faced considerable barriers. Black physicians were barred from training in medical schools and hospitals where internships and residencies were obtained. Town hospitals were usually segregated, and the only source of opportunity for black professionals for practicing and graduate nursing care was a few designated "colored wards." As a result, black physicians had access only to lower income facilities and practice environments.[3] Segregation also resulted in a critical shortage of black allied health professional workers, who were not allowed training in white institutions or hospitals.

Hospital segregation had implications for care as well. The lack of adequate hospital facilities over the decades meant that black patients received care in crowded surroundings that were often second rate. In the 1940s the mortality rate of blacks in U.S. cities was 180 percent that of whites. Blacks had a higher incidence of venereal disease, cardiac disease, malaria, mental illness, tuberculosis, and pneumonia, a pattern that was exacerbated by the low number of charity institutions and black hospitals. In 1942, while the average ratio of physicians to population for the nation was 1 to 750, the ratio for blacks was 1 to 3,810. In Mississippi, the ratio was 1 black physician for every 18,000 black Mississippi residents. There were instances of patients and physicians having to travel 50 or 100 miles to the nearest "Negro hospital" when denied admission by white institutions. In 1947, Edna Griffin, a physician, reported that she could not operate on a black patient who had acute appendicitis because of hospital segregation rules in California. In 1964, as a result of meetings of the American Public Health Association and other bodies, the Medical Committee for Human Rights was formed to teach and ensure access to health care for all people, especially those in lower socioeconomic groups.

During this period of hospital segregation, a number of renowned black hospitals were established. These hospitals served as teaching institutions for nursing and allied health professionals, including respiratory therapists and X-ray technicians. Shaw University's Leonard Medical School opened in 1882, two years after Meharry Medical College was established with its Hubbard Hospital. Freedman's Hospital, in Washington, DC, has operated a school of nursing since 1894. St. Agnes Hospital and Nursing Training School was opened in 1896 in Raleigh, North Carolina. Lincoln Hospital was opened in 1904 in Durham, North Carolina, and is one of the many institutions that were funded by white philanthropists in support of black self-help initiatives to improve health care for the black community. Other famous black hospitals include Provident Hospital in Chicago, Homer G. Phillips in St. Louis, Flint-Goodridge in New Orleans, John A. Andrews Memorial Hospital in Tuskeegee, Alabama, and Milton Community in Michigan.

Many of these hospitals were founded or headed by black women. Sarah Fitzbutler (d. 1923), a physician, was superintendent of a small hospital established by her husband, also a black physician, in Kentucky in 1888. This black medical school-hospital had 40 students; however, it was closed because of accreditation problems following the Flexner Report in 1909. In 1916 Millie E. Hale (1881–1930) established the Millie E. Hale Hospital together with her husband, John Henry Hale, a prominent surgeon and medical educator at Meharry Medical College. She also served as nurse and superintendent of the hospital, the first year-round hospital for blacks. By 1923, 7,000 patients had been served and more than 7,000 more were fed and clothed in their homes.[4]

Of the black medical schools forced to close, Leonard Medical School, closed in 1914, was the strongest. This school was the first four-year medical school in North Carolina, preceding the schools of medicine at Duke, Bowman Gray, and the University of North Carolina. Approximately 400 physicians trained at this facility in Raleigh. It would be difficult to estimate the total number of women professional and paramedical students who benefited from this institution, which many say could have been saved with state funding and continued as an important resource to provide care to the one-third of the North Carolina population that was black.

A problem of black hospitals, which continues today, is the lack of funding. Only Freedman's Hospital in Washington, DC, has received substantial financial support from the federal government. Funding for education and equipment was not available, and physician office space was extremely limited. These hospitals that employ large numbers of blacks have been struggling to remain open even during the 1980s. In the years after integration, many hospitals closed because of lower enrollments and also because of Medicare rules, including diagnosis-related groups (DRGs): preset fees did not adequately compensate small hospitals serving patients with multiple advanced medical and social problems. In 1900 there were approximately 200 black-owned hospitals; in 1988 there were fewer than 10.

The story of the integration of hospitals is a long one. In the North as well as the South, blacks—and black women in particular—often received poor medical attention, if any care at all. In 1920, formal charges were made that Harlem Hospital in New York City discriminated against blacks.[5] The mayor and the commissioner inquired about interns' behavior toward black patients. It was decided that black physicians, with involvement from the Manhattan Medical, Dental and Pharmaceutical Association, would help hospital relations. The concept was that the sick would receive better care and not postpone care. Otherwise, the officials concluded, blacks might become sicker and spread communicable diseases within the community instead of using hospital services.

In 1964 Hubert A. Eaton, author of *Every Man Should Try*,[6] a book about combating discrimination, won a lawsuit (after several appeals) against James Walker Memorial Hospital in Wilmington, North Carolina, for its arbitrary denial of hospital privileges to black physicians and the segregation of black patients in the hospital, which received tax funding. Dr. Eaton's writings also remind us that black physicians were customarily not allowed to train beyond the internship or permitted to give orders to white registered nurses. Dr. Eaton commented on the importance of the black hospital institutions in employment and opportunities for black citizens. He surveyed ten hospitals in North Carolina that were built with Hill-Burton funds after 1957 and found that "only one hospital out of nine had a black secretary, clerk, medical record person, X-ray technician, or laboratory technician. None of the ten new hospitals in North Carolina had accepted a black nurse for training or had a black nurse employed as a supervisor."

Physicians, Dentists, and Pharmacists

Although not all were involved with health care delivery, there were approximately 18,084 black physicians and 29,592 Hispanic physicians in the United States in 1989.[7] Although blacks constitute 11.7 percent and Hispanics 6.4 percent of the U.S. population as a whole, black physicians currently constitute 3.3 percent of the total physician population, and Hispanic physicians, 5.4 percent. The former proportion has not changed significantly since 1910, when it was estimated that there were 3,400 black physicians, representing 2.5 percent of all physicians. Before 1985, there were approximately 54 black physicians for every 100,000 blacks in the population and 104 Hispanic physicians for every 100,000 Hispanics. In contrast, there were 220 majority physicians per 100,000 majority population in 1985. There is obviously a sharp difference between the 3.7 percent of physicians and 2 percent of dentists who are black and the 31 percent of nurses aides, patient care assistants, and orderlies who are black. The Native American percentage of the total is lower than that of Hispanics and blacks in medicine as well as in osteopathic medicine, dentistry, podiatric medicine, and pharmacy (Exhibit 2).

In 1989-90, blacks, Hispanics, and Native Americans made up 12.3 percent of all medical school students (Exhibit 3).[8] Between 1980 and 1989, the number of medical students who were black or Native American increased 13.8 percent and 57.6 percent, respectively (Exhibit 4). In 1990, black medical student enrollment was 6.5 percent of the total. For Asians, there was an increase of approximately 263 percent in "allopathic medicine" between 1980 and 1989. The black enrollment in dental professional schools increased by only 1.6 percent in this period. Despite this progress, the rate of growth of minority physicians will lag far behind the rate of growth of minority populations as a whole. The disparity will be particularly great in the Hispanic community in the next nine years.[9]

Only a very small number of remarkable minority women physicians can be noted by name in this chapter. The first black woman physician to be educated in the United States, Rebecca Lee Wright, graduated from the New England Female Medical College in Richmond, Virginia, in 1864, 15 years after the first white female physician. "Others followed Lee and, remarkably, black women were the first practicing female doctors in four southern states."[10] Rebecca Cole became the second black female physician in America when she received her medical degree in 1867 from the Female Medical College of Pennsylvania. Cole "provided her services in the slum area, gave medical and legal aid to women and practiced fifty years in Philadelphia,

Exhibit 2

Total Enrollments in Selected Health Professions Schools and Programs
United States
1980–81 and 1989–90

	Number					Percent				
	All Students	Black	Hispanic	Asian/ Pacific Islander	American Indian	All Students	Black	Hispanic	Asian/ Pacific Islander	American Indian
1980-81										
Medicine										
Allopathic	65,189	3,708	2,761	1,924	221	100.0	5.7	4.2	3.0	0.3
Osteopathic	4,940	94	52	87	19	100.0	1.9	1.1	1.8	0.4
Dentistry	22,842	1,022	519	1,040	53	100.0	4.5	2.3	4.6	0.2
Pharmacy	21,628	945	459	1,035	36	100.0	4.4	2.1	4.8	0.2
Podiatric Medicine	2,577	110	39	69	6	100.0	4.3	1.5	2.7	0.2
Optometry	4,540	57	80	243	12	100.0	1.3	1.8	5.4	0.3
Nursing (RN only)*	219,188	14,365	5,785			100.0	6.6	2.6		
1989-90										
Medicine										
Allopathic	65,163**	4,241**	3,537**	8,436**	277**	100.0	6.5	5.4	12.9	0.4
Osteopathic	6,615	173	246	463	39	100.0	2.6	3.7	7.0	0.6
Dentistry	16,412	983	1,278	2,393	57	100.0	6.0	7.8	14.6	0.3
Pharmacy	22,764	1,301	945	2,130	63	100.0	5.7	4.2	9.4	0.3
Podiatric Medicine	2,397	240	123	156	6	100.0	10.0	5.1	6.6	0.3
Optometry	4,723	132	293	534	16	100.0	2.8	6.2	11.3	0.3
Nursing (RN only)*	201,458	20,789	6,046	5,201	1,064	100.0	10.3	3.0	2.6	0.5

*Based on those students in schools responding to questions on minority enrollment, male enrollment or both.

**Data are for 1990-91.

Source: Health Personnel in the United States, Eighth Report to Congress, 1991, 215.

Exhibit 3
Graduates from Selected Health Professions Schools
United States
1980–1989

Health Profession	1980	1985	1989	Percent Change 1980-89	Percent Change 1985-89
Allopathic Medicine	15,135	16,138	15,398*	1.7	−4.6
Non-Minority	13,462	13,788	12,075*	−10.3	−12.4
Minority	1,673	2,450	3,178*	90.0	29.7
Asian/Pacific Islander	395	750	1,433*	262.8	91.1
Underrepresented Minority	1,278	1,700	1,745*	36.5	2.6
Black	768	828	874*	13.8	5.6
Hispanic	477	807	819*	71.7	1.5
American Indian/Alaska Native	33	65	52*	57.6	−20.0
Dentistry	5,193	5,289	4,312	−17.0	−18.5
Non-Minority	4,673	4,512	3,288	−29.6	−27.1
Minority	520	777	1,024	96.9	31.8
Asian/Pacific Islander	197	378	521	164.5	37.8
Underrepresented Minority	323	389	503	55.7	29.3
Black	190	223	193	1.6	−13.5
Hispanic	119	149	296	148.7	98.7
American Indian/Alaska Native	14	17	14	0.0	−17.6
Pharmacy**	7,432	5,724	6,557	−11.8	14.6
Non-Minority	6,335	4,591	4,561	−28.0	−0.7
Minority	875	829	952	8.8	14.8
Asian/Pacific Islander	292	320	454	55.5	41.9
Underrepresented Minority	534	501	571	6.9	14.0
Black	249	250	310	24.5	24.0
Hispanic	277	245	249	−10.1	1.6
American Indian/Alaska Native	8	6	12	50.0	100.0

*Data are for 1990.

**Includes minority students in categories other than those shown.

Note: Underrepresented minorities include black, Hispanic, and American Indian/Alaska Native.

Source: Health Personnel in the United States, Eighth Report to Congress, 1991, 214.

Washington, DC, and South Carolina."[11] The first women to graduate from Meharry Medical College, in 1893, were Annie Gregg and Georgia Patton Washington. Josie Wells, who graduated from Meharry in 1904, was the institution's first female faculty member. Dorothy Brown, who was raised in an orphanage, became a professor of surgery at Meharry Medical College and the first black American female surgeon in the South.

Over the last eight years, the number of black women physicians has increased more rapidly than the number of male physicians in the United States. In many major medical schools, black women constitute more than 65 percent of the total black medical student population.[12] Projections estimate that of the total of 28,500 black physicians practicing by the year 2000, 11,200, or 39.3 percent, will be women.[13] The number of Hispanic female physicians will also increase, to 5,400, or 22.8 percent of the total Hispanic physicians. The enrollment in health professional schools and data for race and gender show that for Hispanics in medical school, the ratio of men to women will be approximately 65:35, whereas for blacks it will be 30:50. In pharmacy schools, the ratio of males to females for blacks is projected to be 40:60, and for Hispanics, 53:48. In dental schools the male to female ratio for blacks will be 60:40 and for Hispanics, approximately 70:30.[14]

The substantial increase in the number of women physicians has been especially marked in primary care fields. Black health professionals and black women in particular have a unique ability to influence the preventive health and curative behavior of black citizens. Howard University, the paramount center for black medical education, surveyed women who had graduated between 1924 and 1980. A higher proportion of the black women graduates compared to black men graduates practiced in large inner cities, provided primary care, and served younger and poorer patients. However, the proportion of black and female patients served was the same for male and female practicing doctors.

Among the special challenges cited by these women were lack of support from faculty and spouses, sexism, and racism in school, training, and career. Minority women in medicine face double inequities. The average income for women is less than for men, and less for blacks than for whites with the same level of education, productive hours, certification, and specialty. On average, women work fewer hours than men, but compensation is less even when that is considered. Certain surgical subspecialties are much less available as options than primary care fields that have traditionally attracted women. "Jobs concerned with caring, consoling, counseling, nursing and nurturing tend to be poorly paid and female dominated, whereas those dealing with technical procedures and devices are more likely to be highly paid and respected as 'men's jobs.'"[15] Pediatric nursing and pediatric medicine have been the natural fields in which women could combine caring, skills, and scientific thirst for knowledge. Of course, there are notable exceptions, including Alexa Canady (1950–), the first black female neurosurgeon in the United States.

In addition, black women face difficult decisions related to their identities as both blacks and women. Black women often feel that it would be unpopular and perhaps counterproductive to enter the struggle for women's rights, which is politically perceived as competing with the struggle for racial or civil rights. The woman of color is still faced with stereotypes despite her historical role in the health field. For various reasons, the percentage of black male professionals has diminished. The minority woman has had new opportunities to come forward but often is excluded from power and wealth. Of course, Hispanic and Asian cultures also influence women's roles and may have hindered women's upward mobility both professionally and economically.

Minority membership in professional organizations has historically been limited. Organizations with official membership and influence denied black professionals input in health care planning and policy making as well as continuing medical education. In North Carolina and throughout the South, medical societies and paramedical boards limited membership to whites only. A number of minority medical societies were formed, for example, the National Medical Association (NMA), founded in 1895, which today has a membership of approximately 16,000 physicians, most of whom are black. In the past, many minority societies represented dental and pharmaceutical specialties as well as medical specialties in order to increase their numbers and to band together economically and politically for continuing education and scientific sessions. It is only in the last seven years of its 100-year history, however, that a woman has been president of the NMA. Since 1985, there have been three African-American women physicians who have held the presidency: Edith Irby Jones (1985); Vivian Pinn (1989), now the director of women's health studies at the National Institutes of Health; and Alma Rose George (1991). Rosalyn Epps, a black physician, was president of the American Women's Medical Association in 1991. Dr. Gonzales-Pardo followed in 1992. The American Public Health Association has had minority women leaders, including Iris Shannon (1988–89) and Helen Rodriguez-Trias, M.D. (1992–93). Faye Wattleton, a midwife by training and an outspoken advocate for equal access to health care, served as president of the Planned Parenthood Federation of America from 1978 to 1992. Antonia Novello, a Hispanic woman, served as U.S. Surgeon General from 1990 to 1992. She was followed in 1993 by Joycelyn Elders, a dynamic African-American woman.

The wives of black physicians, dentists, and pharmacists formed the auxiliary to the National Medical Association and National Dental Association. By the turn of the century, the auxiliary represented women who volunteered to provide community health education for blacks and to sponsor health campaigns in conjunction with black professionals. These women's outreach efforts targeted hospitals, schools, and communities at large. The auxiliary to the medical society has been instrumental in raising scholarship funds, providing gift shop necessities, consoling the sick, and increasing awareness about health and social issues related to black Americans.

Nurses

Currently, there are 65,304 black registered nurses in the United States. In 1988, fewer than 5 percent of new nurses were black. There was a total decline of nursing school students in all minority groups in the 1980s.

Although documentation of black nurses prior to 1965 is scarce, the early history of black nurses is largely the story of extraordinary women. Biddy Mason (1818–1891), born a slave, became a prosperous nurse and midwife. Mary Eliza Mahoney (1845–1926) was the first black professional nurse in America.[16] She was graduated from the New England Hospital for Women and Children's New England School of Nursing in 1879. Mahoney was a model nurse in New York, Massachusetts, New Jersey, North Carolina, and Washington, DC. She was also active in the women's suffrage movement. Elizabeth Tyler Barringer was a black public health nurse who influenced the health officials in New York City, Philadelphia, Delaware, and New Jersey to improve the health status of blacks and, indirectly, all citizens.

216   An Unfinished Revolution: Women and Health Care in America

As a result of hospital segregation, black nurses had to overcome obstacles in training and employment. There were numerous inadequacies in black nursing schools, for example, lack of endowment for the schools, insufficient supplies, inadequate food, and overcrowding. Nevertheless, their training stood them in good stead.

At the turn of the century, black nursing graduates encountered a severely limited job market. "That she was a graduate nurse when such nurses were a rarity meant nothing. That her skin was colored meant everything."[17] "Colored" nurses were not allowed to participate in the war effort in the Army-Red Cross Nursing Service during World War I. Because of bureaucracy and the requirement for separate housing facilities, the black nurses selected for military nursing services were actually civilians. Of the 2,300 nurses in the U.S. military after the armistice in 1919, only 18 were black.

In many white hospitals, the "Negro wings" were assigned for nurses menially laboring to bathe and feed patients rather than treating their medical condition under doctors' supervision. In 1921 newspaper articles reported that Bellevue Hospital would allow six black graduate nurses to be employed and to continue further professional training. However, by 1929 Harlem Hospital was the only hospital in the entire New York City municipal hospital system to employ black nurses. In 1921, Nurse Hulda M. Lyttle was superintendent of Hubbard Hospital in Nashville, Tennessee; she remained head of nursing for 20 years, and over this span more than 200 black nurses were graduated.

The experience of black public health nurses was only somewhat better. Jessie Sleet Scales, a graduate nurse from Provident Hospital in 1895, became the first black public health nurse after she petitioned the Charity Organization Society for a job combatting tuberculosis in New York City. In North Carolina, where the country's first county public health agency was established in 1911, tuberculosis sanitariums hired black nurses to care for the black community. "Visiting Nurse Services" were established with the assistance of many black nurses "whose genuine altruism and intelligence in social reform work impressed"[18] and were admired by many. Under the New Deal black public health nurses cared for low-income blacks in the rural South and in urban ghettos of the North. The A. Rosenwald Fund established public health centers with black staffing in "colored communities" for a 15-year span ending in 1942. Mabel K. Staupers (1890–

1989), a registered nurse, played a key role in organizing the B.T. Washington Sanitarium, one of the first institutions in New York City to permit black physicians to treat patients. Staupers became a leader and activist for the National Association of Colored Graduate Nurses in the mid–1930s and in 1939 helped pass a national health act related to public health nursing care. Out of 4,986 public health nurses in the 1930s, 730 were "colored."[19]

Although hindered by Jim Crow rules, black nurses served with distinction in the Army Nurse Corps in the last months of World War II. Della Jackson was the first black nurse to be commissioned as a lieutenant in the U.S. Army during World War II; Susan Elizabeth Freeman became a captain in 1944. Margaret Bailey was the first black nurse to attain rank of lieutenant colonel, and Brigadier Hazel W. Johnson-Brown held several major administrative positions and received many awards. Following President Truman's historic order in 1948 to integrate the Armed Forces, black nurses increased in number, rank, and significance. During the Korean and Vietnam Wars, many black nurses received awards for service and heroism. Clara Adams-Ender was appointed Chief Nurse at Walter Reed Hospital in 1987 and served as Chief of the Army Nurse Corps and Director of Personnel for the Surgeon General of the Army.

Black membership in the American Nurses Association was limited, however, as it was in the American Medical Association, partly because of the state membership's rules. For many years, black nurses had their own professional organization, the National Association of Colored Graduate Nurses (NACGN), founded in 1908 by Adah Thoms (1870–1943). As president of NACGN, Thoms met with President Warren Harding and was instrumental in gaining respect for black nurses following World War I and during the great influenza epidemic. The NACGN assisted in getting black student nurses admitted to predominantly white universities in 1936. Also in 1936, the NACGN established the Mary Eliza Mahoney Award for contributions in the nursing field, in recognition of the example Mahoney set in improving race relations; many outstanding nurses, including Carrie Bullock, Nancy Kemp, and Petrie Pinn, have received the award. Mary Elizabeth Lancaster Carnegie (1916-) was a nurse administrator, educator, and writer, who worked for equality of all races.

In 1951, after committee discussions and changes of the American Nurses Association (ANA), the NACGN, which at the time represented 11,000 professional nurses and students, dissolved and was integrated with the ANA.

The National Black Nurses Association, a professional organization of black women and men in nursing, was established in 1971, in response to perceptions that the ANA failed to acknowledge the contributions of black nurses and because there had been no significant increase in the number of black registered nurses. In addition to these professional organizations, the Chi Eta Phi Sorority exists today as an active community group of black nurses. There is also a Black Public Health Nurses Association. Barbara Nichols, a black nurse who as secretary of the Wisconsin Department of Regulation and Licensing was the first black to hold a cabinet-level post in the state, was elected president of the ANA in the early 1980s.

Entry-Level Services

Although women of color are making significant contributions as physicians, nurses, and other health care professionals, the majority of women of color in health care continue to be concentrated at the labor-intensive, low-wage end of the spectrum. In many hospitals around the country, between 75 and 85 percent of the employees are women; the majority are in service jobs and are women of color. In my regional southeastern community hospital, for example, 76 percent of all employees are women and 29.5 percent are women of color.

Few names or notable examples of the many honorable unskilled hospital laborers have been preserved. One exception is Maria Stewart (1803–1879), an educator and activist who in the course of her abolitionist activity worked at Freedman's Hospital. In the early 1870s, she was appointed matron, or head of housekeeping services, a position that had been held earlier by abolitionist and women's rights activist Sojourner Truth (1797?–1883).

Despite their anonymity, these laborers perform an absolutely essential role. As a team, they provide 24-hour service in private, public, and federal hospitals and nursing homes throughout the nation. They serve as patient care assistants, nurses aides, and dietary workers. As part of environmental services or cleaning crews, they provide an essential job in hospitals, where proper hygiene remains in the forefront in combating the spread of bacterial, viral, and fungal diseases. Sterilizing laundry and cleaning up blood, vomitus, urine, and feces are an essential part of keeping a hospital sanitary and operational.

Approximately 300,000 black women and 65,500 Hispanic women fell into the category of nursing aides and attendants in 1988. Health aides, who are slightly more skilled, have higher earnings, and are more service-oriented than nursing aides of the past, numbered 380,000 in 1987; of this total, 15.8 percent were black and 6.9 percent were Hispanic.

These lower-income women workers are also victims of society's problems, including poor health care. Ironically, these women who work in health departments, hospitals, and home health care agencies may not be able to afford health insurance. Dietary workers, some of whom spend their entire 45-year careers in the hospital cafeteria, often prepare healthier foods professionally than they consume domestically. Recent health statistics compiled by the Office of Minority Health show that the health status of black, Hispanic, some Asian, American Indian, and Puerto Rican women is worse than that of their white counterparts, particularly at the low-income level[20] (see Chapter 4, "Health, Health Care, and Women of Color"). Companies, especially those that are health-oriented, should assist women in their understanding of health problems and the preventive measures needed to reduce their risks for chronic and acute medical problems. Low-income health care workers may have very limited knowledge and distorted experience. There are also cultural barriers related to vaccinations and mammograms, which create additional obstacles to health promotion and disease prevention.

Health Care Academicians and Executives

Academic minority health care professionals are few in number. In general, tenured female faculty members are scarce at universities. There are, however, black women on the faculties at the University of North Carolina School of Public Health, Harvard University School of Public Health, Medical Center of Duke University, University of Michigan, and others. The dean of an osteopathic school in Ohio is a black woman. Although their clout in academics is all too often limited, these women are role models for students and exert an influence on the curriculum and moral posture of their universities and communities. Minority women in academia play an important role in influencing studies and providing documentation through written literature for future interventions in maternal and child health, health and public policy, and nutrition. Jane C. Wright, M.D. (1919–), for example, has made notable contributions in cancer chemotherapy at New York University.

There are only a few black women who are chief operating officers of large hospitals in the United States. Hospital executives have organized to discuss opportunities for African Americans and management strategies to improve health care for all Americans. The National Association of Health Service Executives (NAHSE) was founded in 1936 at a meeting in Durham, North Carolina at Lincoln Hospital. Originally an affiliate of the National Medical Association, the NAHSE raised the awareness of the concerns of black administrators and other workers. The NAHSE strives to "provide opportunities for professional development and to eliminate social, racial, and economic barriers in the delivery of health services." Jeanne Spurlock (1921–), a prominent psychiatrist, is both an educator and a superb administrator.

Summary

Racial prejudices have existed in every facet of American society. Women of color within the health care professions face no different barriers.

Because of many biases, minority women pursuing careers in health care have had to fight long, hard, and seemingly unending battles to achieve the proper training, practice, and respect. Blacks were not allowed to participate in white schools, hospitals, or organized professional societies. They were forced to create their own separate organizations to voice their needs, to address the medical issues of their communities, and to provide their own continuing medical education.

Because minority women are heavily represented in the service aspect of health facilities, they disproportionately continue to face social and economic hardships and poor health. They exist in low-income, low-prestige jobs that are essential to the hospital functioning cleanly and efficiently. Yet women of color—be they workers in the laundry, dietary department, or environmental services, or be they nurses, administrators, laboratory technicians, or physicians—have nurtured and cared for all segments of American society. "Valiant and vulnerable, these women were there."[21]

Notes

In addition to the books listed in the notes, the following sources were used in the preparation of this chapter: Irene Butter, Eugenia Carpenter, Bonnie Kay, and Ruth Simmons, *Sex and Status: Hierarchies in the Health Workforce* (University of Michigan Department of Health Planning and Administration and School of Public Health, 1985); Montague Cobb, "The Black American in Medicine," *Journal of the National Medical Association* 73(Dec. 1981): Supplement; Robert C. Hayden and Jacqueline Harris, *Nine Black American Doctors* (Reading, MA: Addison-Wesley Publishing Co., 1976); *Lappa Hospital*, "New Recruitment Efforts Target Minorities," Lappa Hospital 63(20)(1989)64; Judith Walzer Leavitt, *Women and Health in America* (Madison, WI: University of Wisconsin Press, 1984); Herbert M. Morais, *The History of the Afro-American in Medicine* (Cornwells Heights, PA: The Publishers Agency, 1978; Vivian O. Sammons, *Blacks in Science and Medicine* (New York: Hemisphere Publication Corp., 1990).

1. Brian Lanker, *I Dream a World* (New York: Stewart, Tabori & Chang, 1989).

2. Todd L. Savit, *Medicine and Slavery* (Urbana, IL: University of Illinois Press, 1978).

3. James Summerville, *Educating Black Doctors* (University of Alabama Press, 1983).

4. Jessie Carney Smith, ed., *Notable Black American Women* (Detroit: Gale Research, 1992).

5. Allen Schoener, *Harlem on My Mind* (New York: Dell, 1979).

6. Hubert A. Eaton, *Every Man Should Try* (Wilmington, NC: Bonaparte Press, 1984).

7. U.S. Department of Health and Human Services, *Health Personnel in the United States, Eighth Report to Congress* (Washington, DC: U.S. Department of Health and Human Services, 1991).

8. Ibid.

9. Ibid.

10. Smithsonian Institute, *Black Women in Science* (exhibition).

11. Smith, *Notable Black American Women*.

12. Joyce Joyner, "Health Manpower Today and Future Implications," *Journal of National Medical Association* 80(7)(July 1988):717-720.

13. Remy Aronoff, *Estimates and Projections of Black and Hispanic Physicians, Dentists, and Pharmacists to 2010* (Washington, DC: U.S. Department of Health and Human Services, 1986).

14. Aronoff, *Estimates and Projections*.

15. Smith.

16. Helen S. Miller, *Mary Eliza Mahoney, 1845–1926, America's First Black Professional Nurse: A Historical Perspective*.

17. Darlene Clark Hine, *Black Women in White* (Bloomington, IN: Indiana University Press, 1989); Mary Elizabeth Carnegie, *The Path We Tread: Blacks in Nursing, 1954–1990* (New York: National League for Nursing Press, 1991).

18. *Black Women in White.*

19. Ibid.

20. Office of Minority Health, *Closing the Gap* (Washington, DC: U.S. Department of Health and Human Services, 1988).

21. Lanker.

IV

WOMEN AS HEALTH CARE LEADERS

HEALTH CARE HAS MANY MYTHS; *one of the most damaging is that women do not exercise leadership in this field. Faced with statistics showing that women are only a tiny minority of medical school leaders, officials in organized medicine, hospital and health system executives, and trustees of health care organizations, one could easily come to that conclusion. It would, however, be wrong. Health care has produced many women leaders—executives, physicians, and trustees alike.*

Few have trod an easy road to leadership, however. The obstacles are many and awesome, and, given women's historic inequality in other areas of society, tradition and fear often must be overcome as well. Until the current generation, there were few women mentors to inspire or to emulate, and tokenism was more common than truly gender-blind organizations. With hospitals and other providers facing restructuring and probable reduction in size and numbers in coming years, there is also the possibility that recent gains could be erased as competition for top jobs and prestige, which has always been fierce, becomes even more ferocious.

But the fact remains that the number of women leaders in all areas of health care continues to grow, and many barriers—cultural, educational, and organizational—have been brought down. And every time a woman rises to a justifiably high position of leadership, it makes the trip just that much easier for those who hope to follow.

14

Women as Leaders in Academic Medicine

Janet Bickel

THE FULL-TIME FACULTY of U.S. medical schools is the primary source of the medical profession's leaders, and faculty members serve as the primary role models for future physicians. But although women now make up more than 40 percent of those entering medical school, they are still sparsely represented in the leadership ranks of medicine. If women are to help set health care education and policy agendas, the present leaders in academic medicine must work to change the harmful stereotypes and inflexible policies impeding the full participation of women in medicine.

The Picture Today

Women physicians more often than men physicians become medical school faculty members. According to the Faculty Roster of the Association of American Medical Colleges (AAMC), in 1987, 14 percent of the women and 10 percent of the men who graduated from medical school in 1961 were full-time faculty members.[1] In 1993, women made up 23.5 percent of the full-time faculty. Of these 17,642 women faculty members, 52 percent are M.D.s (62 percent of the 57,007 male faculty are M.D.s). Gender breakdowns are not available for part-time or volunteer faculty.

Women faculty do not progress to the rank of professor at the same rate as men. Of all who had their first full-time faculty appointment in 1976, 22 percent of men but only 10 percent of women had gained the rank of full professor by 1991.[2] Another recent study explored the status and productivity of women and men in academic internal medicine. Women had similar job descriptions and allocation of work among research, clinical, and teaching activities, and they had similar numbers of grants funded as principal investigator, abstracts accepted, and papers published in refereed journals. However, women had lower academic rank and received less compensation.[3]

The difference between the genders in attainment of rank is certainly not unique to medicine. Among all full-time university faculty, a full professor is 9 times more likely to be male than female.[4] However, among medical school faculty, a full professor is 11 times more likely to be male than female. Perhaps even more concerning, U.S. medical schools average only 13 women full professors each, including basic science professors. Given students' need for role models of both sexes and given the number of local and national committees on which these senior women are expected to serve, this is a very small number.

Another concern when looking at the supply of future leaders is that women are disproportionately choosing or being appointed to a nontenured clinical faculty track (at least 85 of the 126 medical schools in the United States have developed such a promotion ladder for faculty who are primarily engaged in patient care and teaching). An examination of data from AAMC's Faculty Roster for schools that have been appointing faculty to a clinical track for some years shows that 18 percent of the men but 26 percent of the women at these schools had appointments on the clinical track. Moreover, women's record of promotion on the clinical track is no better than on the tenure track; 55 percent of the men but only 31 percent of the women on the clinical track had progressed beyond the assistant professor level.[5]

Given this disparity in the numbers of men and women reaching the rank of tenured professor, it is not surprising that currently only about 90 (4 percent) of all department heads are women.

Since more than 56 percent of pediatrics house officers are women, it is not surprising that pediatrics has the highest number of women chairs, 11. Next is family medicine, with 9 women chairs. The only major clinical specialty with no woman chair is internal medicine, despite its claiming the highest number of women practitioners (more than 20,000). Traditionally, internal medicine chairs are drawn from the American Society of Clinical Investigators; being principal investigator on major National Institutes of Health (NIH) grants is a prerequisite to membership, and to date only 2 percent of this society's members are women.

A look at the top administrative posts will complete this numerical summary of women as leaders at medical schools. There are currently five women deans of U.S. medical schools (including two interim deans) and one woman dean of an osteopathic medical school. In 1991, approximately 15 percent of associate deans and 25 percent of assistant deans were women.

In its 102-year history, the AAMC has had only one woman chair, in 1985. Of the 87 societies that are members of AAMC's Council of Academic Societies, in 1989 6 (7 percent) had women presidents and 11 (13 percent), women president-elects. Of the 400 chief executive officers (CEOs) named in AAMC's Council of Teaching Hospitals Directory in 1989, 36 (9 percent) were women. In its 20-year history, AAMC's Organization of Student Representatives has had five women chairs.

What about women's participation within specialty societies? A 1986 survey found that of 38 responding societies, only 20 could identify the sex of their members.[6] Only in two was the enrollment of potential women members equivalent to that of male members; in only 12 had women held offices at a national level in the previous 10 years.

Although no new study has been undertaken, it is apparent that some progress is occurring. For instance, the American Academy of Pediatrics recently elected its first woman president, and in 1990 the president of the American Psychiatric Association was a woman. However, while women make up 29 percent of family practice faculty, the only women who have served on the board of the American Academy of Family Practice (AAFP) have been house officers.

In order to meet unaddressed needs and to gain more power, women have organized themselves within or alongside many specialty groups. Independent organizations include Women in Emergency Medicine, the Association for Women Radiologists, and the Association of Women Surgeons. Within the AAFP, the Women in Medicine (WIM) Committee has produced valuable materials dealing with gender harassment and parental leave policies. Within the American Academy of Orthopaedic Surgeons, the Ruth Jackson Orthopaedic Society (named for the first woman orthopaedic surgeon to be board certified, in 1937) has been active for ten years. One of the society's first officers commented, "No woman wanted to be separate from the men in the Academy . . . . What they wanted was to establish a group in which to share common experiences and to set up an information network for women interested in orthopaedics." While urology and cardiothoracic surgery also have active women's organizations, women's networks within other subspecialties have been slower to form. In some cases, the catalyst to focus on women's concerns has been the men's desire to bolster membership.

Women are beginning to appear in the American Medical Association (AMA) House of Delegates, but numbers remain low: in 1991, 8 percent of the 626 delegates or alternate delegates from the states and 3 percent of the 144 specialty society delegates were women. However, an AMA survey of state medical societies, county associations, and national specialty groups found that more than one-third have had a woman president.

Except for the data obtained from AAMC's Faculty Roster, most of the above counts were obtained by tallying first names likely to be female and thus are inexact. This counting method precludes obtaining a count of women from underrepresented ethnic minorities. However, it is known that there are very few. No more than 3 of the 90 women department chairs are from underrepresented minorities. Data on underrepresented minorities from the 1993 Faculty Roster show that only 4 percent of women faculty were black; 1 percent, Puerto Rican; 2 percent, other Hispanic; and less than 1 percent, Native American. Corresponding figures for men faculty are 2 percent, black; 1 percent, Puerto Rican; and 2 percent, other Hispanic. Other underrepresented minorities make up less than 1 percent for both sexes.

So what do the more than 26,000 women medical students see when they look up? They find very few women in senior administrative posts. They notice many women physicians entering careers in academic medicine but comparatively few who have risen beyond the rank of assistant professor. The handful of women full professors they do see are so busy that few of them have the energy or time to be easily accessible to students and young faculty. Moreover, under the stresses of loneliness and the sacrifice of personal life, some of these professors have become too cold and distant or too much like their male colleagues to inspire confidence in young women.

Cumulative Disadvantages
The gender gap in medicine's leadership is the result of many dynamic interrelated features of the medical education and advancement sys-

tem and of differences between women and men. In considering the many variables contributing to career development, it is helpful to think in terms of "accumulating" advantages and disadvantages. For instance, a prestigious fellowship is likely to pay off in multiple ways over the course of a career, for instance, by increasing the total number of articles published. Similarly, having a child during residency and in so doing losing the support of one's mentor will likely have many negative career consequences. In other words, the final picture is never the result of just one set of factors but of many influences that accumulate in force over time.

In Training

Women arrive at medical school slightly older, with slightly lower scores on their Medical College Admission Tests (MCATs), and with slightly higher educational debt than men. They also express somewhat less confidence in their ability to succeed in medical school and report less parental support for their decision to study medicine than do male medical students. Although their academic achievement during medical school equals men's, in response to AAMC's Medical School Graduation Questionnaire (GQ), women express more dissatisfaction than men with their education. In 1992, more women than men ranked as "inadequate" the curriculum time devoted to 25 of the 27 areas named, with the greatest gender differences in levels of satisfaction in the following areas: effective patient education, management of patients' socioeconomic and emotional problems, and cost-effective medical practice. This consistent finding probably reflects a combination of lower levels of self-confidence; higher expectations regarding the quality of their education, particularly in managing patient needs that extend beyond the strictly biomedical; and the likelihood that the predominantly male faculty is more comfortable with men than women students. Moreover, many studies have found that women students experience more gender harassment and role strain than men do.[7] Not surprisingly, then, women students appear to experience more anxiety and depression than men students.

Therefore, from the perspective of "leadership potential," women generally begin their careers with a combination of slight disadvantages.

Strictures of an Academic Career

In medicine as in most other professions, parents are penalized. No pause buttons are built into the educational continuum or the tenure or competence-proving timetable because men do not have babies and have not requested a pause. In medicine, pressures are especially acute because of the length of training and the around-the-clock demands of patient care. If becoming established as a clinical investigator is the goal (and this is the surest route to leadership positions in academic medicine), a physician must train for three or more years after her or his residency, and then often spend two or three more years doing research before substantial extramural funding is obtained. In the face of clinical, teaching, and administrative assignments, this amount of time for research can be very difficult to protect, especially in the present environment of virtually unprecedented competition for patients and research funds. Even the most highly regarded senior researchers are now experiencing cutbacks in their funding and are spending more time than ever writing grant proposals, many of which go unfunded. Junior researchers, especially women without strong mentors or with small children, may see no choice but to give up.

Residency timetables seem to resist alteration. Even though more than 30 percent of residents are women, most of them of childbearing age, between 25 percent and 40 percent of residency programs do not have maternity leave policies. Even at programs that have such policies, the amount of leave time is usually limited to six weeks. An overriding consideration is specialty board requirements, which may be stricter than a residency program's leave policy; for instance, many specialty boards allow only one month off per year for maternity or disability leave.[8] Shared- or reduced-schedule residency positions have not been widely available, but residency program directors looking for the best candidates are becoming more willing to establish such positions, and directors with significant numbers of pregnant residents are experimenting with various sharing arrangements. At the faculty level, only 34 percent of U.S. medical schools have developed specific maternity leave policies, and only 10 percent have written provisions for paternity leave.[9] In the absence of policies, cases are dealt with individually, usually by relying on a combination of sick, vacation, and disability leave.

However, child*bear*ing leave is easy to put together compared to the flexibility needed for child*rear*ing purposes. Although most schools now allow childrearing leaves, the disadvantages usually outweigh the advantages, since the leave is without pay and usually the employee must pay the cost of benefits. Another consideration for tenure-track faculty is the number of years allowed to compile the requisite portfolio of achievements in research, teaching, and service. Although many schools have lengthened their probationary period or allow the tenure clock to be stopped during childrearing leave, the traditional seven-year up-or-out requirement is still the standard and espoused by the American Association of University Professors. Moreover, the challenges of childrearing obviously extend beyond a child's first year; thus, more flexibility is often desirable. For instance, faculty are increasingly interested in part-time options. Although few models are available, at Yale University School of Medicine, faculty may remain on the tenure track while working part-time, and faculty working part-time for three years are given a 12-year probationary period. However, this provision will not serve its purpose if the department chairperson does not scale back expectations for the faculty member's clinical earnings.

Gender Roles

Women's ability to bear children is their only absolute difference from men; however, the socialization process contributes to other related differences. For instance, women's tendency to divide themselves between family and career rather than devote themselves to personal advancement stems in part from their socialization to seek meaning primarily in relationships and in the achievements of those they nurture. Unfortunately, this tendency toward service and self-sacrifice is all too often combined with a readiness to believe messages of disdain. When women curtail the time spent caring for children, students, or patients and devote it to their own career advancement, they often are subject to criticism, which exacerbates self-doubt, which in turn may lead women to adopt a defeatist attitude about their own advancement and to settle for unequal treatment. Self-doubt also causes women who have all the necessary credentials and leadership skills to underestimate their potential for administrative positions; it may not occur to them, for instance, to look at the job advertisements in the *New England Journal of Medicine*. When a woman does apply for a job, she is more likely to appear tentative, even when her curriculum vitae equals those of men candidates. This tentativeness, especially in contrast to the confidence and assertiveness likely in men candidates, may convey the impression that the woman has not made the necessary commitment to academic medicine.

Another outcome of valuing relationships is restrictions on geographic mobility. While such decisions are surely hard for men as well, women more often seem to put ties to their family and community ahead of career opportunities. Approximately 60 percent of women academic physicians are married to other physicians,[10] and many of the rest are married to other professionals. In such dual-career couples, women who have moved because of a spouse's new job have found themselves in a new city visiting possible employers hat in hand—so much for career planning.

Perceptual Bias
Stemming from some of the differences noted above, attitudes based on stereotypes of women continue to contribute to a demoralizing "chill" in the workplace. Although significant erosion of traditional stereotypes of both sexes has occurred in the last 20 years, gender bias remains. A study of corporate chief executive officers found that 82 percent admitted that stereotyping and preconceptions were barriers to women's climbing the corporate ladder; 49 percent admitted a reluctance to take risks with women in line positions. Another study found that female leaders elicit more negative *nonverbal* responses than male leaders offering the same initiatives.[11] These investigators concluded that because women's leadership is unexpected, it evokes negative reactions that are visible to other group members, and that this chain reaction can result in everybody, even other women, concluding that the woman speaking is incompetent or out-of-line.

With regard to medical academia, Carola Eisenberg writes: "The credentials of women are subtly discounted because of prejudice so thoroughly inculcated in men (and in all too many women) that it operates automatically, often altogether without awareness."[12] Women with superb credentials who have been seriously considered for more than one department chair or deanship conclude that they are passed over because they do not look or sound "familiar" enough or because of some personality trait that might in a man be considered a strength. For instance, whereas a man may be called "strong," the same quality in a woman may be considered "overly aggressive," likewise, "reserved" versus "passive." Also, because women in leadership roles are still a rarity, they face more scrutiny than men in similar roles. With so many eyes watching, the pressure to succeed is enormous, and every failure is costly, since onlookers (and perhaps even the woman herself) may assume that little more could have been expected.

All these factors—the structural inflexibilities, the devotion to relationships that leaves no time for oneself, the lack of mentors, the chill in the academic climate—have a cumulative and synergistic effect. One common outcome is isolation, with each woman struggling in a vacuum to make sense of promotion requirements and to patch together arrangements for maternity leave and child care. In addition to exhaustion and bitterness, isolation can lead women to underestimate the importance of organizational culture, politics, and budgets. Certain realities may take them completely by surprise—for instance, that a department chairperson's departure can disrupt their careers, that behind-the-scenes work is necessary to ensure the orderly consideration of their agendas, that negotiations for space and salaries need to be carefully planned.

The cumulative result of these disadvantages is that all too many women either remain in "horizontal orbit" or drop out altogether. Many who do succeed are more bitter and less productive than they would have been if they had had access to the support that men may take for granted.

View from the Top

This inside-out look at women's careers in medical academia must be complemented by an attempt to look from the top down. The twentieth century medical academician holds the derivation and transmission of new biomedical knowledge above all else. Teaching students and caring for individual patients may be important, but the primary bases on which peers determine fitness to lead are scholarship in the research arena and a record of leadership in one's specialty. The only study of U.S. medical school deans examined those appointed between 1960 and 1976, all of whom were men.[13] Of those appointed between 1972 and 1976, 58 percent had completed post-doctoral fellowships and 83 percent had held NIH grants. About 70 percent had held the position of department chair or division head, and 36 percent had held the position of associate or assistant dean.

The search process for both deans and chairpersons is locally driven and reflects the faculty's views of the pool of candidates and its aspirations for the institution. First of all, the new leader must reflect the character of the institution; if the school or department is research-oriented, research achievement will be a dominant characteristic of the winning individual. Understandably, most search committees are looking for someone even better than the previous dean or chairperson, a research superstar. However, if search committees start out with this attitude, even if they later lower their sights, they may not throw the net wide enough to find women candidates.

How hard are search committees looking for women candidates? In addition to formal efforts to fulfill affirmative action requirements, some leaders are mandating that a woman be included on the "short list" of finalists for every post. Some deans are also requiring that every search committee have at least one woman member. While potentially quite useful, some of these efforts may be only marginally effective. The token woman committee member may feel too vulnerable to raise hard questions or to comment on gender bias, fearing that if she identifies herself with a gender issue, she will compromise her credibility on other issues. Also, in the absence of other supports (such as the dean's backing professional development programs for women faculty), the requirement that every short list include a woman may engender more negative than positive responses.

Most leaders in academic medicine say that they would be delighted to see more women in top positions, but that when they look for candidates, they find a very shallow pool. To be sure, 1,600 female professors is not many compared to 17,700 male professors. When a woman is found who meets all the criteria, deans report that usually she is either rooted due to a spouse's job and children's schools or is already overcommitted and unwilling to take on a new responsibility. However, even though they think they have looked hard, search committees may have overrelied on the "old boys' network" rather than advertising in a publication that reaches all medical school faculty (e.g., *Academic Physician and Scientist*). Most search committees may likewise be unaware of women's organizations within specialties as a source of information about potential women candidates and are unlikely to request the assistance of AAMC's Faculty Roster to generate a list of possible applicants.

Search committees and leaders also need to examine their perceptual biases and use the same measuring stick for all candidates. If the institution has never had a woman leader or if a previous experience with a woman administrator was negative, hiring a woman to lead may feel risky. Alternatively, if the institution already has a strong woman at the helm (e.g., as university chancellor), men may conclude that this woman's presence is sufficient and that other women need not be considered for other posts. The bases for such impressions need to be carefully examined. On the other hand, in the name of correcting past wrongs, some deans have overturned promotion committees' recommendations and awarded tenure to women who did not meet the school's criteria; such misguided efforts can only lead to the impression that, based on their own accomplishments, women are unable to pass muster.

Organizations tend to keep reproducing themselves because those in power seem to most effectively mentor and promote people with whom they feel most comfortable. This tendency works against minorities of all types, as well as women, especially those who have a full family life outside of medicine. Some men believe that it is simply unrealistic for anyone to expect to "have everything," and thus they discount women who are mothers because their "loyalties are too divided." It is natural for those who sacrificed time with their families in favor of breadwinning and career advancement to have regrets, but these individuals should not assume that this "either/or" choice is fixed. In fact, working mothers' experiences with managing multiple responsibilities and honoring multiple commitments are likely to translate into administrative skills key to the practice of medicine and into clinical skills essential to the treatment of families.

A central question then is, How can a profession that has traditionally espoused the ideal of single-minded devotion to patients and biomedical knowledge learn to help practitioners to have broader, stronger personal lives as well? As never before, students are interested in "controllable lifestyle" specialties, and men as well as women are seeking ways to combine their careers with responsibility for the care of children and, also, increasingly of aged parents. Medicine cannot afford to write off the leadership potential of all these women and men.

Assuring Access to Leadership Posts

With its wide variety of work settings, specialties, practice styles, and growth opportunities, medicine will continue to attract women in substantial numbers. Academic medicine offers even more scope: opportunities to generate knowledge (for example, on underresearched women's health problems) and to help shape future generations of physicians. Even in the face of their lower rates of promotion and the daily juggling of multiple roles, women in medical academia report a high level of satisfaction with their careers and personal lives.[14]

But in order for women to participate in academic medicine as fully as men, policies and options must reflect women's need for mentoring, their family-care responsibilities, and their longer life spans. A number of questions must be considered. Must a person forego the chance at tenure and academic leadership primarily because she cannot devote herself fully to research training immediately following residency? Can fellowship and research training grants with part-time options be created? Can research training grants be set aside for mid-career faculty? What can department chairs do to help committed but unestablished faculty protect time for research, given the ever-increasing demands on the services of all clinical faculty members? Are promotion standards that reward large numbers of research publications but not excellence in teaching in the best interests of the institution? Are flexible parental leave policies and "stop-the-clock" options in place? If adequate child care facilities are not available, is a plan under consideration to make them available?

Certainly many of the answers to these questions have financial implications, but not all of them. Moreover, if the long view is taken, pay-offs may exceed the initial investment (e.g., a child care center may enhance recruitment, retention, and performance of all types of women health care workers).

Recognizing that representation on medical school faculties does not automatically create equal opportunities for advancement, the American College of Physicians has recommended that all schools implement the following strategies:

1. Wide dissemination of written guidelines for tenure and promotion procedures.

2. Establishment of a formal career counseling program for junior faculty.

3. Establishment of a faculty development program.

4. Development of flexibility in tenure and promotion procedures that allow faculty to tend to personal and family responsibilities while continuing academic work.

5. Encouragement of the involvement of women and minorities on policy-making and faculty recruitment committees.

6. Establishment of a formal monitoring process.[15]

Eisenberg takes one step further: "If there is only one tenure slot and there are both men and women fully qualified to fill it, a woman should be appointed. That is the only way to offset the prevailing pattern of discrimination."[16]

The commitment of deans to such strategies would go a long way toward increasing the number of women mentors and assuring growth in the pool from which future leaders will come. To their credit, many deans now give some financial if not vocal backing to activities organized by women students and faculty, and all have appointed women liaison officers to the AAMC.[17]

Without the full support of the present leaders and male peers, no matter how well organized women are, they cannot accomplish the necessary adaptations—injecting flexibility into tenure timetables, building child care centers, eliminating harmful gender stereotypes, helping men to mentor women, and easing the fear of change, particularly in light of the precarious economic state of the medical profession today.

Awareness is building that medicine needs the strengths that women offer.[18] But women also face special challenges, and unless the challenges are addressed, women's contributions will be greatly diminished. Today's leaders must work to ensure that women participate in agenda setting and policy making as well as in caregiving and teaching. Medicine needs leaders, teachers, and researchers with strong student- and family-oriented values; given the complicated spectrum of policy questions facing it, medicine also needs to tap the leadership strengths of all its members.

Notes

1. J. Bickel, "Women in Medical Education: A Status Report," *New England Journal of Medicine* 319(1988):1579-84.

2. J. Bickel and B. Whiting, "Data Report: Comparative Representation and Promotion of Men and Women on Faculty Tracks at U.S. Medical Schools," *Academic Medicine* 66(1991):497.

3. P. Carr et al., "Comparing the Status of Women and Men in Academic Medicine," *Annals of Internal Medicine* 119(1993):908-13.

4. A.T. Lomperis, "Are Women Changing the Nature of the Academic Profession?" *Journal of Higher Education* 61(1990):643-677.

5. Bickel and Whiting, 1991.

6. D.I. Allen, "Women in Medical Specialty Societies," *Journal of the American Medical Association* 262(1989):3439-3443.

7. M. Bowman and D.I. Allen, *Stress and Women Physicians*, 2nd ed. (New York: Springer-Verlag, 1990).

8. J. Bickel, *Medicine and Parenting: A Resource for Medical Students, Residents, Faculty and Program Directors* (Washington, DC: Association of American Medical Colleges, 1991).

9. J.A. Grisso et al., "Parental Leave Policies for Faculty in U.S. Medical Schools," *Annals of Internal Medicine* 114(1991):43-45.

10. W. Levinson et al., "Women in Academic Medicine: Combining Family and Career," *New England Journal of Medicine* 321(1989):1511-1517.

11. D. Butler and F. Geis, "Nonverbal Affect Responses to Male and Female Leaders: Implications for Leadership Evaluations," *Journal of Personality and Social Psychology* 58(1990):48-59.

12. C. Eisenberg, "Medicine Is No Longer a Man's Profession: Or, When the Men's Club Goes Coed, It's Time to Change the Regs," *New England Journal of Medicine* 321(1989):1542-1544.

13. M.P. Wilson and C.P. McLaughlin, *Leadership and Management in Academic Medicine* (Washington DC: Association of American Medical Colleges, 1984).

14. Levinson, 1989.

15. American College of Physicians, "Promotion and Tenure of Women and Minorities on Medical School Faculties," *Annals of Internal Medicine* 114(1991):63-68.

16. Eisenberg, 1989.

17. J. Bickel, *Building a Stronger Women's Program: Enhancing the Educational and Professional Environment* (Washington, DC: Association of American Medical Colleges, 1993).

18. J. Stobo et al., "Understanding and Eradicating Bias against Women in Medicine," *Academic Medicine* 68(1993):349.

15

Women in Health Care Administration

Rina K. Spence

HEALTH CARE IS UNLIKE other professions—for example, law and business—where women have only within the last 10 to 15 years entered the field in large numbers and where a few more years must pass before they are represented proportionally in the leadership ranks. Women have traditionally played a large role in health care administration, but until recently, advancement to key positions was difficult. In order to examine the role of women in health care administration today, this chapter will examine their historical role in health care, describe the route by which women have achieved their positions, and conclude with some thoughts on the future role of women in health care administration.

A Historical Overview

Historically, employment in the field of health and human services was a great source of career advancement for women. Many women moved into high positions in the field through their wealth and influence, membership in a religious order, or long-standing employment as nursing supervisors. In fact, in the 1920s, the majority of U.S. hospitals were managed by women, most of them Catholic sisters.

The administrator or matron was typically in charge of the nursing department, as well as the cleaning, laundry and linen, dressmakers, and catering departments. The administrator also oversaw the private staff; nursing schools and any nonmedical schools for women attached to the hospital, such as midwifery and massage schools; and the work of volunteers. Such responsibility was similar to the management of a household, a circumstance that gave rise to the belief that running a hospital required no significant decision-making skills.

Despite the early predominance of women in the field and the fact that health care is a major employer of women in the United States today, health care administration has come to be dominated by men, as the management of hospitals and health care facilities has shifted from the "running of a household" to big business. By the 1950s, there had been a significant decrease in the number of women administrators. In recent years, however, women have once again begun to advance to non-nursing managerial positions, and an increasing number of women are entering graduate health administration programs. Nonetheless, the top administrative positions are still held largely by men.

The Current Situation of Women in Health Care Administration
The literature on the subject of women in health care administration is not extensive. Much of the ensuing discussion is therefore based on a national study conducted by the American College of Healthcare Executives (ACHE), *Gender and Careers in Healthcare Management: Findings of a National Survey of Healthcare Executives.*[1] The study sought to obtain an accurate description of the men and women who were practicing health care executives.

The sample consisted of 1,108 affiliates of ACHE, divided roughly equally into men and women. The study compared three groups of administrators:

1. Those who had entered the field between 1971 and 1975 (n=326);

2. Those who had entered the field between 1976 and 1980 (n=398); and

3. Those who had entered the field between 1981 and 1985 (n=384).

In all three groups, there were significantly more men than women who had achieved the position of chief executive officer (CEO) (Exhibits 1 and 2), and more men than women were currently responsible for general management and financial management. Women were more often responsible for clinical services and training programs (Exhibit 3).

The majority of the respondents worked in hospitals or hospital systems (Exhibit 4). Among those who had entered the field between 1971–1975 or 1976–1980, the proportions of males and females work-

Exhibit 1
Study Sample and Response Rates

	Population	Sample	Responses	Percent
1971–1975*				
Females	557	145	106	73
Males	3,616	181	120	66
Total	**4,173**	**326**	**226**	**69**
1976–1980*				
Females	963	205	142	69
Males	3,178	193	120	62
Total	**4,141**	**398**	**262**	**66**
1981–1985*				
Females	757	198	140	71
Males	1,504	186	115	62
Total	**2,261**	**384**	**255**	**66**
All				
Females	2,277	548	388	71
Males	8,298	560	355	63
Total	**10,575**	**1,108**	**743**	**67**

*Year begun first health management position.

Source: American College of Healthcare Executives and Graduate Program in Hospital and Health Administration, the University of Iowa.

Exhibit 2
Current Position

	1971–1975*		1976–1980*		1981–1985*	
	Females	Males	Females	Males	Females	Males
CEO	17	37**	9	24**	7	17***
COO/Associate	32	37	22	29	18	28
Vice President	36	14	40	32	35	34
Department Head/Staff	14	8	22	11	29	17
Other	1	4	7	4	11	4
	100%	100%	100%	100%	100%	100%
n	106	120	139	119	137	113
No Answer			3	1	3	2

*Year begun first health management position.

**Chi square significant p < .01.

***Chi square significant p < .001.

Source: American College of Healthcare Executives and Graduate Program in Hospital and Health Administration, the University of Iowa.

Exhibit 3
Responsibility Area

	Females		Males	
	Rank	Percent*	Rank	Percent*
General Management	1	44.2	1	66.1
Clinical Services	2.5	7.9	2	5.4
Planning	2.5	7.9	3.5	4.2
Ancillary Services	4	5.0	5	3.4
Ambulatory Care	5	4.5	7	2.5
HMO/PPO	6	3.7	6	3.1
Financial Management	7.5	3.4	3.5	4.2
Nursing Services	7.5	3.4		0.0

*Computed on the basis of whether or not this area was considered the primary current area of management responsibility.

Source: American College of Healthcare Executives and Graduate Program in Hospital and Health Administration, the University of Iowa.

ing in hospitals or hospital systems were not significantly different, but women tended to work in larger hospitals, which may help explain their underrepresentation in the CEO ranks, since the route to CEO in a large hospital is considerably longer than in a small hospital.

Among those who had entered the field most recently, significantly fewer of the females worked in hospitals or hospital systems, perhaps because, frustrated by their predecessors' failure to achieve the top positions within hospitals, they opted for routes that seemed to offer more opportunity. Or, these recent entrants may have been more flexible than their predecessors, willing to enter organizations in which the top managerial positions are not either as prestigious or as financially rewarding. Their male counterparts may prefer the more traditional routes, which will eventually place them in line for the position of CEO of a large system. Of course, as the health care system continues to diversify, new organizations and health care services will offer additional opportunities for the exercise of managerial skills.

In examining the differences in career attainments, the researchers analyzed differences in education, training, and experience; differences in work style and environment (e.g., hours devoted to the job, organizational flexibility, perceived autonomy and available resources, and outside socializing with fellow executives); conflicts between demands of work and family; and early socialization processes.

Exhibit 4
**Female and Male Administrators by
Type of Organization**

	1971–1975*		1976–1980*		1981–1985*	
	Females	**Males**	**Females**	**Males**	**Females**	**Males**
Hospital or System	80%	86%	78%	82%	67%	83%**
Other Direct Provider	12	5	7	7	9	3
Education Consulting Association	8	9	15	11	24	14

*Year begun first health management position.
**Chi square significant p < .05.
Source: American College of Healthcare Executives and Graduate Program in Hospital and Health Administration, the University of Iowa.

Education

In all three groups, the proportion of those with master's degrees exceeded 90 percent for both males and females, but in the group that had entered the field earliest, significantly more males than females had a specialized degree in health administration. The lack of such a degree may have contributed to women's exclusion from positions as CEOs and chief operating officers (COOs). For those entering the field between 1981 and 1985, however, the differences were not as significant, with only 9 percent fewer females having obtained specialized training in health administration. This discrepancy may be due to the fact that the early female entrants had not anticipated that they would enter the field of health administration when they obtained their degrees, since, at the time, the field was almost exclusively male.

Interestingly, the study showed that significantly more females than males (45 percent versus 23 percent) had previous clinical experience in disciplines like nursing or physical therapy.

Work Style and Environment

For the most part, men and women worked a similar number of hours per week, but men were significantly more likely to socialize with other executives in non-work activities such as dining with colleagues, meeting for drinks, attending cultural or sporting events, and participating in sports. The discrepancy may be attributed at least in part to numbers: Because more high-level executives are male than female, men are more likely to be invited to social events with other executives. In addition, women's child care responsibilities precluded socializing. After-work drinks and sports were superseded by the need to relieve the sitter or a day care pick-up schedule. There were no differences among the groups in going to informal lunches. In the youngest group, differences with regard to going out to dinner or for drinks disappeared.

Managing the Demands of Work and Family

The study found that 88 percent of the males but only 66 percent of the females were currently married. Women were twice as likely to be separated or divorced, and were four times as likely to have never been married. With regard to children, more of the females than the males had no children under the age of 16 currently living with them 50 percent or more of the time. For those administrators who were married and had children, fewer women than men could rely on their spouses to take care of a sick child. Among men, almost three-fourths relied on their spouse to take care of an ill child.

The study also found that women encountered more career path obstacles than men—taking less desirable or part-time jobs, even voluntarily leaving the work force—so that their spouses could advance their careers. In addition, more women than men took less desirable or part-time jobs in order to care for their children.

In a finding that says a lot about lingering perceptions and stereotypes, the study found that more females than males preferred to work with colleagues of the opposite sex, and preferred to have a boss of the opposite sex. This may be related to the fact that more males than females occupy high-level executive positions, but it also suggests that on some level, women tend to have a greater respect for men in authority than for women in authority, perhaps reflecting an ambivalence or fear of success. The lack of female role models in executive positions also contributes to this attitude. The logic behind the aphorism "I wouldn't want to belong to a club that had me as a member" may be operative here as well, shedding additional light on the relationship between women's self-esteem and their respect for other women in authority. However, it is difficult to draw firm conclusions about this subject since the study did not measure such features as interpersonal skills, persuasive power, and ability to inspire others, all characteristics of successful people in general.

Career Aspirations

In terms of career aspirations, the women seemed to set their sights lower than the men. For example, although for both men and women the desire for greater challenges was the most commonly cited reason for leaving an organization, more men than women described their departure as a step toward career objectives. Men were more likely to leave an organization because they believed that their job had no future or because they were dissatisfied with their salary.

Significantly fewer females than males were willing to move to obtain a higher level position, and fewer females were willing to move to a rural location for a good career opportunity. With regard to relocation to a large city, however, the males and females were quite similar. The reluctance of women to move to a rural location may be related to the fact that despite their desire to attain high-level positions, many women still place a high priority on family and are less willing to risk changes that could possibly hinder their chances to marry and have children. Women who are already married may not move because of their husbands' reluctance to relocate.

Women's tendency to set their sights lower than men with regard to position level and to have less definite plans may be due to their desire to play other roles as well or may simply be due to their accommodation to a perceived lack of opportunity.

Women in Middle Management

As disconcerting as the ACHE's findings about women in the top ranks are, other studies that have focused primarily on women in middle management positions have found that these women are earning excellent salaries, think they have good opportunities for advancement, and are clearly committed to careers in health care. However, the progress of these middle managers will be stalled if the top executive positions do not open up for women in senior management positions.

It should be noted that these studies focus on hospital administration *per se*. With the growth of health maintenance organizations (HMOs) and the ambulatory care sector, new opportunities exist for female leadership. Although as of December 1993 there were no female CEOs of major insurance companies, there are several female CEOs of HMOs. In addition, there are women in senior managerial positions in these sectors who could eventually become CEOs.

I predict that the 1990s will be noted as the decade when women broke through into CEO and COO positions in both large and small hospitals and other sections of the industry: success breeds success, and as women prove themselves, it will become easier for boards and male executives to accept their leadership.

Another area that is not touched upon in the literature is the prospects and problems for women of color. Interestingly, in parts of the health care delivery system, such as community health centers, there are women of color who have achieved the role of executive director. There are also women of color now in CEO and COO roles.

Reflections

Almost everything we read about women and health care administration focuses on the external issues that either support or hinder women in their efforts to attain senior managerial roles, for example, whether a woman receives assistance from her spouse with day-to-day childrearing activities, or, more broadly, whether she is able to gain the necessary support systems to compete on the job.

But the route to power for women is not very different from that for men, and it depends largely on the "presentation of self." Barring external impediments, those people who achieve leadership positions have a set of internal qualities that persuade others to trust an organization to their hands. These qualities are confidence in oneself; a willingness to take risks; perseverance; and, most important, the ability not to take personally the negative consequences of organizational decision making. It is not the technical qualifications that hinder women in leadership positions, but rather that women have yet to develop the self-confidence or the sense of presentation that is essential in these roles.

The glamour of senior leadership positions is often offset by the real problems that one confronts in the daily workings of an organization. And for a woman, gender problems are superimposed on the regular problems one can expect on the job. Women face a tougher time in the organizational mode, partly because of the persistence of discriminatory social stereotypes. The "barracuda" or "ice queen" image reflects both a prejudice and a perceived threat. These stereotypes are often simply a reflection of tough decision making and steadiness, qualities that are essential for leadership and senior managerial positions but not traditionally ascribed to women. It is important to recognize that higher management is not always a gentle or pleasant place to be, and it may require that women develop a tougher side than they are used to. It seems safe to say that most young women in their upbringing were not encouraged to develop their potential as leaders.

Avenues of Action
On the positive side, what is it that differentiates a female leader from her male counterpart? I would contend that women bring less ego baggage to the job than men and tend to be less encumbered by the trappings of senior positions, perhaps because they have more to over-come in achieving these positions and therefore need to have a higher degree of self-confidence to attain them. This ability to put one's ego aside often leads to less hierarchical organizational models. That is, the more self-confident one is, the less one has to depend on the visible trappings of achievement or constant reinforcements of the status of the job. Leaders who are not barred by their need for trappings or bu-reaucracy to define their position are more likely to reach out and work with the broader organization. This ability to put ego aside often enables women to sit down one-on-one with employees, members of the medical staff, and trustees to deal with the issues at hand. Women are less likely to engage in power and authority struggles, which are of-ten detrimental to organizational health. If my theory is correct—that women have less need for power *per se* and achieve their "power" through accomplishment—then it might be this key characteristic that enables women leaders to develop corporate cultures that have strength at many levels of the organization.

Need for Mentors
Obviously, a successful track record alone does not lead people into the key jobs. A mentor—someone who is willing to gamble or take risks on an individual—plays an important role in moving and help-ing people into leadership roles. Mentors are essential for women; studies clearly suggest that more women than men have had mentors "help them along." Mentors serve to offer professional guidance, make introductions, and offer references. At present, because more men than women are in senior positions, most mentors are male, and thus the mentor relationship repeats the traditional pattern in which men are more dominant and knowledgeable than women. This model, be-cause of shared culture, is comfortable for both parties. Since women

are not the norm in leadership roles, some risk is always taken by boards or supervisors in hiring and promoting them, and often a supportive male mentor can be of assistance. Today, however, as women attain senior leadership roles, male mentors may begin to be superseded by women mentors. To the extent that these women have the self-confidence that I propose they must have in order to attain their positions, they will also have the self-confidence to support other women without feeling threatened.

High Visibility

In order to achieve leadership status, women must also become visible—by becoming involved in not-for-profit or community boards, writing on health care issues, and becoming known in the community as spokespersons. Leaders in organizations, especially in health care organizations, must also be leaders in their broader communities regarding health care issues. Women can and must step onto these platforms in order not only to become candidates for jobs, but to enhance their credibility on the job.

Women need not play "old boy" games, but they must carve out some form of socializing, whether it is playing golf, going out to dinner, or some other form of entertaining. If they are to become leaders, they must be visible; leaders cannot be isolated in their communities. Because of family responsibilities, women presumably have more difficulty finding time to socialize, but they must recognize that this socializing time is as important as their work time and carve it out. For women with families, the balancing act seems to be particularly emotionally draining and difficult because women carry, whether emotionally or practically, a larger share of the family burden. More and more couples are sharing responsibilities, which should free women up, but men still seem to be psychologically freer of the family tie than women, and therefore in some sense freer of the conflict and the burden. Women who are not married, or who do not have families, may more easily put in time outside the parameters of the job, but clearly women with families can do so—and are doing so—as well.

The Challenge of Managing a Hospital

Hospitals pose a special set of managerial challenges. For example, because the hospital operates around the clock, senior administrators are on call at all hours. In addition, from a managerial point of view, hospitals run very much on an early morning, late afternoon, and often Saturday morning schedule, reflecting the availability of physicians. Similarly, CEOs, COOs, and chief financial officers often meet with trustees in the early morning or evening. If a woman administrator bears the primary responsibility for the organization and management of her family, these hours are all the more challenging. There is some room for flexibility, for example, if meetings are held in the mornings and the administrator makes herself available by telephone in the evenings and on Saturdays. But overall it is clear that health care administration requires non-family-centered hours to be effective.

On the other hand, the very positive side of health care administration for women with families is the humanistic values of the culture. A senior female administrator being called to attend to a child's needs by telephone is probably more readily accepted in the hospital than in the corporate sector. The health care environment fosters an understanding of the pulls and responsibilities that are inherent in family life.

It may be trite to say that women are more compassionate leaders, but the statement is not irrelevant. In any organization, but most of all in a service organization, the quality of compassion garners the respect of staff and community. Because hospitals deliver care, even staff members in the managerial and financial areas must have sensitivity and compassion with respect to the human issues in the health care environment. Therefore, this quality, which is often easier for women to bring to and express on the job, is very important in generating a trusting work environment.

Conclusion

Both the qualitative and quantitative information suggests that the current state of women in top administrative positions leaves much to be desired. The future looks somewhat brighter, not only because there are more women coming through the pipeline, but because the examples set by successful women administrators are leading to a growing recognition of the special set of skills that women bring to the job, a recognition that will make it more likely that recruiting firms and boards will identify women candidates as their first choices. The confidence and strength of women in leadership roles in health care will be essential to moving and sustaining organizations, and ultimately to the delivery of care to people during these difficult times in the industry.

Note

1. American College of Healthcare Executives and Graduate Programs in Hospital and Health Administration, the University of Iowa, *Gender and Careers in Healthcare Management: Findings of a National Survey of Healthcare Executives*, Research Series 3 (Chicago: American College of Healthcare Executives, 1991).

16

Women as Hospital Trustees, Women as Agents for Change

Carolyn B. Lewis

Trustees are not accustomed to thinking of themselves as designers of change. They are likely to be more present-oriented than future-oriented . . . In a rapidly changing society, the past is no longer a guide for the future.

Leland R. Kaiser, *Education of a Hospital Trustee: Changing Roles for Changing Times*

IN CHARACTERIZING TRUSTEES as "agents for change," Leland R. Kaiser touches on an important element of what women bring to the board-room. Women ought to, and generally do, find the role of "change agent" both rational and comfortable. As trustees, women have no history to defend. By and large, they enter the boardroom wanting, intending, and determined to make a difference.

And they do make a difference. Women come to the boardroom equipped with professional experience and political know-how, seasoned with well-learned lessons about "a woman's place." They bring first-hand knowledge of the community and a storehouse of community contacts; moreover, they are determined to make the delivery of health care more responsive to the needs of the community, needs with which women usually can, and do, more easily identify. These women appreciate the full measure of caregiving and its applicability to the provider setting. Many have strong organizing and leadership skills, untested or unappreciated in other quarters, waiting to be tapped; others become involved as a matter of self-interest. And like all people, women enjoy being an effective part of meaningful endeavors, and the opportunity to be an active part of the leadership and to respond to the challenge of providing quality, affordable health care for a community of people is enormously rewarding.

Given the range of these imperatives (and the list could go on), what difference do women on hospital boards of directors make? What do they bring to the job? What do they do right and wrong? What obstacles do they face? What about women of color? Where do they fit into this picture?

Changing Roles

Before 1970, hospital boards of directors, in general, did not make a notable difference in shaping health policy. Any influence associated with hospital boards was more perceived than real. And, before 1970, women were a rarity on boards of directors, hospital or otherwise.

Now, the picture is changing on both counts. In commenting on the role of hospital boards, Barry S. Bader says, "Powerful changes in the economic, social, and political environment have turned Boardsmanship from a prestigious pastime into a serious endeavor of heavy responsibility."[1] Other indicators bear this out, from court rulings to new standards for hospital accreditation. As a colleague on a health care board reminds me, "The buck stops here and the bucks start here." Indeed, the board bears the ultimate legal and fiduciary responsibility for the performance and accountability of the hospital.

The scarce data that are available show a measurable (albeit not dramatic) increase in the number of women on hospital boards of directors. What does this trend portend? And what factors will influence and facilitate further movement in this direction?

Serving on a hospital board of directors was not on my list of "things to do when I grow up," for some rather obvious reasons. There were no role models—nobody I knew was a director; there was no compensation—being a director did not pay anything; and there was no output—being a director did not produce anything that I could measure. But a traumatic experience in 1960 at the birth of my second child gave me a valuable, if subliminal, lesson about the importance of health care as a matter of public policy, a lesson I was to recall years later when asked to serve on the board of a local community hospital.

Faced with premature labor pains while stopping over in an unfamiliar town, I was brought face to face with some troubling realities. Because black doctors were not admitted to practice in the one hospital in town, my options were to be admitted by a white doctor to a segregated floor in that hospital or to go to a nearby town where the clinic was owned and operated by a black doctor.

I went to the clinic in the neighboring town. Once admitted, however, I realized that I was expected to be a silent partner in decisions about the delivery. As "the patient," I was being discussed, decisions and preparations were being made, and I was either hushed or ignored every time I tried to tell the decision makers important, relevant matters about my medical history. Other women in the labor room spoke up to tell me, gently, not to worry and not to fuss. But I did make a fuss. Through sheer force, I did not accede to a procedure that my regular doctor had advised against. In the process of my physical resistance, my second child was born.

I applauded and appreciated the fact that there was a clinic to go to. The services available were indeed adequate for normal procedures. A staff of well-trained professionals was on hand, and I never doubted their good intentions or questioned their professional competence. But the status quo was simply overwhelming. The relationship between the women at the clinic and the "system" was both caring and crippling, a kind of well-intentioned paternalism. Roles, well defined and entrenched, were not challenged.

That experience, buttressed in the late 1970s and early 1980s by my volunteer service on community boards and governmental commissions dealing mainly with women's rights issues, gave me helpful insight into the importance and validity of having my perspective represented in the hospital boardroom.

An Open and Shut Case

The case for increasing the presence of women of all racial and ethnic backgrounds on the boards of hospitals is as simple as the numbers. More than half of the population and the work force in this country now consists of women and minorities. Women comprise more than 80 percent of the health care work force. The case is as basic as common decency or good public policy. The world outside the boardrooms of our hospitals is very diverse. Yet the people in our country who are falling into the gaps are not very visible inside our boardrooms. Exclusion is neither good policy nor good practice. People barred from the front door simply find another point of entry—one that costs more in dollars, dignity, and human suffering. And the case is as pragmatic as marketplace imperatives. Survival for health care providers in today's marketplace, and in the future, will require much greater attention to patient and consumer satisfaction, and women are the primary consumers of health care. From any point of view, the case for increasing the numbers and the influence of women on hospital boards of directors is easily made and incontrovertible.

However, the best case, in my view, is the participation of women on a multicultural board of directors, where the presence of women is a natural by-product of the institution's search for good directors, a relatively gender-blind, color-blind approach. I have witnessed this best-case scenario in the system with which I am most familiar: the Greater Southeast Healthcare System in Washington, DC.

A Case Study: Greater Southeast Healthcare System

In 1975, the 21-member board of directors of Greater Southeast Community Hospital looked a lot like the boards of directors of other urban community hospitals around the country. The snapshot was one in which white men from the local business community predominated. Hospital boards, like the rest of the country's corporate power structure, lived (and reproduced) by the mirror image concept. The demographics of the service area or patient population and consideration for diversity simply were not factors in board selection, and nowhere was this more graphically demonstrated than at Greater Southeast.[2] The 21-member board included only one white woman and one black male.

Nineteen years later, the Greater Southeast board has a very different look. This urban health care system has grown horizontally and vertically; restructured; expanded its operations; broadened its mission; and, in the process, diversified its boards of directors.

The single most important impetus for change at Greater Southeast was the drive to excel as a community institution. The population base served by Greater Southeast included some of the poorest, most underserved citizens in the city, a fact that underscored the importance of drawing on the best leadership available. And the best governance team, as a matter of logic, could not ignore half the population.

In 1994, the Greater Southeast boards (there are now five) are rich with diversity in terms of race, gender, ethnicity, profession, and geographic distribution. By charter, at least 80 percent of the board members must come from the service area. Seventeen (or 40 percent) of the 42 Greater Southeast board members are women—professional women, retired women, housewives, former auxilians, community activists. Ten of the 17 women are African-American. Sixteen African-American men and nine white men complete the picture. Each of the principal subsidiaries has been chaired by a woman. Currently, three of the five boards in the system are chaired by women: the board of trustees of the parent company and the boards of directors of the system's two hospitals, Greater Southeast Community Hospital and Fort Washington Hospital.

There is no artificial screen through which Greater Southeast board candidates must pass. We look, simply, for men and women who

> Have a stake in the communities we serve and knowledge of community needs;
>
> Can demonstrate a commitment to the system's mission;
>
> Are familiar with health issues generally and their relationship to other societal issues;
>
> Are willing to commit the time and energy to board service;
>
> Have standing with a constituency that affects or is affected by Greater Southeast; and
>
> Agree to advocate, provide leadership, and build bridges on behalf of the system.

In the process, we get the broadest possible range of involvement from men and women who are truly representative of and care about the community. We heighten our system's sensitivity to different points of view, different approaches to problem solving, and different market needs. We learn from one another. An intrinsic value of this diversity is the creative tension, the energy that seems both inherent in and not possible without the interaction of women and men around the board table. The pay-off is this: the broad-based board composition works to create and maintain a balance between community values and institutional, or corporate, imperatives—a kind of synergy of purpose, resources, and outcomes that advances the collective well-being. Or, as Barry Passett, former chief executive officer of the Greater Southeast Healthcare System, put it, "The more balanced our board became (by race and gender), the more dynamic it became." And the more dynamic the board became, the more relevant our system's programs and services became.

There is a liberating significance in this best-case scenario. Women who serve in a welcoming, gender-friendly boardroom, with other women in leadership roles—on the board, in senior management, in nursing, on the medical staff—can get on to the task at hand. Energy need not be dissipated staking out the right to be present, to be heard, to be taken seriously. A board that adopts and promotes a philosophy of respect for differences creates an environment in which everyone is free to do her or his best work. Diversity becomes a strength. It's a win-win situation.

What is the observable, tangible outcome at Greater Southeast? Has board diversity made a difference? And how reliable are these observations for broader application? These are not easy questions to answer, considering that a board's "product" or contribution to a hospital's outcome generally is not quantifiable. On the other hand, one author has observed that "When you find a corporation in trouble, you find a board of directors either unwilling or unable to do its work."[3]

By objective measure, the Greater Southeast Healthcare System has made a profound difference in the communities it serves. The hallmark of the system—an organizational mission tied programmatically, directly and visibly, to the needs of the community—was introduced and advanced by a woman trustee. Building on this foundation and with strong leadership and support from men and women on the board, Greater Southeast has distinguished itself, locally and nationally, as a financially sound organization *and* a trend-setter in community health, health care for the elderly, and programs designed for the health and health-related problems of children and young people.

To set the tone, Greater Southeast board members typically ask three questions: "What are the health and health-related challenges facing the community?"; "What can we do to help?"; and "How can we afford it?" The discussions that follow often generate the "doing good versus doing well" or "mission versus bottom line" tension. The important point is that with diversity on the board representing a community as well as a business focus, and with a mission and organizational culture influenced and reinforced by trustees with solid, legitimate, relevant experience in the community, both sides of the issue are argued, passionately and persuasively. An interview with former Greater Southeast CEO Thomas Chapman in the *Harvard Business Review* presents a good account of this process.[4]

This deliberative process takes us beyond the hospital walls, beyond acute care, and into a network of partnerships with churches and schools, business and government, young people and elderly people, other nonprofit organizations, and other providers. Examples of the system's reach into the community include community health partnerships with local governments and others that embrace wellness, social, and recreational programs for the elderly; school-based health centers; community youth initiatives offering health promotion and health education; elderly-teen linkage programs; and breast cancer education programs.

These collaborations, formal and informal, frequently originate at the board level. The concept behind the Ballou High School Adolescent Health Center, the first of its kind in Washington, DC, was proposed by a woman trustee who was active in the school's Parent Teacher Association and grappling with problems that pointed up the need for such a center. Another woman combined her role as a Greater Southeast trustee with her presidency of a local chapter of a leading national social organization to develop a major glaucoma screening program. On an ongoing basis, yet another trustee identifies ways to connect programs associated with her work as executive director of the local Commission for Women with community outreach projects at Greater Southeast. The leveraging effect works to the betterment of the overall community. In all cases, the diversity, reach, political acumen, and clout of our board empower and direct the CEO to make community service intrinsic to the system's operations and to be innovative and aggressive in designing programs to meet community needs.

Greater Southeast's reputation as a facility with a heart and a conscience, one that practices what it preaches—that the health of a community is as important as the health of an individual and that a hospital should strive to heal both—is well established. National recognition includes the 1989 Foster G. McGaw Prize for distinguished community service and the 1992 Community Benefit Recognition award from the Hospital Community Benefit Standards Program for continuing efforts to develop and expand effective programs to address community needs. Walt Bogdanich's harsh criticism of hospitals in his expose *The Great White Lie* notes, by way of exception, that "Greater Southeast Community Hospital showed it had a passion for its neighborhood, not just its bottom line, when it renovated or built 600 housing units in its drug-ravaged Washington, D.C. neighborhood."[5]

On the local level, this reputation resides not only in the institutions' programs and community outreach. It is associated very closely with the work of system trustees, notably women, whose track record in community service is well established. The credibility the system has established, the expectation that Greater Southeast will "do the right thing" in the community, and the willingness of others to partner with and support the community outreach initiatives are all tied to the people who make up the leadership of Greater Southeast. And that leadership has had the strong influence and presence of women trustees.

The Greater Southeast motto, "Caring enough to try. Smart enough to succeed," practically announces the influence of women in the Greater Southeast hierarchy. It reflects the nurturing approach that permeates the board's philosophy and captures the system's determination to employ all available resources to create a healthier community. This is further borne out by Chapman, who notes, "There has been an assumption for some time in healthcare that the (health) professionals know best. We've undermined ourselves by making the provision of healthcare a club that's almost exclusive to the professional ranks."[6] Not so at Greater Southeast; using "all available resources" means being inclusive, expansive, open-ended, and diverse, beginning with a board that mirrors the community it serves, to the benefit of both the community and the institution.

At Greater Southeast and in the overall equation, women can and do make a difference. They bring a different perspective, a "freshness," an added dimension. They strengthen and enrich the board's overall performance. And, yes; women also bring some of the same qualities as men—they are not a monolithic class unto themselves. The importance of women trustees is as imbedded in the value of diversity as it is in the unique qualities of women.

What Women Bring to the Job
What are the unique qualities associated with women and, by extension, with women trustees? Some givens: through the process of socialization, women develop a different set of insights. Societal values have defined certain gender expectations. Men are "competitive, strong, dispassionate, objective, controlling." Women are "cooperative, supportive, caring, sensitive, interactive." (Not such bad traits, in my opinion, particularly in light of the purpose for which hospitals exist:

to serve the patient and the community, to heal, to restore and promote health.) In fact, of course, these characteristics are not so discretely distributed, just as they are not so easily labeled the "right" or "wrong" traits for effective board performance. Still, these perceptions persist, and unless women can gain entry into the boardroom, there is no way to confirm or dispel these perceptions.

Directly or indirectly, women acquire a different set of survival skills and, in many cases, a different set of values than men. Women, relatively new to positions of power, generally see the ability to share power as an asset, not a liability; and women generally require less appeasing when a point or battle is lost. The average woman plays multiple roles in her day-to-day existence—demanding that she be a quick study, a careful listener, and an astute negotiator with a clear understanding of the value of "smart" compromise. Anyone who can cook and wash and clean house and tend restless children and pay bills and help with homework and patch up cuts and bruises after "a day at the office" is a talent to be reckoned with. A few years on this track and a woman develops an amazing ability to cut through minutiae, line up her priorities, understand the demands of the moment, and get the job done. Women are also given, perhaps by default, a wider latitude to make and admit mistakes. This may make it easier for them to ask questions and reach out for help. These are all valuable leadership skills.

Beyond these intuitive traits is a host of other lifestyle and gender-related factors that must be considered. Most women are the primary caregivers in their families. Of necessity, they come to understand the needs of their families and children and learn how to balance these needs with competing interests. Routinely, women live with budgets and income limitations and develop an acute sense of outrageous cost and waste. Women tend to take volunteer service more seriously than men and give it more time and effort. In fact, women have more experience as volunteers and are generally more at home with the notions of inclusiveness and interchange that are fundamental to meaningful board exchange.

On the gender-specific front, women live longer and consume more health care than men, and they have different health needs, health needs that have historically received relatively little attention compared to those associated more closely with men. There are some encouraging signs that this is changing, as a result, perhaps, of the growing number of women in national and local policymaking roles. The aging of the population will only accentuate the dominance of women as consumers of health care, as older women tend to have more chronic illnesses than older men.

Minority Women

Despite success stories like Greater Southeast and the modest increases in the number of women trustees generally, we live in a society that tolerates tokenism and perpetuates stereotypes about women, and which is especially skeptical and unwelcoming about the role of African-American women and other women of color. Proceedings of the 1986 National Conference on Women's Health paint a picture that, in my view, has worsened in the years since:

> As a group, minority women suffer disproportionately from socioeconomic disadvantages and discrimination that impact on their health. Many must also overcome ethnocultural barriers in gaining access to the health care system. In addition, in sharing these common obstacles, each minority has its special problems and needs. Today, minority women bear a disproportionate share of diseases, homicides, and unintentional injuries. Their special health care needs present an important challenge to persons in all facets and at all levels of the health care system. Becoming aware of and sensitive to the plight of minority women is a crucial first step for policymakers and service providers. There should be a concerted effort to educate both health service providers and consumers about ways to break down ethnocultural barriers . . . Lastly, there should also be a sincere effort to increase participation by minority women in all aspects of health care.[7]

The imperative is clear. Hospitals exist to serve their communities; they are accountable to the public for spending resources prudently and in the community's best interest. If the board does not resemble the community, the community and the institution are at risk. The history of the breakdown in social services around the country is filled with glaring examples—more than we can afford—of how not to plan and of what does not work. Throughout our social service delivery system, there is, at best, a fragile connection between the policymakers and a large and growing segment of the consumers. Those who make the decisions do not feel the pain of their inaction or bad decisions but they, and we, are paying the cost. Whether the result of altruism or self-interest, there appears to be ample impetus to open the boardroom to those who have been systematically excluded.

What Are the Pitfalls?

Because of their relatively sparse numbers, many women bring a kind of tentativeness to the role of director. If we are not careful, we can slip into or buy into popular stereotypes about inexperience or ill-preparedness, or accept marginal roles on the board. In such an environment, a woman must be very clear about who she is, what she wants to accomplish, and how she expects to get the job done. She must define herself and value her difference.

Once in the door, a woman can unwittingly perpetuate the syndrome of recycling the same few women. It is an easy trap to fall into, linked as it is to ego and prestige, but it must be resisted. We have a responsibility to spread the opportunities around, to open the door to more women—young women, women with perspectives and backgrounds different than ours. History will not view us kindly if we walk through the doors that others have opened for us, only to close them behind us.

How Can We Get More Women Involved as Trustees?

First, be a model of good trusteeship! Do the right thing. Exercise the power vested in you prudently and in the best interest of the institution and its mission. Do your homework—understand the system you are trying to influence and the issues you want to advocate; become the expert. Identify your friends and adversaries; know your natural partners and know whom you need to influence. Learn how to diffuse dissent and how to structure compromise. Perfect the task of follow-up—reliability builds supporters. Understand the power in you and in solidarity; build alliances with other women and with other like-minded board colleagues.

Establish your right and, by proxy, the right of other women to be at the table; educate others about the value women add. Hold on to your own uniqueness by recognizing and emphasizing your strengths; there isn't much currency in becoming, simply, a custodian of male power.

Educate yourself and those you represent about the essential elements of the systems within which you work so that you can make them more representative of women's and families' health needs. Encourage and help others to get involved in board service. Work within existing networks and groups to educate the community in matters of health policy and equitable distribution of resources. And work to connect your hospital to other community groups with more diverse leadership. Leadership skills are fungible. Spread the word!

Learn to leverage your political base. Expand your contacts and your clout through the use of networks. Challenge the notion that hospital boards are the domain of the privileged and the powerful.

Advocate for diversity, *for the sake of the institution and its public purpose,* not as an end in itself. Governance and community must be connected in a meaningful way. A board's jobs of setting the mission, establishing the vision, and ensuring accountability work best when the players have a stake in the outcome.

Where Do We Go from Here?
Health care reform is at the top of today's agenda. And governance is coming of age. While the intense interest in solving the country's health care problems is being driven, largely, by cost considerations, there is an equally compelling need to transform the delivery of health care to a publicly accountable, integrated, and coordinated system able to address the needs of the population. Our physical and financial well-being demands it. I believe that this bodes well for the involvement of more women as trustees. I also believe that as we start to construct the sweeping social change that health reform promises and that we so desperately need, we cannot afford to slight or ignore the value that women bring to the debate.

Women are uniquely suited to be agents for change in the delivery and reshaping of health care. Women are accustomed to working in structured, collaborative relationships; getting things done through other people; and working through defined processes. Ultimately, the number of women directors—of all ethnic and racial backgrounds—will increase because women are becoming more visible, more vocal, more political, and more influential. These women, with their contributions and their possibilities, represent a reality and a vital dimension in the health care equation; they are a strength and a force to be reckoned with. Finally, the number of women directors is sure to increase because smart leadership will look to strengthen itself with the best talent it can find, and it will find it without regard to gender or race.

Notes

1. Barry S. Bader, "Five Keys to Building an Excellent Governing Board," from *Keys to Better Governance through Better Information* (Hospital Trustee Association of Pennsylvania and Bader & Associates, Inc., 1991),1.

2. Located on the dividing line between Washington, DC, and Prince George's County, Maryland, Greater Southeast's service area spans the two jurisdictions. The population on the DC side is primarily African American; the service area in Prince George's County is predominantly white.

3. Kenneth Dayton, *Corporate Governance: The Other Side of the Coin.*

4. Nancy A. Nichols, "Profits with a Purpose: An Interview with Tom Chapman," *Harvard Business Review* (November-December 1992):87-95.

5. Walt Bogdanich, *The Great White Lie: How America's Hospitals Betray Our Trust and Endanger Our Lives* (New York: Simon & Schuster, 1991), 28.

6. Healthcare Forum case study.

7. U.S. Department of Health and Human Services, Public Health Service, *Proceedings of the National Conference on Women's Health,* June 17-18, 1986: 12.

About the Editor and Authors

Emily Friedman is a writer, lecturer, and health policy analyst based in Chicago. She is section editor for health policy of the *Journal of the American Medical Association*, contributing editor of *Hospitals and Health Networks*, *Healthcare Forum Journal*, and the *American Journal of Medicine*, and a contributing writer to *Health Management Quarterly*, *Health Progress*, and other publications. She is also currently an adjunct assistant professor at the Boston University School of Public Health.

George J. Annas, J.D., M.P.H., is Edward R. Utley Professor and Chair, Health Law Department, Boston University Schools of Medicine and Public Health. He writes a regular feature on health law, "Legal Issues in Medicine," for the *New England Journal of Medicine*, and is the author or editor of a dozen books on health law, most recently, *Standard of Care: The Law of American Bioethics* (Oxford, 1993).

Laurie J. Bauman, Ph.D., is codirector of the Preventive Intervention Research Center and associate professor of pediatrics at the Albert Einstein College of Medicine in New York City. She is associate editor of the *Journal of Developmental and Behavioral Pediatrics* and recently co-edited a special supplement to that journal on psychosocial issues in pediatric HIV.

Janet Bickel is assistant vice president for institutional planning and development, and director of Women's Programs of the Association of American Medical Colleges (AAMC). She serves as faculty on George

Washington University Health Sciences Center's Issues in Health Care course and on AAMC's Management Education Program on the evaluation of medical students.

Elaine M. Brody is senior research consultant at the Philadelphia Geriatric Center, clinical professor of psychiatry at the Medical College of Pennsylvania, and adjunct associate professor of Social Work in Psychiatry at the School of Medicine at the University of Pennsylvania. She is the author of *Women in the Middle: Their Parent-Care Years* (Springer-Verlag, 1990). Mrs. Brody is a past president of the Gerontological Society of America.

Karen Davis, Ph.D., is executive vice president of The Commonwealth Fund. Previously she was chairman of the Department of Health Policy and Management in the School of Hygiene and Public Health at Johns Hopkins University. Dr. Davis served as deputy assistant secretary for planning and evaluation/health at the U.S. Department of Health and Human Services and administrator of the U.S. Public Health Service. She is a fellow of the Institute of Medicine, a member of the Kaiser Commission on the Future of Medicaid, and a member of the Physician Payment Review Commission.

Andrea Boroff Eagan was a writer and advocate who focused on women's rights and health care. She was the editor of the National Women's Health Network Series for Pantheon Books and president of HealthRight, a nonprofit organization. She taught about health and women's issues at New York University and La Guardia, Manhattan Community, and Hunter Colleges.

Claire M. Fagin, Ph.D., R.N., is the Leadership Professor and dean emeritus of the University of Pennsylvania School of Nursing. She recently completed a term as interim president of the University of Pennsylvania. She is chair of the Division of Health Promotion and Disease Prevention at the Institute of Medicine. She is the author of many books and articles, most recently, *Charting Nursing's Future Agenda for the 1990's*, with Linda Aiken (Lippincott, 1992).

Eli Ginzberg, Ph.D., is director of The Eisenhower Center for the Conservation of Human Resources, Hepburn Professor Emeritus of

Economics at the Graduate School of Business, Director of the Revson Fellows Program for the Future of the City of New York, and special lecturer at the School of Public Health, Columbia University. He is the author of more than 100 books, including *The Medical Triangle* (1990), *Health Services Research: Key to Health Policy* (editor) (1991), *The Road to Reform: Future of Health Care in America* (1994), and *Critical Issues in U.S. Health Reform* (editor) (1994). He is a member of the Institute of Medicine, National Academy of Sciences.

Jeane Ann Grisso, M.D., M.Sc., is associate professor of obstetrics and gynecology at the University of Pennsylvania, and associate professor of medicine at the University of Pennsylvania School of Medicine, where she is also course director for the women's health seminar series. She is director of the Women's Health Clinical Research Program at the Center for Clinical Epidemiology and Biostatistics, and serves on the advisory board of the University of Pennsylvania's Center for Aging.

Elaine Hart-Brothers, M.D., M.P.H., is an internist in Durham, North Carolina. Practicing with Metropolitan Durham Medical Associates, she is also medical director for employee health services at the Durham County Hospital Corporation. Dr. Hart-Brothers is clinical assistant professor at the University of North Carolina School of Medicine, vice chairman of the Durham County Board of Health, and director of the Community Health Coalition Project. She is board-certified in internal medicine and preventive medicine.

Dorothy Jones Jessop, Ph.D., is director of research and evaluation for the Medical and Health Research Association of New York City, Inc., and is a visiting associate professor of pediatrics at the Albert Einstein College of Medicine and associate research scientist in sociomedical sciences at the School of Public Health of Columbia University.

Phyllis Kopriva is director of Women in Medicine Services at the American Medical Association (AMA), which represents almost 300,000 physicians. The department was created in 1989 to address the special concerns of women physicians and medical students in organized medicine and the profession.

Risa Lavizzo-Mourey, M.D., M.B.A., is associate executive vice president for health policy, associate dean for health services research, and the Class of 1970 associate professor of medicine and health care systems at the University of Pennsylvania. From 1992-1994, she served as the deputy administrator of the Agency for Health Care Policy and Research. A board-certified geriatrician, Dr. Lavizzo-Mourey is a Fellow of the American College of Physicians, the American Geriatric Society, and the Association of Academic Minority Physicians.

Carolyn B. Lewis is assistant director of the U.S. Securities and Exchange Commission. She is chairman of the board of trustees of the Greater Southeast Healthcare System in Washington, DC, where she has served as a trustee for 18 years. She also serves on the boards of the D.C. Hospital Association and National Forum of Women Health Care Leaders, and she is a commissioner on the Joint Commission on the Accreditation of Healthcare Organizations.

Joan E. Lynaugh, Ph.D., F.A.A.N., is associate dean, director of graduate studies, and professor of nursing at the University of Pennsylvania School of Nursing, where she directs the Center for the Study of the History of Nursing. She edits *Studies in Health, Illness and Caregiving*, a book series at the University of Pennsylvania Press, and is editor of *Nursing History Review*, the official journal of the American Association of the History of Nursing.

Charlotte Muller, Ph.D., is Professor Emerita at Mount Sinai School of Medicine and in the Economics Doctoral Program at the City University of New York. Dr. Muller is Associate Director for Economics of the International Leadership Center on Longevity and Society at Mount Sinai. Most recently, Dr. Muller is the author of *Health Care and Gender* (Russell Sage Foundation).

Diane Rowland, Sc.D., is the senior vice president of The Henry J. Kaiser Family Foundation and the executive director of The Kaiser Commission on the Future of Medicaid. She also serves as associate professor in the Department of Health Policy and Management at the School of Hygiene and Public Health of the Johns Hopkins University. Dr. Rowland is the co-author of *Medicare Policy: New Directions for Health and Long Term Care of the Elderly* and *Health Cost Containment: Lessons from the Past and a Policy Proposal for the Future.*

Rina Spence, M.P.A., is president of RKS Health Ventures Corporation, which is developing innovative approaches to women's health services. For ten years, she served as president and chief executive officer of Emerson Hospital. Ms. Spence serves on several nonprofit boards and two corporate boards.

Ruth E.K. Stein, M.D., is professor and vice chairman of the department of pediatrics, director of general pediatrics, and director of the Preventive Intervention Research Center for Child Health at Albert Einstein College of Medicine in New York City. She is also pediatrician-in-chief at Bronx Municipal Hospital Center.

Index

Current Publications

At the Bedside: Innovations in Hospital Nursing *Paper Series*

Drawing on the findings of the Fund's Nursing Initiatives Program, this paper describes strategies for increasing the efficiency, productivity, retention, and satisfaction of nursing staff.

32 pp. 1991 $10

Better Jobs, Better Care: Building the Home Care Work Force *Paper Series*

This paper defines the specific challenges concerning home care workers, including their need for more defined career opportunities, improved supervision and support, and better training.

56 pp. 1994 $10

Building Bridges: Community Health Outreach Worker Programs *Practical Guide*

Through descriptions of seven model programs in New York City and elsewhere, this guide presents innovative techniques for training and deploying community residents as health outreach workers.

40 pp. 1994 $10

Caring for Neighbors: An Examination of Nonresident Use of New York City Hospitals *Paper Series*

Approximately 10 percent of the patients in New York City hospitals come from beyond the city limits for care. This paper presents a profile of these patients and compares their usage patterns, case mix, and length of stay with those of residents.

32 pp. 1993 $10

The Changing Role of Volunteerism *Paper Series*

Based on a Fund conference, this paper describes strategies for recruiting, training, supervising, and motivating volunteers. Model programs are described.

40 pp. 1993 $10

A Clearing in the Crowd: Innovations in Emergency Services *Paper Series*

Drawing on the Fund's Emergency Services Initiative, this paper describes eight projects designed to reduce overcrowding in hospital emergency departments.

48 pp. 1994 $10

A Death in the Family: Orphans of the HIV Epidemic

Based on a Fund conference, this 17-chapter book considers the plight of children who have lost a parent to HIV/AIDS. Among the issues discussed are custody and placement, bereavement and mental health, confidentiality and disclosure, and new service models.

176 pp. 1993 $10

Facilities for the Aging: How to Choose a Nursing Home, 1994 Guide

This consumer's guide contains information about the capacity and services of 163 nursing homes in New York City. It describes the nursing home placement process, as well as alternatives to nursing home care, and offers suggestions about selecting a nursing home.

48 pp. 1993 No charge

In Sickness and in Health: The Mission of Voluntary Health Care Institutions

This eight-chapter book traces the evolution as well as the sociological, philosophical, and legal basis of voluntary health care organizations.

256 pp. 1988 $35.95

Mediating Bioethical Disputes *Practical Guide*

This publication provides background information on bioethics and dispute resolution strategies and outlines a process for mediating disputes in hospital settings.

104 pp. 1994 $20

Poverty and Health in New York City

This volume explores the link between economic circumstances and health in New York City and includes chapters on general health status and disability, infant morbidity and mortality, the elderly residing in low-income areas, and avoidable disease and death among disadvantaged groups.

224 pp. 1989 $40

Simple Acts of Kindness: Volunteering in the Age of AIDS

In moving first-person narratives, volunteers relate their personal experiences and the rewards and challenges involved in working with people with AIDS. Model programs are described.

76 pp. 1989 $5

The Tuberculosis Revival: Individual Rights and Societal Obligations in a Time of AIDS *Special Report*

This report, the product of a distinguished working group, examines the legal and ethical issues that must guide a response to the tuberculosis epidemic.

64 pp. 1994 $10

To order, please write to the Publications Program, United Hospital Fund, 55 Fifth Avenue, New York, NY 10003. Checks should be made payable to the United Hospital Fund and include $3.50 for shipping and handling. For information about bulk orders or for a complete list of publications, please call 212/ 645-2500.